YOUR LITERACY COACHING PLAYBOOK

What to Know, Say, and Do

IRENE C. FOUNTAS & GAY SU PINNELL

Library of Congress Cataloging-in-Publication Data is on file.

Library of Congress Control Number: 2025938080

Printed in the United States of America on acid-free paper

ISBN-13: 978-0-325-02872-9

1 2 3 4 5 6 7 8 9 10 VP 29 28 27 26 25

4500910873

Editors: Kerry L. Crosby, Debra Doorack, Sue Paro
Production Editor: Angel Lepore
Cover and Interior Designer: Kelsey Roy
Typesetter: Gina Poirier, Gina Poirier Design
Manufacturing: Jaime Spaulding

Contents

List of Online Resources

How to Access the Online Resources

To access the Online Resources for *Your Literacy Coaching Playbook*:

1. Go to http://hein.pub/FPCoachPlaybook-login
2. Log in with your username and password. If you do not already have an account with Heinemann, you will need to create an account.
3. On the Welcome page, choose **"Click here to register an Online Resource."**
4. Register your product by entering the code **COACHBOOK** (be sure to read and check the acknowledgment box under the keycode).
5. Once you have registered your product, it will appear alphabetically in your account list under "My Online Resources."

Note: When returning to Heinemann.com to access your previously registered products, simply log in to your Heinemann account and click on **"View my registered Online Resources."**

Our Sincerest Appreciation

The creation of this book reflects its underlying theme—collaboration and teamwork. This is a most important book for us—one that focuses on the growth and dignity of teachers, who are the bulwark of teaching children to understand, enjoy, and use literacy all of their lives. Our Heinemann team was outstanding in supporting the conceptualization and production of this book, and we have long valued their partnership and long-standing dedication to teachers.

Our incredible editorial team, which included Sue Paro, Kerry Crosby, and Deb Doorack, played key roles in conversations about the writing and substance of ideas, harnessing decades of our experience and content in the process of collaborating with us to bring our thoughts to paper. We thank Kerry for her vast knowledge and meticulous attention to ways of making the content informative and practical for coaches. We thank Deb for her artful editing to make the volume come alive through her extraordinary ability to shape language to engage the reader. And this book would not have been brought to completion without the leadership of Sue Paro, who was the guiding light. Her patience, management skills, and considerable editing skills brought this to the finish line.

One of the most expert teachers and literacy coaches we know, Wendy Mattson, offered her thoughtful guidance. We thank her for reading chapters and offering feedback. We also thank Wendy Vaulton, a gifted researcher, for giving feedback on the data chapter as we value her extraordinary expertise. We want to extend our sincere appreciation to Nicole Drury for her collegial generosity in sharing her practical experiences as a coach in organizing for her school year. Cindy Downend, our valued colleague at Lesley University, was also invited to read and give feedback on the book. A gifted scholar and coach herself, Cindy gave us the gift of taking our work seriously and offered insightful and constructive feedback (which we paid attention to) on every chapter.

And we owe our sincere appreciation to our team of generous colleagues at Lesley University and The Ohio State University who have been our passionate partners in learning about the impact of coaching on teacher expertise and student outcomes through our collaborative research, development, and implementation efforts for more than three decades. We also want to acknowledge the exciting and impactful learning opportunities our teams were afforded through their participation in visionary research on the systemic impact of coaching on school culture, teacher expertise, and student outcomes. We learned a great deal from the research team, led by the distinguished researcher Dr. Anthony Bryk through his work at the University of Chicago, Stanford University, and the Carnegie Institute for the Advancement of Teaching and Learning.

As always, the staff at Heinemann applied their excellent talent to the production of this book. Kelsey Roy brought her creativity and brilliance in design to the creation of the interior and cover, and Mark Tricca and Angel Lepore handled the production with their usual level of care and competence. We thank them for their utmost patience and support throughout the process.

We are grateful that leaders at Heinemann and HMH supported our work and believed in the value of this book in transforming schools for children through the expertise of its teachers. In a time of great changes in education, Samantha Garon, Roderick Spelman, and Maggie DeMont believed in our work and this new direction, dedicated to the professional learning of teachers, reflecting the deep roots of Heinemann's distinctive brand.

Back at home, we are grateful to Cheryl Wasserstrom, who is herself a highly competent manager as well as a skilled research librarian and professional creator of documents. We also thank Kris Kennedy for her broad range of excellent editing, organization, and technical skills right when they were needed.

Finally—and this may be most important—we thank the thousands of literacy coaches all over the world who engaged as true partners with us over several decades, generously sharing the successes and challenges in their work to improve schools for all of our children. Their unwavering commitment to every child and every colleague in their schools are the inspiration for the content of this book. For decades, they have demonstrated what it means to advocate tirelessly for the kind of long-lasting improvement that gives children and families hope for a bright future, and we are proud to be part of that effort.

We dedicate this book to them.

Irene *Gay*

PART 1

Start **Strong**

Get a handle on your role

Do what's needed to succeed

Use the right words every time

Chapter 1

What Is Your Role—**Really?**

Let's talk about titles. Maybe yours is *coach*. Or maybe it's *professional learning leader*, *instructional coach,* or *literacy specialist*. Regardless of what you are called, your role is to support the continuous development of teacher expertise with the goal of better teaching and better outcomes for students. In this book, we use the term *coach* to mean a leader of professional learning in a school or district, but the title is hardly the point. It's how you embody the role that really matters.

Effective coaches position themselves as thinking partners, colleagues, advocates, problem solvers, and active participants in working with teachers to support a strong culture of continuous professional learning in the school. Effective coaches are collaborators, bringing together people who share common goals, interests, or problems of practice and putting them in touch with each other and with other sources of professional knowledge, such as current research on teaching and learning as well as professional magazines, organizations, and books. Although they have broad expertise to share, effective coaches make it clear that they do not think of themselves as "experts," but as thought partners who facilitate the continuous professional learning of their colleagues. They position themselves as learners who draw understandings from their observations of and interactions with colleagues.

If all that sounds like a lot, take heart. The coaching role *is* multidimensional, but after a while, you will see that the individual components work together to produce a kind of synergy. And little by little, you will begin to learn that your role is not to take on a set of discrete responsibilities, but to weave them together in a coherent way. When that happens, you will notice a change taking root in your school as it becomes a vibrant learning community.

Meaningful change happens when teachers are inspired by a clear sense of purpose and a collective commitment to excellence, when they willingly help one another solve problems and celebrate successes, and when they are offered compelling professional learning opportunities, including one-on-one coaching, that they trust will keep them working at the top of their game.

Meaningful improvement in teaching and learning doesn't happen overnight, however. It takes time, and it requires at least one person in the school to be an agent of positive change. If you are that person, the pages that follow will help you get a handle on your role.

The Multidimensional Role of Coach

The coaching role—and the amount of time allotted to it—varies greatly from school to school. Some schools are staffed with multiple coaches, each of whom concentrates on a different content area or a span of grade levels. In these cases, coaching tends to be a full-time role. In some districts, a single coach serves multiple schools. Others have school-embedded coaches who also teach students for a portion of the day. Some coaches have flexibility to provide coaching support across an entire school day, while others have only a few hours a day on a few days of the week. But the one thing all coaches have in common is the multidimensional aspect of their role.

Be Clear About Your Role

Be sure your job description doesn't imply that you are in any way an evaluator (unless you do have a role in evaluating teachers, in which case you need to be clear that you do). Use language that expresses your role as a thought partner and a collaborator in the school-wide pursuit of continuous professional learning.

Your impact as an instructional coach has the potential to reach deep into the heart of your school's community because of the multiple roles you play in supporting the various dimensions of professional learning within the school. Whether you are called *coach* or by another title, you know that you must juggle all the parts of your role, often within a single day.

Coaches typically fill multiple roles simultaneously. One of the most challenging and rewarding aspects of being a coach is balancing the range of responsibilities while serving different personalities, varying levels of experience, and diverse needs within a group of teachers. Though you have an official job description, and you might clearly communicate your role to your team, it is difficult to capture the element of coaching that we describe as "taking a coaching stance all day long." How do you capture the hundreds of brief, supportive interactions that you have with colleagues across a day, month, or year? The answer is you don't.

You are spontaneously supporting teacher learning all the time—when you have a conversation at lunch about a student's work, when you send a text about a book you know a class will love, when you write an email responding to a question, and when you have an impromptu conversation in the corridor about a problem of practice. For some coaches with limited time, these brief interactions comprise most of their coaching opportunities. Regardless of the amount of time you are given, you can make the most of even your briefest exchanges, so don't underestimate how small moments can have a big impact. When you make personal connections with teachers, take time to check in, and support them with small gestures, you make a difference in the way your colleagues perceive you as a member of the team. You inspire them, and they in turn inspire their students.

Regardless of the amount of time you are given, you can make the most of even your briefest exchanges, so **don't underestimate how small moments can have a big impact.**

Your Role Description

We trust you were provided with a general description of your role when you applied for the position. We recommend that you take the time to work with your supervisor (e.g., principal, district-level leader) to discuss and write a more detailed description that outlines clear expectations and the full scope of your responsibilities because the coaching role can vary quite a bit depending on the expectations of the school or district. It is helpful for you and your supervisor to have a common understanding of the details of this complex role.

This is important: without a written document that summarizes your role and responsibilities, you will have nothing to refer to if you are challenged by misunderstandings of how you are expected to support teacher learning in the school. Although urgent situations may arise that cause you to temporarily take time away from your role to do whatever needs to be done, in general, your job description should specify a high priority for working with teachers.

Take time at the beginning of every school year to clarify your role with your administrator even if you've been in that role for a long time. Reflect on what has worked well in the past and how you each see the role continuing in the future. Talk together about how much actual time you get to provide structured professional learning and coach teachers. The more work you put into clarifying your role for yourself and others, the more effective you will be in building trust and meaningful partnerships.

The more transparent you are about the many dimensions of your role with all members of the school community, the more successful you will be. When you revisit your role with your supervisor at the beginning of each new year, make any revisions you think are needed. Your goal in doing so is to maintain a current document that expresses, in clear language, the expectations of your role in supporting professional learning in your school. Figure 1–1 may be helpful in discussing the broad categories of your responsibilities. Some of these may apply in your school and others may not.

Your Attitude Toward Your Role

As an expression of your mindset and approach to working with others, your coaching stance conveys your attitudes about professional learning, collaboration, growth, problem-solving, self-reflection, and more. The way you see

THE MULTIDIMENSIONAL ROLE OF COACHES

Teacher of Students	Teaching children is critical to build literacy knowledge and skill and enables the coach to maintain credibility with colleagues.
Professional Learning Leader	The coach is responsible for designing collaborative, job-embedded, standards-based professional learning.
Instructional Coach	The coach works directly with teachers through modeling, co-teaching, and observing, and provides feedback for the purpose of improving instruction and promoting teacher knowledge, agency, and independence.
Partner with School Principal	The coach works closely with the principal to create a culture of continuous collaboration and teamwork to implement a coherent design for school improvement.
Coach on the Run	The coach provides teacher support all day through informal professional conversations, taking advantage of opportunities to interact with teachers in the nooks and crannies of the day.
Mentor for New Teachers	The coach orients new teachers to the building, the school team, the curriculum, and the assessment materials, and provides an overview of the professional learning opportunities.
Coordinator of Curriculum and Professional Resources	The coach is responsible for all aspects of coordinating the use of curriculum and assessment materials, the school's book room, other supplies for literacy teaching, and professional resources.
Data Coach	The coach oversees the administration, analysis, and interpretation of the school's assessments, including high-stakes literacy assessments, as well as assessments that inform instruction.
Curriculum and Instruction Specialist	The coach keeps up with the latest literacy research and standards, reads and shares professional books and articles, and attends professional learning opportunities for coaches and other school leaders, to assure the highest quality literacy instruction.
Learner	The coach models a learning stance by continually demonstrating curiosity and reflecting on all dimensions of the role.

Figure 1-1

yourself feeds directly into your stance, which is the way you form relationships with and present yourself to teachers, other coaches, students, and administrators. Your stance will also be reflected in the language you choose when you communicate with others.

As a coach, you help colleagues see where they are in their thinking, articulate where they want to be, and develop a plan to get there. When you consult with a teacher, your stance requires more listening than telling. It means bringing the individual into the interaction to make decisions and seek solutions. Each time individuals make a decision and analyze its impact, understanding expands—and that's what you want for the teachers you coach.

The coaching stance is not a rigid, single way of being. It is fluid, multifaceted, and responsive to each teacher's unique needs. In general, you can think of your coaching stance as a composite of multiple stances that you will move in and out of, often unconsciously, in response to what's called for in the moment.

Collaborative Stance

A collaborative coaching stance requires movement away from a top-down distribution of information and toward a collaborative learning relationship as shown in Figure 1-2. You thrive on being helpful and believe almost anything can be accomplished when you think and work together. Though the comparison is certainly not a rigid one, you can see how a collaborative stance honors co-constructing, co-planning, and valuing the voices of all professionals involved. Because your role as coach might appear to place you in a position of power, it is important to clarify from the beginning that teachers will be working *with* you, not for you. Of course, there will be times when a coach will model or demonstrate a lesson, focus on procedures, or provide information, but even those acts happen in a context that values collaborative thinking.

Coaching is about supporting your colleagues in being reflective. It is not about fixing people and behaviors, judging others, or telling teachers what to do. There is no right or wrong, just collaborative analysis of evidence that shows the impact. If the coach views coaching as fixing a situation, then the coaching becomes evaluative and judgmental. If teachers see the relationship in this way, they begin to ask the coach, "What am I doing wrong? Tell me whether I am doing this right." They put themselves in the position of individuals who need fixing instead of valuing their own experience and expertise, working collaboratively with the coach to reflect on the impact of their teaching,

FROM

Take Role of Expert

- Give information
- Tell what to do
- Focus on use of procedures
- Provide a model
- Provide evaluative feedback

→

TO

Think Together

- Set goals
- Seek information together
- Engage in reflection and analysis
- Share noticings and evidence of learning
- Pursue questions together
- Solve problems collaboratively
- Lead by example
- Learn from others
- Take role of learner

Figure 1-2

and finding solutions to what they see as problems. A collegial coaching stance conveys the view that teachers are lifelong learners who are capable of expanding their expertise with a little guidance and support.

It may be helpful to think of your coaching stance as an umbrella over all you do as a coach and leader of professional learning. Your stance reflects a spirit of genuine collaboration.

A collegial coaching stance conveys the view that **teachers are lifelong learners** who are capable of expanding their expertise with a little guidance and support.

Reflective Stance

A reflective stance conveys a focus on genuine inquiry and exploration that leads to new understandings. Conclusions are tentative and subject to testing. You show genuine curiosity and engage in wondering to learn more. This means your statements are not absolute and are adjusted continually as you discover new evidence. You are critical while reading research. Is it sound or based mostly on opinion? Such a stance can serve as a model for teachers as they observe children engaged in new learning and form tentative hypotheses that are tested by the actual behaviors of the students. When you enter a coaching experience or observe children without a preconceived idea of what will happen and how you will respond, you are more open to being surprised by the learner. As a coach with a reflective stance, you collect data and information that influences your response instead of forcing the data to fit into an established, rigid view of the situation. This stance allows you to be flexible, tentative, and responsive to your colleagues.

Your reflective stance extends to the way you read professional resources and learn new information. Keep an open and wondering approach so that you can critically evaluate the information and decide whether or how it applies to your situation.

Inclusive Stance

When you take an inclusive stance, you show that you value teachers and students for their unique identities inclusive of their cultural backgrounds, languages, diverse experiences, and perspectives. This stance also means you actively coach teachers to embrace culturally responsive practices that provide access to high-quality education for *all* children. Aguilar (2020, 6) explains that "educational equity means that

Coaching for Equity and Inclusion

Canaday (2023, 192) describes inclusive coaching by saying, "The coaching relationship provides a perfect platform for two people with diverse backgrounds to connect on a meaningful level and invest the time to understand their different or even opposing viewpoints." She goes on to explain that "developing an ongoing relationship with someone whose background and life experiences look nothing like yours can expand your worldview . . . and may also allow you to uncover any unconscious areas of bias and begin working to eliminate those."

every child is seen for who they truly are, and their unique interests and gifts are surfaced and cultivated." Apply this asset-based mindset to your work with both teachers and students. An inclusive stance encourages teachers to reflect on their own biases and beliefs and to work collaboratively to identify and interrupt policies and practices within the school that contribute (even unintentionally) to inequities for particular groups of students.

When you draw on an inclusive stance, you show that you understand that social and emotional learning are essential in providing educational equity. When you coach with this stance, you help everyone in the school community approach teaching and learning with empathy and a focus on relationship building. You get to know and value the teachers in all their uniqueness, the teachers build strong bonds with students and their families, and the students develop meaningful and respectful relationships with one another.

Responsive Stance

A responsive stance reflects your desire to meet teachers where they are and support them by building on their unique experiences, expertise, and knowledge. With a responsive stance, you continually adjust your feedback to fit the responses you observe. When you take the stance that all teachers can learn, your responses show a belief in their professional capacity. This stance builds trust because you listen and respond genuinely to the teachers you coach. It also shows your interest in getting to know the people you coach. You value who they are inside and outside the classroom and respond to them as individuals with their own unique identities.

Whenever you interact with teachers in whatever context you find yourself, remember that your stance as a coach reflects the way you see yourself and how others see you. It is important that every interaction conveys "learning together" as you position yourself as a thought partner and draw individuals into the conversation. Later in this book, we describe and offer examples of language that can help you communicate your stance to others.

Up **Next**

You can't be successful in your role unless you have the right supports. In Chapter 2, you'll learn how to help individual educators in your school become a team, develop the team's vision for literacy teaching and learning, build a school-wide culture of collaboration, and form sustaining relationships with teachers, your principal, and other coaches.

Chapter 2

What You Need to **Succeed**

If you are a full-time coach and leader of professional learning, you probably spend upward of 1,000 hours in your school each year (not to mention the time spent preparing and problem-solving outside of school). Multiply that by the number of years you've been working with students and teachers, and you will quickly see that your job consumes a big chunk of your life. No doubt you want every one of those hours to count—to be satisfying to you and your colleagues because you are making a positive difference in the culture of the school and the expertise of its teachers.

This chapter will help you work productively in your role by laying a foundation for success. That means crafting the conditions for success: establishing a shared vision for literacy teaching and learning, building a culture of collaboration, and developing strong, affirming relationships with your principal, with teachers, and with other coaches.

Help the Group Become a Team

A group may form for reasons as random as having the same ZIP code or riding the same subway line to work each day. But a team? That's something different. When you join a team, you implicitly agree to support common values and beliefs, to help others thrive so the team will excel, and to do what is needed to achieve stated goals. On a team, everyone wants the same outcomes and everyone is pulling in the same direction. All schools consist of a group of educators working in the same building. Your job is to help that group become a team.

This important process will better enable educators to achieve coherence in curriculum goals and instructional practices so students and teachers can benefit from the collective efficacy that drives long-lasting change and transforms the school culture. When you foster teamwork, you begin to notice an important

All schools consist of a group of educators working in the same building. Your job is to help that group **become a team.**

language shift by the teachers—away from "my" students and "my" scores to "our" students and "our" scores. Additionally, team members come to realize that they are smarter together. As members of a team, the teachers in your school not only make the commitment to their own professional growth but also value and enjoy contributing to the learning of their peers.

Develop the Team's Vision for Literacy Teaching and Learning

When you have a common vision to guide your decisions, then all the different ways you interact with teachers will have a greater sense of purpose and cohesion because everyone wants the same outcomes for the students and each other. We recommend that, early in the year, you and your school principal bring together the classroom teachers and specialists in the building to revisit and amend their shared vision for literacy teaching and learning. In the following text, we briefly describe a process we have used for creating a shared vision in schools across the country. We invite you to use it in your own school. To guide the process, download Resource Tool: Authentic Literacy Classroom (available as **OR 2.1** in the Online Resources).

ONLINE RESOURCE 2.1

RESOURCE TOOL

AUTHENTIC LITERACY CLASSROOM		
WHAT DO YOU SEE AND HEAR THE CHILDREN DOING?	**WHAT MATERIALS ARE NEEDED IN THE CLASSROOM?**	**WHAT WILL TEACHERS NEED TO TEACH THIS WAY?**
▪ listening to books and poems the teacher is reading aloud ▪ sitting in comfortable places to enjoy their independent reading ▪ reading and talking about books in a small group with the teacher ▪ recommending books to each other ▪ choosing books from a classroom library ▪ talking with each other about their books and their unique perspectives (in pairs, in small groups, and as a whole group) ▪ sharing their thinking about texts through drawing, writing, performance ▪ keeping a record of books they have read and a list of books they want to read in their reader's notebook ▪ participating in explicit, systematic, and structured phonics/word study lessons using a variety of manipulatives ▪ applying phonics/word study principles in reading and writing ▪ playing games with letters, sounds, and word parts ▪ listening to books individually at a listening center ▪ reading enlarged-print books, poems, and songs with the support of the teacher ▪ reading print and digital texts ▪ writing for a variety of real purposes and audiences ▪ writing in a variety of genres or forms ▪ writing in a reader's notebook to express their thinking about books ▪ collecting their writing ideas in writer's notebooks ▪ making sketches in their writer's notebooks ▪ creating multimodal presentations ▪ using printed and digital research tools to learn about a topic	▪ beautiful picture books for reading aloud ▪ multiple copies of books for book clubs ▪ multiple copies of leveled books for small-group reading ▪ some decodable books for skills practice as needed ▪ enlarged-print versions of books, poems, and songs for shared reading ▪ hundreds of books in the classroom for the children to choose from, arranged by titles, genres, authors, and topics ▪ baskets or tubs for a classroom library ▪ high-quality books and other media that represent a variety of people ▪ personal book boxes for each student ▪ devices for collaboration, research, reading, writing, creating, and presenting ▪ a reader's notebook and a writer's notebook for each child ▪ two easels; unlined chart paper ▪ pocket charts ▪ individual whiteboards and dry-erase markers for each child ▪ pocket folders to organize and store word study activities ▪ letters in a variety of textures, styles, and sizes ▪ variety of manipulatives for phonics learning ▪ sticky notes ▪ long, thin pointers for shared reading ▪ magnetic letters and word cards ▪ various writing tools ▪ variety of paper for writing ▪ pocket folders to collect and organize pieces of writing ▪ markers, pens, art paper ▪ bookmaking materials ▪ rug for meeting area ▪ comfortable seating for meeting area ▪ tables that can be arranged flexibly ▪ movable seating (e.g., chairs on wheels)	▪ a written document that clearly articulates the literacy competencies that children need to be successful (curriculum goals) ▪ a strong understanding of the research on language and literacy development (including phonological awareness) and its implications for instruction ▪ a clearly articulated vision of every student's literacy learning opportunities ▪ a collaborative culture that supports risk-taking and continuous improvement ▪ professional books and resources ▪ many professional learning opportunities: workshops, institutes, seminars ▪ opportunities to observe each other teach and reflect with each other ▪ opportunities to work with a literacy coach or teacher leader ▪ time to plan and reflect together ▪ assessments that measure students' authentic reading and writing ▪ collegial partnerships with school leaders ▪ expertise for making instructional decisions that are responsive to students' needs ▪ tools for reflecting on teaching ▪ time to collaborate

Your Literacy Coaching Playbook **Online Resource 2.1 | Resource Tool:** Authentic Literacy Classroom **Version 01**

Figure 2-1

Process for Developing a Shared Vision

The questions below correspond to the three columns in Figure 2-1. Create a three-column chart that everyone can see, so on chart paper, an interactive white-board, or a computer. Title your chart *Ideal Literacy Classroom.* As the team begins to call out answers for each category, enter each one in the appropriate column. Wait to move on to the next column until you have finished filling out the column you are working in.

- **Column 1:** *In an ideal classroom, what would children be doing during literacy time? What would this look and sound like?*
  - List concrete, observable evidence of what team members most want to see and hear children doing in an ideal literacy classroom. Ask the team what they notice about the descriptors. Are there any that feel at odds with the team's collective vision?
- **Column 2:** *What books, resources, and materials would teachers need to make this vision a reality in their classrooms?*
  - Ask the team to imagine the school has an unlimited budget to purchase all the materials needed for this ideal classroom. What materials are needed for systematic phonics and word study? What resources will help students build their knowledge of the world? What books are needed for whole-group, small-group, and individual reading instruction? What writing supplies and tools are essential? What furniture and technology are needed?
- **Column 3:** *What professional learning will teachers need to teach this way?*
  - At this point in the process, change the name of the chart from *Ideal Literacy Classroom* to *Authentic Literacy Classroom* as you have likely described students engaged in real reading, real writing, and real learning.
  - Ask the team to imagine stepping into the authentic literacy classroom and picture what they will need from their professional learning experiences to be able to teach this way and for students to engage in authentic learning and achieve excellent outcomes.

Our experience indicates that this exercise will help you and your colleagues gain insight into what you truly value as a team. This shared vision will serve as a foundation for your discussions related to common values, beliefs, and goals for your team. To move from this shared vision to an articulated set of set of core values that guide your work, we encourage you to take the next step in your leadership and refer you to a detailed protocol for developing core values with your team (see sidebar).

Getting from Your Team's Vision to a Set of Common Values

Using the brainstormed ideas generated for the authentic literacy classroom as a foundation, engage your team in a process of articulating the few essential values and beliefs they hold for the students and for themselves as members of a team of educators. The set of common values will guide decision-making around instruction, materials, assessment, and professional learning. We offer you a step-by-step protocol to create the set of core values in *Leading for Literacy* (Fountas and Pinnell 2022, 30). The time you spend working collaboratively for coherence and excellence will have a long-term impact on the outcomes in your school.

Build a Culture of Collaboration

In a positive school culture, educators believe in themselves, their team, and every student. They not only value and promote the identities and perspectives of all the children they serve but also of one another. Diverse voices are welcomed, actively invited, and sought out. When all members in a community feel valued and trusted, everyone is all in, and people are more willing to put in the hard work of problem-solving together and raising expectations for continued school improvement.

Teacher learning is facilitated when the school in which they work is a "learning place" (Fullan and St. Germain 2006). By that, we mean a school where students, teachers, coaches, and administrators are learning all the time, every day. If you want your school to be a learning place, or just a better version of the learning place it already is, be advised that radical transformation in your school culture or even small improvements in collaborative learning can take time. But the payoff is well worth the effort, because in learning places, the following statements are true:

- People are willing to share with trusted colleagues their successes as well as their difficulties.
- Conversations about everyday topics and professional topics flow through the day.
- People expect to and take delight in learning something new.
- Learning is shared across the school.
- The school community sets goals for their professional learning every year and actively seeks the resources needed to boost their expertise.
- Nobody is afraid to identify a problem and work with colleagues to solve it.
- Everyone welcomes coaching (including the coach!) and the opportunity to have another person's eyes on their teaching.
- Everyone seeks out opportunities to expand their expertise through a variety of professional learning opportunities.
- Individuals take responsibility for their own learning and for helping others.

As a coach, you can promote this positive school culture by setting up situations in which colleagues have opportunities to learn alongside and from one another. Though you might be the only person in the school with the title of coach, you'll also want to encourage capable colleagues to take on leadership roles. For example, you might ask a colleague to lead a professional book club or work with you to design a professional learning session. Because when everyone believes that each person has something to offer, and people believe they have more to learn, collaboration is inevitable. Educators are then more willing to open their doors and share with one another. If everyone is invited to share expertise and everyone also invites feedback (again, including the coach), the playing field is leveled, and trust develops genuinely. Singh (2024) writes, "A culture which reflects that everyone deserves a coach because everyone deserves to grow, transform, and support the positive impact of student achievement is an imperative message that must be made loud and clear in order to help make shifts in teacher practice."

Don't Take Trust for Granted

Galinsky and Schweitzer (2015, 197) warn that trust should not be taken for granted. "In an age where it's all too easy to get lured into a sense of false intimacy created through social media and email, real trust can be a rare commodity." The pair go on to point out that people who inspire the most trust possess two important traits–warmth and competence.

We offer these principles for building trust:

- Always keep your word.
- Follow through on your promises, but don't over-promise.
- Don't share confidential information.
- Always be respectful.
- Assume positive intentions.
- Have difficult conversations in person, not by email or on the phone.

Strengthen or Build Relationships

Even if the culture in your school is highly collaborative, you'll still need to nurture relationships that can influence your thinking about teaching and learning and strengthen the learning outcomes of the adult learners in the building.

Coach-Teacher Relationships

Fostering a culture of collaboration built on trust begins with the way you interact and talk with your colleagues. If you communicate and work as a true partner, you can be another set of eyes and ears in the classroom and someone who promotes confidence, risk-taking, agency, and the pursuit of continuous learning. To make this partnership work, it is essential that you develop trusting relationships with your colleagues. Singh (2024) also writes, "When coaching is utilized in its truest form, the coach works to develop a plan with the teacher based on student and teacher needs and engages in a cycle of goal setting, inquiry, and improvement which is grounded in partnership and trust. Teachers will resist when coaching is done 'to them' versus it being done 'for them.'" Teachers need to see coaches as nonevaluative and as a support in reaching their own professional goals.

Both the coach and the teacher need to work at developing the coaching relationship. When teachers and coaches work side by side, they are truly partners working to make positive changes for students. They aren't afraid to take risks together and learn from one another because it is a learning experience, not a test of whether the teacher is implementing the coach's ideas. Teachers should never feel like they have to put on a show for you. One coach we know tells her teachers, "Bring me your messiest; let's work through it together. I won't necessarily have answers, but two heads together will be better than one." It is in the "messy situations" that real collaboration and real change happen.

You and the teacher need to trust each other to be vulnerable to work on real issues together. To develop this trust, the teacher-coach partnership needs to be nurtured. Trust requires face-to-face discussions and demands that each party offers feedback on how the coaching experiences are going. Establish from the beginning that you want to hear feedback, and then provide opportunities for it. You can also nurture this partnership by proactively thinking of ways to support teachers outside of professional learning situations (Figure 2–2).

Ways to Nurture the Coach-Teacher Relationship

- Send encouraging emails and texts or leave short messages on sticky notes.
- Share a book or an article with an individual teacher who could benefit from reading about a topic that you know is of interest.
- Recognize small things that took a lot of work in the classroom by asking permission to share the work with colleagues. Take a quick photo on your phone and send it around by email or text.
- Invite teachers to attend a conference or workshop with you even if it can be only one teacher a year.
- Engage in conversation as you travel to workshops, eat meals together, attend social events, etc.

Figure 2-2

Coach-Principal Relationship

Your relationship with your principal is another collaborative partnership that supports effective coaching. A successful partnership is built on a clear foundation of each other's values, beliefs, and goals and on an understanding of your respective roles. In schools where coaching is effective, the coach and principal work together to create a culture that supports enthusiasm for professional learning opportunities. Much of the preparation to create and support that culture will be done in one-on-one meetings (Figure 2-3). You and your principal should help each other understand school-wide conditions that affect teachers and address problems and progress. The administrator must set the tone by emphasizing that every professional has more to learn and that everyone in the school (including the principal and the coach) will be coached in some capacity. Coaches are then left to concentrate on supporting the teachers and are removed from setting expectations for teacher participation.

Following are some other things you can do to ensure that the relationship you have with your principal is positive and productive.

Invite the principal to watch you work. This one packs a one-two punch—first, by visibly showing that everyone in the school will be observed and coached, including you; second, by giving your principal the chance to better appreciate your skills and the impact of your work with teachers.

Invite the principal to attend professional learning sessions. Nothing says "everybody is a learner" better than the sight of the school's leader engaging in a learning opportunity along with everyone else.

Share the self-reflection tools from Chapter 26. Identify a section you are working on, and ask your principal to observe you and discuss their observations.

HOW TO HAVE PRODUCTIVE MEETINGS WITH YOUR PRINCIPAL

Try to schedule short, efficient meetings (thirty to forty minutes) every two weeks or at least monthly to establish continuous coach-principal communication and collaboration around your professional-learning goals. Here's how to make sure the meetings go well.

Prepare an agenda with teacher input.

Being organized for the important issues you'll discuss at these meetings promotes productive collaboration.

Discuss important issues such as:

- updates on progress toward learning goals,
- plans for future professional learning,
- priorities the teachers are working on,
- trends in the data,
- resources needed, and
- policies that need revisiting.

Send a summary containing specific action items.

Maintain confidentiality.

- Provide updates on the kinds of work teachers are doing.
- Never name teachers without their express permission.

Figure 2-3

Check in to discuss needs for coverage in classrooms during out-of-classroom learning sessions for teachers. Try to provide your principal with a long-range view of the plans you've made for professional learning experiences that will require classroom coverage. It would be great if your schedule could always be the same—but things do happen. If you find yourself needing to cancel a session and reschedule, make sure the principal is aware so you can get some help with adjusting schedules.

Don't be afraid to ask for resources. Your principal may have a budget line for professional resources—books, journals, online subscriptions, and the like—but you may not know that unless you ask. Advocate for even a small amount of funds to support the purchase of professional resources. A library of current professional books is always helpful. There may be one book each year that every teacher should read or discuss in a professional book club (see Chapter 17).

Encourage the principal to be on the lookout for professional opportunities for teachers. There may be district meetings a few teachers could attend or school-wide projects that would foster collaboration. There may be opportunities for teachers to observe in other schools or to make presentations at local, state, or national educational conferences. We don't want teachers to be out of the classroom for more than a few days a year, but occasional opportunities like those we've described here can help develop the leadership potential of your colleagues.

Clarify with the principal your understanding of confidentiality. As you partner with your principal, be sure to politely but firmly maintain your commitment to teacher confidentiality so your colleagues can trust that you will not discuss their teaching with others. Think about language that might make your point clear if you find yourself in a situation that calls for you to restate the importance of your trusting relationships with the colleagues you coach (Figure 2-4).

YOU MAY BE ASKED	YOU MIGHT RESPOND
How are the fourth grade teachers dealing with behavior management?	*We have been working on time and behavior management in our professional learning sessions and in coaching sessions. You might want to observe in those classrooms and ask the teachers how that is going.*
Has Teacher X started to pull together small groups of children for differentiated instruction?	*As you know, I am not comfortable talking about a specific teacher, so if you have a question I suggest you ask the teacher directly.*

Figure 2-4

This value also applies to positive statements about a teacher. When you say Teacher X is doing really well in using a writers' workshop structure, you are talking about a teacher's performance and compromising confidentiality.

Stick to communicating the names of the teachers you are currently coaching and the content the team is working on. Your ability to communicate gracefully and clearly with your principal and teacher colleagues will provide a strong foundation for creating a positive learning culture resulting in long-term improvement in teacher expertise and student outcomes.

Coach–Coach Relationships

It takes time to build a network of other coaches with whom you can connect when you're feeling the need for support, but it is worth the effort. After all, who better to give expert advice, offer a different perspective, or celebrate your triumphs than another coach? Let's face it: coaching can be isolating. But if you take the time to build even a very small network of coaching colleagues within your school, district, or region, you will always have someone to call when you might benefit from another voice. Not only that, but a network of coaches can be a source of professional growth, effective instructional practices, shared resources, and friendship.

We urge you to find a partnership or a larger group that will nurture and sustain you as a coach. If there are no coaches to work with in your own school or district, seek other ways to connect with people who do what you do. Building a network of coaching colleagues is one of the best ways to keep growing as a coach.

Ways to Connect with Other Instructional Coaches

- Reach out to coaches in your district, even if they work in a different grade-level band.
- Look for virtual coaching networks. Many blogs and professional organizations host professional learning opportunities for coaches.
- If you are the only coach in your district, reach out to coaches in other local districts:
  - Offer to host monthly or quarterly meetings.
  - Read and discuss professional books and articles together.
  - Share ideas based on a topic or theme.
  - Share information from conferences or workshops you've each attended.
  - Try to attend conferences or professional learning sessions together.

Up **Next**

Chapter 3 provides essential information that will add to the knowledge base you already bring to your interactions with colleagues. We'll discuss the difference between professional development and professional learning; how adults learn best; coaching for equity; what every coach must know about curriculum, instruction, and assessment; and why it's important to celebrate success.

Chapter 3

What to **Know**

Effective coaches continually reflect on their craft, use data to inform their practices, and keep current with the latest research on teaching and learning as part of their continuous growth. Most important, they recognize that there is always room to improve and always more to know about literacy instruction and teacher development.

On the following pages we briefly describe areas of essential information that will help you build on or expand the knowledge base you bring to your professional conversations.

Call It "Professional Learning"

Why is the term *professional development* gradually being replaced by *professional learning*? Hicks and Sailors (2018) explain that the change in language signals a shift in stance from top-down, expert-delivered formats to more authentic and personal experiences that engage teachers' thinking and view of themselves as professionals. Figure 3–1 summarizes how the two terms can be interpreted.

Notice that unlike traditional professional development, today's concept of professional learning (described in the second column of the chart) puts teachers at the center of their own learning and emphasizes collaboration and variety in the ways teachers are treated as capable learners. Learning experiences are designed to engage the team in authentic, relevant inquiry and develop a sense of agency in teachers' growth as professionals.

We strongly advocate for the kind of curriculum-embedded learning that is described as professional learning because of the promise it holds for the sustainability of continuous improvement in schools and because we have seen schools come alive when teachers, coaches, and school leaders see their learning as relevant and work together in this way.

Professional Development	Professional Learning
▪ Content usually comes from "the top" ▪ Little or no say in topics on the part of teachers ▪ Teachers are seen as receivers of knowledge ▪ Usually performed by "experts" ▪ Uses traditional formats (workshops, lectures, webinars) ▪ Sessions often disconnected from each other and from the classroom ▪ Often presented as "one shot" ▪ Little attention to implementation with regard to fidelity ▪ Seldom includes concrete follow-up ▪ Often based on someone else's judgment of what teachers need ▪ Often focused on sets of instructional materials	▪ Content comes from the top *and* from teachers ▪ Considers teachers as active, competent, adult learners who construct their understandings ▪ Uses multiple formats and learning structures (e.g., learning walks, lesson study, data meetings, peer coaching, and workshops) ▪ Is embedded in high-quality curriculum, focusing on the integrity of implementation of high-quality instructional materials ▪ Is interactive because teachers learn from each other as well as from the facilitator ▪ Engages teachers in collaborative inquiry using evidence of student learning ▪ Is process-based, recognizing change is gradual and difficult ▪ Focuses on the importance of professional decision-making and reflection with explicit links to student outcomes ▪ Always includes follow-up and reflection of growth over time ▪ Builds knowledge of both curriculum content and instructional practices ▪ Is built on current language and literacy research and its implications for teaching and learning

Figure 3-1

Adult Learners

If you are a newly minted coach, aka professional learning leader, you may struggle with the transition from teaching children to teaching adults (although it will serve you well if you continue to teach children as part of your day or week). All human learners share common characteristics, but teaching adults is far more complex. As Knowles, Holton, Swanson, and Robinson (2020) acknowledge, adult learners need a form of adult education.

Most adults have a far greater ability to sustain effort even when the learning is frustrating. They are willing to perform some tasks they think are tedious or very challenging in the pursuit of new knowledge, skills, information, or personal achievement. Adults who fit this description have a repository of childhood experiences telling them that learning pays off and also provides satisfaction. The following understandings describe adult learning and methods that will better ensure that adults in your school will have positive and productive opportunities to learn and grow.

Coaches Need Coaching Too

Like all teachers, coaches need the support of professional learning. They need to go further in their understanding of literacy learning but also understand adult learning and approaches to coaching. Too often, coaches are appointed, rather than developed. There is an assumption that just being a good teacher is enough qualification to be a coach. But that is simply not true. Even highly expert literacy teachers of children may find coaching adults more challenging, and some may even experience a feeling of failure in the role. Don't let these feelings fester; instead, talk with your principal or another trusted colleague about getting some guidance and support.

- **Adults have accumulated a large amount of life experience and teaching experience, sometimes leading them to hold strong opinions and beliefs.** They bring all that into their professional learning, and they need to know that their knowledge and views are respected. They usually respond well to a collegial approach that respects their experiences while also offering new insights.
- **Adults may have experienced a variety of positive and negative outcomes from certain instructional approaches and curriculum materials.** For some, the same may be true of their previous experiences with professional learning sessions and coaching. New and veteran teachers alike may be either eager for professional learning or apprehensive because they are worried about being evaluated.
- **Adult learners respond well to professional learning they find relevant and that meets their perceived needs.** They need to understand the "why" in the professional learning opportunities in which they will be expected to engage.
- **Adults construct their own learning.** Most adult learners actively construct their knowledge, bringing their unique experiences and understandings to the process. They develop their understandings from the inside, rather than being told. In this way, they use prior knowledge as the foundation upon which to build new learning.
- **Adults can expand their capabilities with assistance from others.** With the support of a skilled teacher, children can stretch themselves to create new understandings beyond what they could achieve independently. Adults are no different; they benefit from the advice and support of colleagues who may be more experienced or skilled in certain areas of practice.
- **Adults learn through social interactions.** Collaborative inquiry for students and for adults requires an environment that promotes social interaction. When people work alongside and collaboratively with other people, learning is easier. And when professional learning takes place in a supportive social context, adults feel more comfortable asking for and giving help, and they can build their own understandings on the ideas of other teachers.
- **Adults learn when they are actively engaged.** Some forms of professional development require teachers to be passive recipients of knowledge that is delivered to them by an expert other. But teachers, like all learners, need to engage directly in the practices they are learning as well as opportunities to participate in small- and large-group activities involving analysis, writing, talking, role-playing, and problem-solving.
- **Adults learn in emotionally supportive and culturally responsive environments.** All learners need an emotionally supportive learning environment that enables them to take risks, admit what they don't know and share what they do, ask questions, and make personal connections with their colleagues. An emotionally supportive environment for adult learners is comfortable, free of distractions, uncluttered, and arranged in a manner that is conducive to conversation and collaboration. And like the children they serve, adult learners

need to know that their diverse backgrounds and lived experiences are honored and supported.

- **Adults are willing to reflect on their learning.** Examining one's own learning can be risky. Providing learners with the time, opportunity, and encouragement to look back on what they are learning and reflect on how it can be helpful to them in classroom practice builds confidence and sheds light on future goals.

Curriculum, Instruction, and Assessment

At the top of your list of things to know as a literacy coach is a deep understanding of your school's literacy curriculum, instructional practices, and assessment system. Here's what you need to know about this powerful triad.

What to Know About the Literacy Curriculum

- **Alignment to State and National Standards:** You'll need to be very familiar with your state's academic standards as well as any other standards that are used in your school and how your school's current literacy curriculum aligns to them. And, because assessments—especially standardized assessments—are designed to test how well students are meeting grade-level expectations, you'll need to have a good grasp of those expectations in the areas of reading, writing, speaking, and listening. You will need to stay abreast of new standards as they are published.
- **Content Knowledge:** To be current on evidence-based research related to literacy, you need to have a thorough understanding of the essential components of literacy (oral language development, phoneme awareness, phonics, fluency, vocabulary, comprehension, writing, engagement, and motivation) as well as the content of literacy curriculum materials, including the texts students will read and the genres they will explore.

Be an Eye on Equity

Equity does not mean equality. In essence, while equality aims for treating everyone the same way, equity strives for fairness and justice by giving every student what they need to succeed academically and in life. As a literacy coach who regularly observes classroom teaching and learning, you are in a unique position to see the positive effects of equity in action—as well as areas in which equity is lacking or improvement is needed. Here are just some of the ways you can keep an eye on equity for your school and its students:

- Do some identity work to unpack potential biases and become more aware of them.
- Collaborate with teachers to select curriculum materials so students, in all of their diversity, see themselves represented.
- Work with other school leaders to raise awareness of unconscious bias and systemic barriers that affect groups of students in the school.
- Support teachers in differentiating instruction.
- When observing in classrooms, notice where children are seated, who gets the most attention from the teacher, who gets called on the most, and other observations that might indicate unconscious bias.
- Use data and other forms of evidence to help teachers identify achievement gaps and suggest appropriate interventions. Teachers should never predict achievement by membership in any group.
- Provide teachers with professional learning opportunities about culturally responsive teaching practices for diverse learners.

- **Differentiated Instruction:** As a literacy coach, you should have a strong understanding of how the curriculum can be adapted to meet students' diverse needs, including those of multilingual learners, students with learning or physical disabilities, neurodivergent thinkers, and children who are working above grade level. You also should be experienced in selecting or adapting curriculum to meet the standards of a culturally relevant curriculum.

What to Know About Evidence-Based Literacy Instruction

- **Understanding of Literacy as a Complex Process:** You need to develop a strong understanding of behaviors that show evidence of students' strengths and needs in literacy processing, the demands of different types of texts on readers, and the characteristics of effective writing. Your deep knowledge of how the sounds of language map onto the letters of the language is essential in supporting teachers' understanding of phonics and word study across the grades. And your deep knowledge of literacy processing will ground all professional learning in teachers' understanding of reading and writing development and how their teaching decisions influence learning.
- **Instructional Approaches:** Stay abreast of research-based instructional approaches so you can help teachers learn and apply them with students. While tried and true approaches, such as direct instruction, project-based instruction, inquiry-based learning, and cooperative learning, are still quite useful, the research base is always evolving. You should also be well versed in emerging technologies like artificial intelligence (AI) so you can respond knowledgably to teachers' ideas about integrating technology in their instructional plans.
- **Intervention Practices:** Be sure you know how to help teachers implement frameworks for Multi-Tiered Systems of Support centered on equity, early intervention, and social-emotional supports for students who are struggling with reading and writing.
- **Technology:** Technology capabilities change by the day and have many implications for literacy and learning. Many teachers working in schools today are digital natives, who grew up using technology in their daily lives. These teachers are likely familiar with digital tools and resources such as software, apps, and online platforms for teaching reading and writing. If using technology doesn't come easily to you, it might be a good idea to take an online course or read up on emerging technologies and their implications. You might need to consult with your district technology specialist to support teacher learning related to literacy implications.
- **Professional Learning:** As a leader of professional learning in your school, you need to understand standards for professional learning and how to provide ongoing, job-embedded,

Using AI

Although there are legitimate concerns about its ethical use, how to provide adequate training for teachers, and what the ideal balance of human and machine interaction looks like, AI can have a powerful impactful on student learning if used in the right ways for the right reasons.

As a literacy coach you have an obligation to understand both the risks and the payoffs of integrating AI with the instruction in your school. Educators are already engaging with this powerful tool to

- support personalized learning and differentiated instruction,
- provide instant feedback on students' writing,
- introduce students to interactive and engaging content and modes of learning with technology,
- save time, and
- receive more detailed data on student progress.

content-based professional learning opportunities for teachers. You also need to know how to model effective instructional practices and how to provide guidance and feedback that can expand the expertise of all teachers.

What to Know About Assessment

- **Diagnostic Assessments:** These assessments are designed to identify students' literacy strengths and needs, which can inform instruction. You should understand how to administer and interpret a variety of diagnostic assessments—reading, writing, phonics and word study, language competency—so you can help teachers learn how to use them efficiently and use the information to tailor their teaching decisions.
- **Progress Monitoring:** It's important for you to be very familiar with the techniques and tools for monitoring students' learning progress over time, including students who are receiving intervention services.
- **Formative and Summative Assessments:** Be sure you understand the differences between and the application of formative assessments (ongoing, informal checks on student learning) and summative assessments (end-of-year or end-of-unit evaluations).
- **Standardized Tests:** Standardized tests are currently required of all public-school students in state and local jurisdictions. These externally validated measures of achievement help schools rate the progress of their students compared with other students locally and nationally. Although imperfect in some ways, standardized tests do hold schools accountable for improving student outcomes. As literacy coach, you need to know how to prepare both students and teachers for these assessments, though not at the expense of broader literacy teaching.
- **Data Monitoring Tools:** These tools include detailed records of oral reading, observation notes, data walls, and various software programs. We have helped schools implement the use of data walls and find them to be very effective in analyzing individual and group data for needs, strengths, and patterns among students (see Chapter 19). They are especially helpful in identifying achievement disparities among particular groups of students and determining what actions are required to ensure that all children are academically successful. As a literacy coach, you'll want to share trends in data regularly with administrators, grade-level teams, and individual teachers, though not at the expense of broader learning, deeper understanding, and professional application.

Hard or Soft Data?

The answer is "both." Hard data is quantitative and measurable, while soft data is more subjective but can reveal qualitative insights about students' reading and writing that hard data doesn't capture. When you look at both hard and soft data, you get a fuller picture of student progress.

Celebrate Successes Large and Small

Your school team brings many strengths. Early career teachers bring fresh new thinking, blossoming energy and positivity, and familiarity with cutting-edge research. Your experienced colleagues bring energy, commitment, and extremely valuable insights from their wealth of experience with a diverse population of students. Think of the assets each team member brings, and don't lose sight of the need to recognize and celebrate them. Success breeds renewal, and your continuous attention to the positives will go a long way toward keeping the staff learning and working collaboratively. When you believe in every member of the team, you can support all of them to become the best version of themselves.

Look for opportunities to celebrate teachers (and, of course, students and their families). Create a culture of celebration, bringing colleagues together for a quick get-together (with a few refreshments) around milestones, such as birthdays, or special accomplishments. Send thoughtful notes when there is something to celebrate, and perform random acts of kindness when a genuine opportunity arises. If you think about your colleagues as people first and then as professionals, you will foster positive relationships.

Up **Next**

You won't want to miss Chapter 4, which contains an extensive role-play of one coach's annual start-up meeting. It's chock-full of helpful language you can pick right up and use in your own first coaching conversations of the year.

Chapter 4

Your **First Coaching Conversation** of the Year

At the beginning of the school year, pull together your colleagues to talk through the broad dimensions of your role and the many ways you will interact with them to support their professional growth and their work with children. In your meeting, keep the focus on your work as a team and describe your understanding of how you will work together on professional learning across the year in many different contexts. Be sure to allow enough time for questions at the end. This will leave no room for misunderstanding or lack of clarity later on. Taking this informative stance each year will contribute to school improvement, support your common goals, and foster the kind of teamwork you need to be a school that educates all of the children.

Depending on the situation in your school, your colleagues may be more or less familiar with the scope of your role. Those who have already worked with you as a coach might benefit from a refresh to start the year on a positive note. But if you are the first coach in the school, it's likely there will be much curiosity about your role. First, we offer some actions you can take to help everyone feel comfortable with the school's professional learning goals right from the start. Then we will share an example of a role-play that shows how one coach introduced herself to the school team, clarified her role, and thoughtfully responded to teachers' questions.

Do a Morning Walk-About

The time when teachers are working in the building to ready their classrooms, before the official school year has begun, is a great time to personally welcome each of your colleagues. Introduce yourself to new team members, greet

Stream the Video

Show short clips from a video of an individual coaching session with a teacher you have coached in the past. Hearing and seeing what a coaching session sounds like and looks like establishes the tone for what the coaching relationship can be. Knowing what to expect reduces teacher anxiety and helps teachers get a better understanding of your role as their thought partner.

Circle Time Tips

- Teachers and leaders sit shoulder to shoulder with no empty chairs or breaks in the circle.
- All participants are focused on one another. No one is tempted to slip off task to look through materials or check email or texts.
- Participants can see and hear each other to communicate effectively.
- Participants look at each other to talk instead of all facing you as the person running the meeting. This levels the playing field and emphasizes a collegial, collaborative stance.
- People can turn and talk in pairs or threes for a quick chat and then talk again as a whole group, allowing everyone to share their thinking.

colleagues you haven't seen for a while, and get a quick sense of how they are organizing their classrooms and what professional learning topics might be relevant to all. Of course, if you are new to the role of coach or new to the school in general, this first personal interaction is a good opportunity to show your warmth and support. We have found it helpful to engage in morning walk-abouts not only at the beginning of the year but also throughout the year as time allows for quick, spontaneous conversations and to remain visible and available to colleagues.

Schedule a Start-Up Meeting of the Team

We strongly recommend that you work with your school administrator to dedicate about thirty minutes to meet with the whole team, all the educators in the building, just before the first day of school when teachers are in the building without students. This unique kind of professional learning session can set the tone for collaborative teamwork all year long.

Realizing how busy the teachers will be with getting ready for opening day, be flexible about the timing of this important team meeting. If it's not possible to schedule it before school opens, consider asking for thirty minutes of the first faculty meeting, or ask your school principal for other suggestions. And don't forget that your principal will be an important participant in the meeting whenever it takes place.

The coaching start-up meeting is an opportunity for your colleagues to hear straight from you (with your principal sitting shoulder to shoulder with the teachers) what you understand about your role and how you will support them throughout the year. In just a few minutes, you can educate new colleagues or remind your experienced colleagues of your mutual goals, your school's common curriculum, and the overall vision of the school as a learning community for children *and* adults.

Meeting Tips

Here are a few things you can do to ensure the meeting will be enjoyable and productive.

- **Plan to have refreshments on hand.**
- **Arrange the chairs in a circle,** making sure that the number of chairs matches the number of expected participants. Your goal is to have a continuous circle of communication, so push any empty chairs out of the circle before you begin. If there are any stragglers, tell them to push a chair in and join the circle. It is important not to let anyone sit outside the circle. A circle will also ensure that each person can see everyone and that everyone is sitting shoulder to shoulder beside two other teachers. Circle meetings like this support collaboration, and we have used them with great success too many times to count.

- **Make a list of the key points you want to discuss.** As you make your list, you might want to consult the school's core values and beliefs and its articulated vision statement or reread the broad areas of your job description (which you cleverly reviewed with your principal beforehand to prevent any ill-timed surprises). You might also find it helpful to review the local teachers union guidelines with your principal to ensure you will not violate them, particularly regarding the amount of time teachers spend in the building before or after school. Don't be afraid to remind people of key understandings that everyone should have in mind. And, most important, think about how to show your positive energy and generous support of the school team.
- **Finally, be sure to start and end on time!** Incorporate stragglers quickly and quietly, but don't wait until everyone is there. Be respectful of everyone's time by ending when promised.

The Coaching Role-Play

We offer the following example to help you get a feel for what a start-up meeting might sound like. The particular setting is a school that has never had a literacy coach before, and some of the teachers are quite anxious because they are aware that coaching did not go well in another school in their district. The coach is new to this school, although she does have previous coaching experience. If your context is different, think about how you would adapt the content and language to fit your situation. The meeting begins where every successful meeting begins, with a warm welcome and refreshments.

Welcome: *Good morning, everyone. I hope you all got a chance to grab some coffee and a snack. Feel free to take more on your way out.*

Thank you for taking the time to meet, and special thanks to Principal West, who had some unexpected challenges this morning and still took the time to join us. I do want to get started so we can end on time because I know you all have so much to do. I'm going to talk for ten to fifteen minutes, and then I'll open it up to your questions.

As you know, my name is Catherine. I'm glad I had the chance to meet each one of you, though briefly, on my walk around the school yesterday. It was so exciting to see the rich, welcoming environment the team has provided for our students and their families.

I wanted to have some time with you today to share information about professional learning opportunities in our school this year. I am honored to join this team of educators and this community of students and families. I took a look at the values and beliefs that guide your literacy instruction and knew right away that I would enjoy being a member of this team. I especially look forward to embracing the invaluable opportunity I've been given to serve so many students, families, and educators who represent such diverse cultural backgrounds with their languages and experiences.

The Coach's Beliefs: *I believe in the importance of authentic and proficient literacy and know I will enjoy working with others who clearly value real reading and real writing, along with systematic phonics and word study instruction. Your curriculum framework shows that you offer students rich content knowledge and culturally sustaining instruction, which is at the very core of what is essential in today's schools.*

The Coach's Background: *I'm sure you'd like to know a little about me. I taught in the classroom for several years, spanning primary- and intermediate-level teaching. I enjoyed my collaborative work with colleagues so much I knew I wanted to become a coach. I am relatively new to the role as I coached for only three years in my previous district. I have so much more to learn about literacy and coaching teachers, and I know I will learn so much from you. I am committed to improving my professional practice in every way I can, so I certainly will appreciate your honest feedback. I make it a point to participate in a wide variety of professional learning opportunities for coaches, am part of a network of coaches in the state, and am an avid reader of professional books and articles on the topic. Sometimes it all feels pretty overwhelming but, at the same time, very energizing.*

The Coach's Role: *I want to say a few things about my understanding of my role, particularly since you have not had a coach at your school in the past. My understanding of my role is that I am responsible for supporting all aspects of professional learning in literacy in the school. That would include a variety of opportunities such as professional learning sessions, grade-level meetings, coaching of individual teachers or small groups in their classrooms, professional book clubs, study groups, and any other opportunities that support your professional growth. I see all of you as highly competent professionals, and I see myself as your thinking partner. My goal is to support you in becoming the best version of yourself you can be while also learning more about teaching and learning from each one of you.*

It's very important for you to know that I will have no role in evaluating or judging your teaching. I am your colleague and see myself as a thought partner—another set of eyes and ears as we think together about students' literacy progress. I also want you to know that I will never talk about your teaching with anyone else—not our school principal, not another teacher, not an intervention specialist—without asking your permission. You can count on the confidentiality of our work together.

Coaching Sessions: *Now let's talk about our individual coaching sessions as one type of professional learning for all of you this year. I know these sessions will be new to most of you, and you'd probably like to know what to expect. First, when we need to be out of the classroom together, Principal West has offered to arrange for coverage so you won't need to worry about your students.*

Our individual coaching sessions will have a general three-part structure. We will meet briefly for a pre-observation conversation so I can learn about your students, your goals, and what you want me to notice during the lesson. Then I will come into your classroom for the observation, and I will sit behind the students so as not be in the way. I will not speak with any of the students except to say "hello"; I will simply be a silent observer. You will notice me taking notes so that we will have a written memory of the lesson that we can refer to when we meet in our post-observation conversation. I'll also note the time in segments so we will have that to refer to as well.

Following the lesson, we will meet at a scheduled time to think together about the lesson. At the end of our time together, I will ask for feedback on how the session went for you. I hope you will feel comfortable giving honest feedback so I can continue to refine my practice and make our time together as helpful as possible.

Scheduling Coaching Sessions: *We will set up a schedule beforehand, but because I will need to schedule time with so many of you, I would appreciate any flexibility you can offer. I will always try to schedule our time together during your literacy time, but occasionally I may need to ask you to move something and would really appreciate your flexibility if a change is necessary.*

Principal-Coach Meetings: *I want you to know that I have a monthly meeting with Principal West—the first Wednesday of the month for thirty minutes—to keep her updated and to get support for our literacy work. In those meetings I will update her on the focus of our professional learning and what the team is working on in their teaching so she is aware of this when spending time in classrooms. I will never talk about individual teachers. I will discuss any policies or data requirements or any other topics she has or I have that should be addressed. Please feel free to suggest any items you think I should bring up at the meeting. I see my role as representing all of you in our literacy efforts at these meetings.*

Request for Feedback: *I would like to ask something of you. If you ever have any concerns about how I engage in my role in this school, I would appreciate it if you would come and tell me personally. It doesn't help me—or you—if people have a concern and talk to each other about it, but I am not aware so that I can do something to improve it. So, thank you for thinking about that.*

Questions: *I promised I would save time for questions so I will stop here. We'll have more time together in the future to talk about our work. Now, who has a question? Don't be shy, because others may be wondering the same thing.*

Teacher: *I am retiring in a year, so you don't need to waste any time coaching me. You can spend your time with the new teachers instead.*

Coach: *Congratulations on your retirement plans! I am sure you are looking forward to a change of pace. And thank you for all you have contributed to the education of children. I am pleased that you will be a member of the team for one more year because you bring such a wealth of experience to your colleagues. Since my understanding of my role is to coach every teacher on the team as part of their professional learning, I will have time to work with you. I especially look forward to our time together since I know I will learn a lot from you.*

Teacher: *If I already know about the topic of some of our professional learning sessions, can I skip them and focus on my other work?*

Coach: *Thank you for your question because I am sure others are wondering the same. I know you are very busy, and I will always try to make every bit of professional learning time valuable to you as you continue to refine your practice. Our work as a team will include some topics familiar to each of you. When a topic is very familiar to you, I hope you will support the learning of your colleagues by sharing your knowledge with your colleagues at our sessions. I also hope you will find the session will offer layers of new learning to everyone. Be sure to provide feedback at the end of each of our sessions so I can address any concerns.*

Teacher: *I am not a supporter of small-group instruction. Do I have to work with small groups in reading?*

Coach: *As you know, your entire educator team engaged in a thoughtful process of articulating their values and beliefs and the instructional practices that are aligned with them. By consensus, you adopted the curriculum document, meaning that every team member agreed to provide whole-group, small-group, and individual instruction as part of a comprehensive and differentiated literacy program. Our professional learning time will include opportunities to refine our instruction in small groups, and I am hopeful that when you see the impact on your students, you will be excited to spend more time with them in a small-group context.*

Teacher: *Will you be the one who assesses our students? That would be helpful because our schedules are so full.*

Coach: *You ask a good question. Time is always so challenging. The person who assesses the student is the one who learns the most for instruction. It is my understanding that the teacher who provides the literacy instruction to the child will conduct the assessments of that child's literacy skills. It is such a good opportunity to build a relationship with each student when you conduct individual assessments, such as a benchmark assessment. I will certainly find ways to support you–we can make a schedule together, and as a team we can find ways to provide coverage to make the assessment administration as efficient as possible. Our goal can be to complete the individual assessments in no more than two or three weeks when you assess two or three individuals a day.*

Teacher: *Will you be working with the students in my room who need help with reading or writing?*

Coach: *It is my understanding of my role at this time that it does not include providing direct services to students. Having said that, I do want to support every teacher in working with students who find literacy difficult, and that topic will be a high priority in our workshops and in coaching support.*

Teacher: *I had a coach in another school, and the situation was not helpful to me or to my students. I'm hesitant about working with a coach again.*

Coach: *I am sorry that you did not have a good experience and understand how you might feel skeptical about working with a coach again. Your time is very valuable, and I will always honor that. I hope you will find that our work together is enjoyable and productive, and I will do everything I can to rebuild your confidence in coaching. At the end of our time together I will always ask for feedback, and I hope you will feel more positive and see the time as well spent.*

Teacher: *My students' test scores are always strong, so I don't feel like I need to be coached. Do I have to?*

Coach: *It is good to hear how well your students are performing. You must be providing them with strong teaching! It is my understanding of our school's professional learning plan that every teacher will have the opportunity to be coached and that I am responsible for providing coaching support to every literacy teacher. And therefore, it is my role to coach every teacher. I hope you will find your coaching time very productive as you refine your understandings. I will certainly look forward to learning from you.*

Teacher: *No offense to you, but I am not interested in attending the professional learning sessions this year. I just have too much else to do.*

Coach: *It is my understanding that every teacher is expected to participate in professional learning, but I know how very busy you are and will work very hard to make our time together highly productive. I hope you will see that our time together is an investment in all your students. I also hope you will give me your honest feedback at the end of each professional learning session we have together.*

Teacher: *Will you be able to model lessons for me? I learn better when I watch someone first.*

Coach: *I understand what you are saying. Seeing what teaching looks like and sounds like is so helpful when taking on new practice. I will provide you with many demonstrations of instructional practice through video that we will all have time to view, and you will also be able to view them again if you choose. You will also have opportunities to observe each other teach. Though it may be appropriate for a demonstration of some aspect of teaching in your classroom, it is not ideal as I will not know your students as well as you do, and the teaching will tend to be superficial. But, it might be possible for us to co-plan or co-teach a lesson. So let's talk about that when we plan our coaching time.*

Teacher: *Will I have to be out of my classroom a lot for this? I already don't have enough time with my students.*

Coach: *I agree. The amount of instructional time is limited and every minute out of the classroom is challenging. We will work together to schedule times that are as convenient as possible and minimize time out of the classroom. I hope you will find the whole process so valuable that it will impact all your students and be well worth your time.*

Teacher: *Will you initiate coaching with us, or do I ask you when I want some coaching?*

Coach: *I will talk with each of you to schedule a time that works for you. I would appreciate as much flexibility as you can because it is challenging to schedule so many coaching times.*

Teacher: *How often will you work with me?*

Coach: *It will vary, but on average, I hope to be able to schedule each of you about once every two or three weeks.*

Teacher: *Will you have the topics to work on, or do I come up with what we work on?*

Coach: *Sometimes the topics will be a follow-up to our professional learning sessions or other forms of professional learning, such as lesson study or learning walks, but we can decide together what to work on when we make the schedule. You may have some other priorities for our time together.*

Teacher: *Can we watch other teachers teach lessons?*

Coach: *Yes! It will be wonderful to have the opportunity to observe in each other's classrooms and learn from each other. As a team, our goal is to open our doors to support each other.*

Teacher: *Do you work with just classroom teachers or all teachers in the building?*

Coach: *It is my understanding of my role that I will coach every teacher who teaches literacy–that would mean classroom teachers and specialist teachers.*

Teacher: *What about paraprofessionals and volunteers in the building?*

Coach: *Yes, I look forward to supporting all teachers of literacy as my time will allow. It is likely that I would need to prioritize paraprofessionals as they are on staff but will do all I can to support the volunteers. We are so appreciative of them.*

Teacher: *Will you be helping me with just my trickiest students? I just need help with those kids.*

Coach: *Yes, I will certainly help, as will all your colleagues. As a team, we will all learn from and support each other. We must commit to the success of every child, and it is going to take all of us.*

The Debriefing

In the short meeting captured above, the coach has set the stage for a year of coaching and professional learning. We recommend that a refresh meeting like this one take place at the start of every school year as a way to get the team fired up for new learning opportunities and to welcome any new teachers to the team and answer their questions. Now let's talk about what the coach said and did during the meeting.

A Follow-Up Exercise

It is probably clear to you that the coach's values and beliefs about her role are evident in her choice of words. Reflect on your observations of the interactions.

- What, specifically, did you notice about the coach's stance and language?
- What do you think the team took away from the meeting about her values, beliefs, and understandings?
- How might the meeting attendees be thinking about how the coach's plan for professional learning will impact them?
- Jot down in the margins or highlight key words that stand out for you.

You may have noticed that the coach did the following:

- Prioritized taking time to build relationships with her colleagues
- Showed transparency regarding her role and her values
- Treated her colleagues as competent professionals
- Saw the teachers as her valued colleagues
- Saw herself and the principal as part of the team responsible for all the students
- Showed that she values cultural and linguistic diversity
- Saw multiple languages and cultures as assets
- Conveyed that she would learn from them, and they would learn from each other
- Demonstrated humility and the ability to listen to people's feelings
- Remained positive regardless of what people said to her
- Positioned herself as a lifelong learner
- Invited constructive feedback
- Made confidentiality absolutely clear
- Showed that she values reading professional literature
- Unmasked the structure of a coaching session
- Unpacked the mystery of the principal-coach meeting and invited agenda items
- Made clear the expectation that all members of the team will attend professional learning sessions and participate in one-on-one coaching
- Continually reinforced the school's description of her role and made clear that it reflects her own understanding of her role

- Reinforced the school's common curriculum goals
- Committed to improving learning outcomes for all teachers and students

Refer to this example frequently as you reflect on the language you use in professional conversations. Your careful language will impact your colleagues' view of your role and their own roles as members of a team and will model the kind of transparency that builds trust and contributes to your success as a leader and a coach.

Up **Next**

In Chapter 5, we turn to the subject of language, the most important tool you have as a coach. In this overview chapter, we explain what we mean by the term *facilitative language* and describe its characteristics.

Chapter 5

All the **Right Words** for All the **Right Reasons**

Ask a group of people to name the greatest invention in all of human history, and some might say "language." After all, we'd be nowhere without it. There would be no easy way to communicate complex ideas, to collaborate, or even to build civilizations. There'd be no literature, no philosophical discourse, and only very limited forms of art. And, because language shapes thinking and even the contours of the human brain, our cognitive abilities would be decidedly low level. So, even if you don't believe it's the greatest invention of all time, you have to give language its due.

Talk is your most important tool. Through your choice of words and phrases, you mediate educators' professional activities and experiences, enabling them to build their identities, knowledge, agency, flexibility, and independence. For example, through a simple response like "What could you try?" or "You figured that out," you confirm the teacher's confidence and sense of agency.

Language positions people in relation to each other. It operates within and influences collegial relationships. As a professional learning leader, you are not the expert, the fixer, or the giver of knowledge. Your colleagues are your collaborators and thought partners. Your choice of language can convey this dynamic and influence the social, emotional, and intellectual culture of your school. This chapter will help you find the right words when you need them.

What Is Facilitative Language?

The intentional and skilled facilitation of professional conversations between teachers and coaches is the surest way to promote and sustain the learning and expertise of teachers. As the coach, you steer the process of job-embedded professional learning, enhancing each teacher's capacity and success. Your language is the most important tool for expanding your colleagues' understandings of their students, the curriculum, instructional approaches, and assessment. Use language that invites teachers to think about the curriculum or evidence of student learning and the impact on their instruction. Remember that your goal is not to get your colleagues to do what you want or tell them what you think they should do. Your goal is to think together about literacy teaching and learning and reflect on the decisions that lead to improved student outcomes. Mastering the art of facilitative talk—language that promotes productive conversation—requires that you understand your own agendas, biases, and assumptions in order to approach the thinking of others with humility and genuine interest in diverse perpsectives.

In this chapter, we discuss five principles for using facilitiative language (Figure 5–1). In addition to supporting your colleagues' decision-making, your language constantly drives the conversation to teacher reflection, which deepens their understandings about teaching and fuels continued growth and expertise.

Five Principles for Using Facilitative Language

Here are five language principles to keep in mind in all your interactions with teachers, no matter what the context.

1. **Facilitative Language Conveys Collaboration, Not Judgment**
   Interactions with teachers that are constructive, collegial, and helpful will amplify your collaborative stance. They convey your belief that with appropriate levels of support everyone can grow more competent over time. When you convey a collaborative stance, you communicate that you are not a judge or an evaluator. Here are some characteristics of language that is truly collaborative:
   - The interaction is conversational and invites multiple perspectives.
   - Both you and your colleagues listen to understand, offer information, and learn from each other.
   - Mutual respect and curiosity permeate the interaction.
   - No one dominates the conversation.
   - You pause and listen closely, rather than waiting for another chance to speak, because you know that what teachers say reveals what they currently believe and understand.
   - Your colleagues talk about what is real and important to their work, and together you arrive at co-constructed understandings.

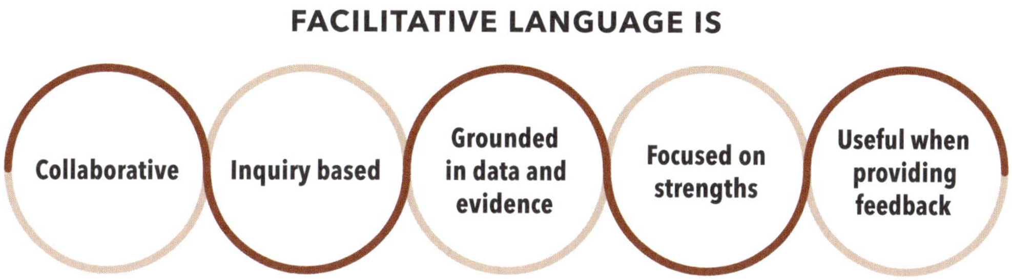

Figure 5-1

2. **Facilitative Language Promotes Genuine Inquiry**
   When facilitative talk is used to promote genuine inquiry, the goal is to learn more about the teacher's rationales for decision-making, that is, the evidence or detailed knowledge of individual students that underpins the instruction. Your choice of language promotes analytic thinking so your colleagues are actively engaged in pursuing answers to meaningful questions by analyzing data and other relevant information.
3. **Facilitative Language Is Grounded in Data and Evidence**
   When coaching conversations are rooted in data and behavioral evidence, you bring objectivity into the discussion and set the stage for your colleagues to analyze their own effectiveness in accomplishing their goals. Questions about the "why" of certain teaching decisions are very useful because they prompt teachers to articulate their own thinking and focus on sound rationales for their decisions.

   Some teachers are natural observers of children, but others may need practice learning how to notice what is important. You can help by providing systematic ways of gathering evidence of student successes and challenges. When teachers identify and name specific learning behaviors, allow time for them to talk about those behaviors and what they reveal. The right language can encourage the regular use of data and other forms of evidence to guide their teaching decisions.
4. **Facilitative Language Builds on Your Colleagues' Strengths**
   As a coach, begin your thinking with an eye to the assets your colleagues bring to teaching. You might begin your coaching conversations with a descriptive comment that does not evaluate the teacher but does show that you were observing closely; for example, "I noticed that you invited (a quiet or shy student) into the conversation, and the student immediately contributed to the conversation." If teachers feel that their skills have been noticed and valued, they are more likely to be

Developing Soft Skills

Soft skills are interpersonal skills that make it easier to read people, interact with them more effectively, and handle tricky social situations. Soft skills include intuition, communication, and flexibility. Bates and Morgan (2018) examine three soft skills that are central to effective coaching: listening, establishing trusting relationships, and structuring constructive conversations. They explain that these skills are interdependent and should be part of every coach's repertoire.

receptive to your support and willing to try new approaches. But recognizing and building on a teacher's unique strengths is also a form of differentiated support. It's easier to tailor your coaching to individual teachers' needs if you are aware of their unique strengths and use them to promote additional growth in adjacent areas of teaching. Focusing on strengths creates a strong foundation for continuous improvement and contributes to teachers' increased confidence, effectiveness in the classroom, and professional satisfaction.

5. **Facilitative Language Invites Honest Feedback**
   There is no better way to reinforce the idea that everyone in the school is a learner than to solicit feedback on your interactions with colleagues. Asking for honest feedback also shows that you value their input, which helps build trust and makes it more likely that teachers will want to engage with you in growing and improving their instructional practices. The number one reason for soliciting feedback on your coaching? You can use the information to ensure that the support you provide is effective, responsive, and tailored to individual needs.

Better Language for Better Conversations: A Self-Assessment

The tone of your interactions and your choice of words are equally important, as they will make a difference in how you are perceived by your colleagues. Be careful to communicate as an equal rather than talk down to your colleagues or imply that you have all the answers.

As Figure 5-2 makes clear, your goal is to help teachers reflect on their own teaching by leading them to analyze the impact of their decisions. When you make statements or ask questions that lead teachers to analyze their own teaching, they learn how to do the same when you are not there. Here are some general principles to keep in mind as you consider your language.

- Maintain an exploratory, inquiring stance that shows genuine curiosity.
- Make your points about teaching and learning clear by using concrete examples.
- Ask genuine questions to understand better.
- Offer rationales and other useful information.
- Paraphrase and extend the teacher's comments.
- Avoid the use of judgmental terms or making either/or conclusions.
- Make statements or ask questions that help the teacher confirm effective decisions and reflect on decisions that did not influence student learning.
- Use language that promotes the teacher's self-analysis and independence.
- Summarize key points that you have concluded together.

ASK YOURSELF	EXAMPLES OF FACILITATIVE LANGUAGE
Does your language communicate a tentative stance?	*That's one hypothesis. Another reason might be_________.* *I was wondering if another explanation might be_________.*
Are you genuinely seeking to discover more about the teacher's thinking?	*What did the child do that made you think that?* *Let's talk about your decision to_________.*
Are you using language that supports collegial problem-solving and inquiry?	*Let's look at the evidence to see what we notice.* *I have found that children often_________. What do you notice about your students?*
Does your language demonstrate your desire to clarify and understand more?	*Talk more about that.* *When you said _______, what was your thinking?*
Do you listen attentively and empathetically?	*I can understand that those comments would make you think that.* *I have never thought about it that way. Let me think more about it.*
Do you paraphrase occasionally to show that you are seeking to understand the teacher's precise comments and questions?	*This is what I hear you saying: _________.* *By that, do you mean _________?*
Do you summarize at appropriate points to be sure you are both thinking the same?	*So, I think we are at the point where we both ____.* *What are the big, important ideas we talked about today?*

Figure 5-2

Your goal in professional conversations is to bring your experience and knowledge together with the teachers' experience and knowledge. Using language that opens the conversation and facilitates inquiry will help you achieve this goal. Entering the discussion from an inquiry stance is an important element in the coaching relationship (Lyons and Pinnell 2001; Rodgers and Rodgers 2007).

Up **Next**

In Chapter 6, we introduce you to four essential language skills, one superpower, and a few good questions, all supported by ready-to-use language.

Chapter 6

Four **Core Skills**, One **Superpower**, and a Few **Good Questions**

Throughout this book, we provide coaching moves and language for all kinds of purposes in many different professional learning contexts. Each of them will be useful at one time or another as you engage your colleagues in reflecting on their practice. However, we begin this chapter by focusing on four essential skills—asking questions, clarifying, paraphrasing, and summarizing. These language techniques are so helpful in coaching conversations that you really must learn to use them. In fact, if you *only* master these four skills, we're certain your professional conversations will be more productive.

Why are we so enthusiastic about these four? Because they are easy to learn, useful in many different contexts, and so dependable in steering meaningful conversations that you will rely on them over and over again. And not only in coaching contexts. Eventually, you will apply these skills whenever you are speaking to your colleagues (and maybe even your friends and family!) because they have simply become an unconscious part of how you interact with others.

In addition, we've included another essential skill that's less about what *you* say and more about what other people say. We're talking about the skill of listening, which just might become your superpower if you learn to use it effectively.

Finally, we end with advice on crafting questions that rise to the level of art. As an instructional coach, your questions should be genuine wonderings, relevant to the teacher's instructional practices, reflective, and nonjudgmental. You'll find out what makes good questions great toward the end of this chapter.

First, let's look at the group of four essential skills we call "The Core Four."

The Core Four

As a coach, you want to create a learning environment that is emotionally, intellectually, and physically safe for all learners. Be aware of your language, your tone, and your body language in your interactions with others. Keep these essential skills in mind and practice them until they feel natural to you. And remember that simply pausing and giving wait time creates space for a teacher to think.

1. Asking Questions

- **The Why:** Skillful coaches are purposeful in their use of questions to broaden, focus, and clarify thinking. Asking a good question opens thinking through the collaborative exploration of information and ideas grounded in behavioral evidence. Your questions invite teachers to think in new ways about their teaching decisions through analysis, reflection, and problem-solving.

QUICK TIP

Avoid asking a question when you already know the answer. To the teacher, it will feel like a test.

- **The How:**
  - *What were you thinking when . . . ?*
  - *What do you think would happen if . . . ?*
  - *What ideas have you considered to help with this challenge?*
  - *How did you decide . . . ?*
  - *Talk about another way you might . . . .*
  - *What would it look like if . . . ?*
  - *Is it possible that . . . ?*
  - *What was your thinking about . . . ?*
  - *Why do you think . . . ?*
  - *Is there another way to think about that?*

2. Clarifying

- **The Why:** By making a comment or asking a question to check your understanding when you think you might not have fully understood what was said, you will gather more information and learn more about the teacher's thinking.
- **The How:**
  - *So, are you saying . . . ?*
  - *What do you mean by . . . ?*
  - *Let me check my understanding.*
  - *I am puzzled by what you said when . . . .*
  - *Talk more about . . . .*
  - *Talk me through your thinking about that.*
  - *So what do you mean when you say . . . ?*
  - *Can you talk more about your thinking?*

3. Paraphrasing

- **The Why:** By putting what your colleague said in your own words, you provide evidence you were listening and ensure your understanding was accurate. You reflect your colleague's thinking back to them for further consideration and give the teacher the opportunity to clarify thinking. You might also use the speaker's exact words and state them back. Be sure to avoid using too many words or paraphrasing so often that it slows down the conversation. Also, teachers might begin to think they are being parroted or manipulated. Still, paraphrasing is a great way to check your understanding and interpretation of an individual's comments or a group discussion. Use it when you really need to know.
- **The How:**
  - *In other words, ... Is that right?*
  - *It sounds as though . . . . Is that right?*
  - *From what I hear you saying, ...*
  - *So, you are saying . . . . Is that right?*
  - *You seem to be concerned about . . . . Is that accurate?*
  - *If I understand that correctly, ...*

4. Summarizing

- **The Why:** When you summarize, identify the big ideas or insights and confirm shared understandings. Summarizing helps you and your colleagues consolidate the discussion, ensure accurate understanding, and set priorities for next steps. And, as a bonus, it helps teachers organize their thoughts and bring clarity to their thinking.
- **The How:**
  - *So, what do you think are the big, important ideas from our conversation today?*
  - *Let's quickly review the important ideas together from our talk together.*
  - *So, you are saying that your next priorities are . . . ?*
  - *The important ideas we want to talk more about next time are . . . .*

Try Hmmm or Uh-huh

Think about all the ways you show that you are present and listening to your colleague and how your tone matters. Toll (2005) describes the two phrases—*Hmmm* and *Uh-huh*—as ways of showing you are listening but should not be overused. She emphasizes using the phrase in a neutral voice that is encouraging to the teacher instead of a rising pitch that sounds as though you are surprised or a decreasing pitch that sounds like disapproval. So add that to your language moves!

The Superpower: Listening

Effective coaches don't just *seem* to listen when teachers talk, they hang on every word. Great coaches know that when teachers respond to genuine questions or offer rationales for their teaching decisions, they open a window on their thinking. And that's something you don't want to miss. Yet, focused listening doesn't always come easily. Here are some situations you may have found yourself in during coaching conversations:

1. You are formulating a response in your head while the teacher is still talking.
2. You become distracted by planning what you and the teacher will do next.
3. It sounds like the teacher has misunderstood something you said earlier, so you interrupt to make yourself clear.

Covey (2020, 275) advises, "Seek first to understand, then to be understood." You can't really understand another person and their thoughts, actions, emotions, decisions, and rationales if you're busy trying to make yourself understood. If that's your agenda, we can almost guarantee you won't be listening.

How to Be a Better Listener

QUICK TIP

Listening skills can improve through regular practice—and it doesn't have to be in the context of coaching. A family dinner, an outing with friends, even an argument with a loved one can provide an opportunity for you to practice listening more and talking less.

Listening is the foundation of productive coaching conversations, so you need to be very good at it. When you listen attentively, you convey to your colleagues that you value them and their thinking and are open to their ideas. You engage in a dialogue, not a monologue, and relate to them as equals. You can develop specific listening skills that will enhance your ability to understand and engage with the teachers you coach. Here are nine important listening skills and behaviors to practice and perfect.

1. **Give the speaker your full attention.** This means turning off or putting away your phone for a starter.
2. **Sit side by side, eye to eye.** This subtle move goes a long way toward conveying your belief that you are equals engaged in thinking together.
3. **Use positive body language.** If culturally appropriate, maintain eye contact. Lean in, nod your head, smile in agreement, etc. You might utter sounds like *uh-huh* or *hmmm*, or smile to encourage your colleague's thinking aloud or to confirm the person's insights.
4. **Maintain a neutral stance.** Listen without judgment or criticism.
5. **Avoid interrupting.** Remember: listening and interrupting are incompatible behaviors.

QUICK TIP

Don't forget to pay attention to body language too. Note your colleague's facial expressions and tone of voice. Both can help you gauge the speaker's emotional state.

6. **Manage your emotions.** Remain calm even if the teacher does not. When emotions are high, people can't truly hear one another.
7. **Be aware of unintentional biases in your listening.** Listen to what is actually said, not what you expect to hear based on your attitudes about the teacher's character, professionalism, or competence. Also be aware of implicit biases related to generalizations about age, gender, attire, ethnicity, etc.
8. **Engage in regular practice.** Take advantage of every opportunity to practice listening during collegial interactions and in your life outside of school.
9. **Give listening a do-over.** You definitely will get distracted. Don't panic when you realize you've lost the thread of the conversation. You could just resume listening, but it might be best to admit it and say something like, *"I'm sorry, I got stuck thinking about ____. Would you please repeat that last part so I clearly understand you?"*

Listen to the Sounds of Silence

You know the feeling: A coaching session is going well, and the conversation is moving along. But then you ask a question—it could be any question—and an uncomfortable silence follows. If you're like most people, you immediately jump into that silence and try to fill it, maybe by posing the question a different way or prompting the teacher with a statement you think might draw out an answer. But what if you *didn't* do that? What if you just waited? That's exactly what author Michael Bungay Stanier recommends.

Stanier (2016, 130) says, "Silence is often a measure of success." He goes on to explain that when coaches leave time for silence, thinking deepens and the resulting conversations are more productive.

During your first session with a colleague you have not coached before, you might make it known that you are a strong believer in wait time, not just for kids, but for adults, too, and that a little bit of silence can help both of you think more clearly and more deeply about what you want to say or do next.

The next time silence arises in a coaching conversation, go with it—even if only for a few seconds. That brief silence might allow the teacher to produce a more thoughtful or coherent answer, which will help move the coaching forward.

Perfecting the Pause

Lipton and Wellman (2024, 60) describe four types of pauses that will help you focus on your colleagues and encourage thoughtfulness.

- Pause after a question for three to five seconds of think time.
- Pause after a colleague's initial response to allow the person to say more.
- Pause before paraphrasing so you can think and construct thoughtful language.
- Pause after paraphrasing to allow your colleague to consider whether your paraphrase accurately represents what was said.

A Few Good Questions

Many of the world's greatest discoveries began with a simple question: Why does an apple fall from a tree? What makes the night sky dark? What if computers could talk? These questions and others like them have led to discoveries that have changed the course of history. While the questions you ask in your work with teachers may not have quite the same level of impact, they certainly can inspire purposeful inquiry into teaching and learning. And that will lead to better academic outcomes for students.

Crafting just the right questions to yield the results you seek is, indeed, an art. Even so, some guidance for what to strive for in your questioning and what to avoid might be helpful. Figure 6-1 offers such guidance.

Better to Ask Than Tell

The more you ask and the less you tell, the more impactful your colleagues' learning will be. Your ability to ask the kind of questions that get teachers to reflect enables them to articulate their thinking and come to their own conclusions. You are the co-inquirer and the co-constructor of your colleagues' understandings, not the expert delivering information. Although there are certainly times when providing information *is* the right move, your role is not primarily to tell or give advice. When you ask good questions, you shift the thinking and problem-solving to your colleagues, which will improve their ability to analyze and reflect on their teaching decisions when you are not there.

QUICK TIP

When you sit shoulder to shoulder with your colleagues, you convey the idea that you are equal partners. If you speak in a tone of voice that is calm, and if you pause and provide wait time for thinking, your colleagues will learn more, develop a sense of agency, and build self-confidence.

QUESTIONING DO'S AND DON'TS

Do	Don't
Encourage deeper thinking that will inform you both. ▪ *What are some ways you think you can get _____ more engaged?* ▪ *What did you notice about your students' responses to the book?*	**Ask yes or no questions.** ▪ *Do you think this was a good lesson?* ▪ *Do you want some suggestions on how to make the lesson better?*
Aim to find out more about the teacher's understanding and perspectives. ▪ *What information was most helpful to you in planning this lesson?* ▪ *Share what you hope for in this lesson.*	**Make questions feel like a test.** ▪ *What does the guide say about where to start?* ▪ *Do you remember my suggestions from last week?* ▪ *What was the article about?*
Make way for genuine conversational give and take. ▪ *What would you like to talk about?* ▪ *What did you think about as you planned this lesson?* ▪ *What parts of the lesson felt most productive?*	**Put the teacher on defense.** ▪ *How do you think your lesson went?* ▪ *Do you know the parts of the lesson? What did you leave out?*
Add space in the conversation to provide thinking time. ▪ *Let's look back on the lesson. When do you think students were most engaged?* ▪ *I'll look through my notes and then we can share what we both noticed.*	**Ask questions in rapid succession.** ▪ *Were the students engaged throughout the lesson? What made you realize they weren't? What are you going to do about it tomorrow?*
Invite the individual to engage in collaborative inquiry. ▪ *Let's analyze _____'s responses to think about what they show. Take a look and then let's share what we both noticed.*	**Give information disguised as a question (ask rhetorical questions).** ▪ *And what do we know about stopping to ask for questions during the lesson?* ▪ *What happens when there are interruptions?*
Engage your colleague in thinking with you about the rationales for instructional moves. ▪ *And you decided to _____ because?* ▪ *What was your thinking about asking the students to _____?*	**Lead the learner to the "right" answer, communicating that you need to remind the teacher of what was taught.** ▪ *Do you remember the purpose of _____? It's _____.* ▪ *What will you do when that happens?*

Figure 6-1

It all starts with the understanding that, although asking questions is an important skill (as noted earlier in this chapter), crafting just the right question is more like an art form. We begin with a few helpful questioning techniques.

Ask authentic questions. Real questions about your genuine wonderings will land better with your colleagues than questions for which you already think you know the answer. When questions come from your genuine curiosity, you communicate that you don't have all the answers and that you and your colleague can think and learn together. And, asking a real question about something you want to know shows your respect for the other person and is not likely to come across as a test or manipulation.

Avoid long strings of questions. Asking questions one after another in rapid succession can feel like an interrogation. Instead, allow space for the teacher to think by providing brief pauses or wait time at the end of questions or statements. Although it may be tempting to fill the silence, you'll get a a better answer if you provide time for your colleague to think and frame a coherent response.

Every Question Needs a Purpose

The questions you ask in coaching are important; but don't forget their purpose: to elicit a response that reveals a teacher's thinking, understandings, and attitudes. If one of your questions doesn't get a revealing answer, or if it's clear that the teacher has misunderstood what you were asking, try rewording the question and asking it again.

Ask open-ended questions. Questions that can be answered with one word, such as yes or no, can leave you and your colleague with nowhere to go next in your discussion. Open-ended questions, on the other hand, have a much better chance of resulting in a substantive conversation in which there is healthy give and take. If you do get a short or one-word response, be prepared to invite further thinking with prompts such as, "Talk more about that," or "Can you talk me through your thinking?" Questions like these can help teachers think aloud and, in the process, become more thoughtful about rationales for their teaching decisions.

Couch questions in a tentative stance. Your job is not to have all the answers but to engage in collaborative thinking. Just adding words like *maybe* or *I wonder if* shows your willingness to wonder along with your colleagues. Your tentative stance reinforces the message that you are not the expert, but you are reflecting on evidence to learn together.

Use questions that invite deeper thinking. So that your colleagues will develop strong noticing and naming skills and learn how to use those observations to ground their teaching decisions, pose questions that invite them to name and analyze their observations. Use questions that will facilitate your colleagues' attention to interpreting behaviors and noticing patterns.

Use questions to generate new learning. Every instructional coach wants to help teachers think about how to take the points made in a coaching session to future teaching decisions. We call this generative learning because it changes how teachers think about their work and helps them apply new understandings gained from working with one student to many other students.

Generative learning is promoted through *generative language*, which invites exploration, critical thinking, and innovation and tends to include open-ended questions and statements. On the other hand, specific language is narrow and focused on concrete information, actions, or facts. Most of the time, you'll want to use generative language. However, sometimes, it will be beneficial to use specific language to gain necessary information. Take a look at the examples below that

QUICK TIP

We've often said that there are no magic words in coaching. But maybe there is one. When posed as a one-word question, "Because?" can help you uncover a colleague's current thinking and rationales for decisions made in the classroom or draw the teacher more deeply into discussing the whys of their instructional practices. For example, to keep the focus on rationales, you can use "because" as a follow-up to questions like these:

What was most helpful to you in our talk today? . . . Because?

What are your teaching priorities? . . . Because?

I got the impression that you were thinking ______. Because?

You said ______. And that's because?

Record Your Questioning

With your colleagues' consent, you might want to record yourself asking questions in a coaching or other professional learning session. This way, you can notice the kinds of questions you typically ask, and–even more important–the types of responses they typically elicit.

illustrate the differences between generative language and specific language.

Specific: *What were you teaching Mia about adding detail to her writing?*

Generative: *What are some things you want students to understand and be able to apply in terms of adding detail to their writing?*

Specific: *Why did you focus on words with vowels influenced by* r *in this reading lesson?*

Generative: *How do you select the phonics elements students need to learn when planning your lesson?*

Did you notice how the generative language provides jumping-off points from which to engage in a discussion that leads to new understandings? At the end of each professional conversation, aim to make the generative learning explicit by asking the teacher to share how the new insights will affect future teaching.

How to Recognize Great Questions

- They show your caring and genuine curiosity.
- They are authentic.
- They demonstrate that you value your colleagues' thinking and experience.
- They encourage teachers to think more about a topic.
- They empower teachers by showing confidence in their ability to think for themselves.

Add these questions to your repertoire and use them often. The following questions are designed to promote reflection, identify areas for improvement, and encourage your colleagues' ongoing professional learning.

What has been challenging in your teaching?

What would you most like me to notice during the lesson?

Given our time together, how can I be most helpful to you?

What kind of support do you most need from me?

What areas of your teaching are you most focused on improving?

What surprised you?

What's in the way of ____?

With practice and a few hints from this chapter, you will be on your way to crafting great questions that will lift the expertise of the teachers you coach.

Up **Next**

Chapter 7 is where language and purpose come together in what we call Your Coaching Prompting Guide. Because we know you'll use these pages a lot, the prompts are available in the **Online Resources**. Download them and keep them in your coaching notebook.

Chapter 7

Your Coaching **Prompting Guide**

Whatever your purpose—whether to offer encouragement, provide feedback, or facilitate reflection—your use of precisely matched language brings focus and clarity to your work with teachers. Not only that, but when your language is carefully chosen to suit a particular goal or purpose, it is more likely to hit the mark. And so, this chapter is all about how to use specific language to achieve your purposes.

On the pages that follow, you'll find many examples of coaching purposes and the facilitative language you might use to shape professional conversations and open teachers' thinking so you can get at what's behind it. Your goal as a coach is to internalize the kind of language that shapes the learning culture in your school. Later in the book, we provide additional language and prompts that are particularly useful in specific coaching conversations related to instruction.

You will notice that the language examples may fit more than one category, but they all promote respectful, professional inquiry that results in improving practice.

KEYS TO SUCCESSFUL COMMUNICATION IN PROFESSIONAL CONVERSATIONS

1. **Say less, ask more.**
2. **Listen more, talk less.**
3. **Play back your understandings.**
4. **Summarize mutual understandings, actions, and goals.**

Keep the Prompts Handy

Before you enter a coaching situation, take a look at the prompts that you think might be relevant. Download Prompting Guide Tool: Coaching Prompting Guide, available as **OR 7.1** in the Online Resources. Download it and keep it in your coaching notebook (Chapter 23) so that you can access it easily.

ONLINE RESOURCE 7.1

PURPOSE: Foster Noticing and Naming

Responsive teaching rests on the teacher's ability to observe individual students closely and name what they see in students' reading, writing, and language behaviors. Teachers who recognize the value of careful observation and rely on it regularly and systematically in their daily work develop their ability to make moment-to-moment teaching decisions based on students' precise strengths and needs in relation to the goals of the curriculum. In short, they are able to recognize evidence of learning—or challenge—and act on it. The closer teachers observe, the better they will understand what students know and are able to do.

When you help teachers learn how to notice and name (Ray 2002, 18, 21) what they see in students' literacy behaviors and discuss what those behaviors mean, they develop a deeper understanding of literacy development. When your colleagues discuss observations and name them, they not only develop greater awareness and expand their content knowledge but also develop a common language about teaching and learning that becomes part of their common vocabulary and pool of literacy knowledge. They learn what kinds of things are worth noticing and develop a lens for attending to those literacy behaviors.

Prompts

- *What did you notice?*
- *You noticed ____. Any other noticings?*
- *I noticed that you ____.*
- *What else was important to notice?*
- *What did you notice about the author's messages in the text? Are any perspectives missing?*
- *What did you notice about the students' responses? Were there any surprises for you?*
- *What are you noticing? Are there any patterns?*
- *What did you notice about the students' body language?*
- *Given how the children responded, what is your thinking now?*
- *What did you think when you saw ____?*
- *I noticed that ____. What do you think that meant?*
- *What did you see happening at that moment? What did that tell you?*

PURPOSE: Confirm or Expand Knowledge

Confirmation of successful teaching decisions goes a long way in building confidence and opening teachers up to taking more risks in their learning. As the saying goes, "Knowledge is power." When you confirm your colleagues' knowledge base and support them in taking on new learning, you increase their power as professionals and help them expand their knowledge and develop a thirst for continuous learning. As their knowledge grows, so does their confidence–and both can lead to improved teaching and learning.

Prompts

- *You knew that.*
- *You noticed that.*
- *How did you know?*
- *Can you say more about that?*
- *What was your thinking?*
- *That's an interesting way to think about that.*
- *Thanks for helping me understand that.*
- *You expressed your interest in learning more about ____. Here's an article that may be helpful in learning more about those issues.*

PURPOSE: Support Teacher Identity

Your choice of words influences the way your colleagues view themselves. Through your choice of words in professional conversations, teachers come to see themselves as people who are competent and continually growing as professionals. They become confirmed in their strengths and build new insights. Your words show respect for your colleagues' unique identities, experiences, and cultures and their assets as humans and as professional educators.

Prompts

- *You were resourceful in how you went about figuring that out.*
- *What do you think is important about that?*
- *What a generous colleague you are.*
- *What have you learned as a teacher of reading (writing, phonics)?*
- *What would you like to work on next?*
- *I think your colleagues appreciate your flexibility.*

PURPOSE: Promote Teacher Independence

You can promote the growth of independence in your colleagues by encouraging them to take charge of their professional learning, helping them hone their problem-solving skills, and asking questions that lead them to self-reflect on their recent experiences in the classroom. Once they know how to learn from their own teaching, they become self-extending learners. You will be able to observe that they have developed the ability to reflect independently on their teaching decisions to gain new insights.

Prompts

- *You know your students much better than I do. What do you think you should try next?*
- *I'm thinking about a journal article I recently read that might be helpful to you. I will send you a link to it when I'm back at my desk.*
- *Trust your instincts. You've got this!*
- *What do you think is causing ____ to behave this way? What are some ideas you are thinking about that will change that behavior?*
- *What do you think will be the best decision? And that's because . . . ?*
- *What information will you need to make a new plan?*
- *What else would be helpful for us to talk about?*

PURPOSE: Foster Teachers' Sense of Agency

A sense of agency is a fundamental human desire that persists throughout life. Your colleagues need to believe in themselves as professionals and work to solve problems. They need to feel rewarded when their teaching decisions have a positive effect on student learning and puzzle out what's in the way when students are not successful. Through your responses, they learn that they are capable of solving problems and accomplishing their goals. They learn that as professional educators they are the kind of people who can engage in genuine inquiry and solve problems.

Prompts

- *What do you hope to accomplish with your teaching today?*
- *What information will you need to make a plan?*
- *What's important to you right now?*
- *What part are you confident about? What are you less confident about?*
- *What are you planning to do about that?*
- *What have you learned that you might want to try in your next lesson?*
- *How are you going to figure that out?*
- *Why did you decide to do that?*
- *What are you working on in your teaching of reading (writing, phonics)?*
- *Why do you think that happened?*
- *And that was because . . . ?*
- *How else might you do that?*
- *What are your priorities for helping your multilingual learners become more effective at ____?*

PURPOSE: Ground Conversation in Data

When you ground your professional conversations in specific data, you put the focus where it belongs: on the data and what evidence reveals about student outcomes. Teachers learn to value all kinds of data (hard data and soft data) as information that is essential to guide their instruction.

Regular use of data also reduces the potential for unconscious biases to enter the picture because the data is what tells the story. Then, with your colleagues, you can analyze and interpret it to make sound instructional decisions. This use of evidence keeps teaching grounded in rationales. Knowing the whys of their teaching approaches and being able to express them clearly will not only strengthen their confidence but also enable them to give explanations to colleagues, administrators, and families. Finally, focusing attention on data leads to new insights, more precise discussions, and more effective instructional decisions.

Prompts

- *What data did you use to plan for your teaching?*
- *How will you assess your students' learning?*
- *Let's look at a running record and see what it shows about this child as a reader.*
- *How will you know students processed the text with understanding? With accuracy?*
- *How can you tell that your lesson was effective?*
- *What information about your students as readers and writers did you use to plan for today?*
- *What was your rationale for ____?*
- *What patterns in the data or evidence point to possible inequities?*
- *What information should we look for to assess the quality of the writing?*
- *How do the scores fit your knowledge of your students as readers?*
- *When you look through their notebooks, what do you notice about most of your students' writing?*
- *How are the reading records helping you identify your teaching priorities?*

PURPOSE: Support Culturally Relevant Teaching

In today's classrooms, it is more important than ever for teachers to understand and nurture their students' cultural backgrounds, unique identities, and perspectives if they are to create truly inclusive and supportive learning environments. This means helping teachers identify and examine their own biases and expanding their knowledge of every child's assets.

Prompts

- *I can see that you are using information about the children's cultures (histories, languages, lived experiences) in your teaching. What steps did you take to learn more about each student?*

- *How are you using information about the children's cultures (histories, languages, lived experiences) in your teaching?*
- *Let's think together about how to build on the richness of the experiences you and your students bring. Maybe we can find ways to bring more diverse voices into discussions.*
- *How are you promoting the sharing of varied perspectives?*
- *Would you like me to observe particular children for evidence of their active participation (understanding, engagement)?*
- *Talk about how you are planning adjustments to the lesson to support multilingual learners.*
- *What voices have not been part of the discussion?*
- *What implicit and explicit biases are you becoming aware of as an educator?*
- *How do you think your own background and experiences have shaped your teaching?*
- *What are you learning about your students' unique identities that you have not thought about before?*
- *How might you work with and learn from your students' families?*

PURPOSE: Reveal Teachers' True Challenges

Teachers, especially those who are new to the profession, often feel overwhelmed by competing priorities, too much to learn, and not enough time. Often, they may tell you that they can't do it all, and in many cases, that is perfectly true. After a while, they may begin to feel like everything is an insurmountable challenge. Of course, you can't help with every challenge your colleagues face, but you can use language to lead them to identify the real challenges that are getting in their way.

Prompts

- *What are you most concerned about?*
- *What I am hearing you say is ____.*
- *What have you tried so far?*
- *Where in your teaching were you feeling challenged to make the best decision?*
- *What is preventing you from doing your best work?*
- *When you saw ____, what choices did you have?*
- *I'd like your insights on this challenge so I can ____.*
- *This is what I've tried. What suggestions do you have?*
- *What challenges are you finding in your teaching of reading and writing?*
- *What made you think you were not clear?*
- *So it seems like ____. What ideas do you have for moving forward?*

- *Another one of the teachers I coach expressed a similar challenge and eventually arrived at a way around it. I can ask that teacher if the two of you might connect on this.*
- *How might I be of support?*

PURPOSE: Promote Flexibility

Not every teacher you coach will be open to change, experimentation, or new thinking at first. But coaching can help teachers who are set in their ways become more open-minded and flexible, which may lead to more responsive and reflective teaching. Your precise language influences their teaching decisions and their ability to develop flexibility and make more productive teaching decisions for their students. In addition, your modeling of flexibility will impact the learning of your colleagues.

Prompts

- *Another option might be ____.*
- *What do you think might happen if ____?*
- *Talk about another way you might ____.*
- *What would it look like if ____?*
- *That was your plan, but what changed your thinking?*
- *How else might you have done that?*
- *What else were you thinking when you observed ____?*
- *When you saw ____, what choices did you have?*
- *If you had decided ____, how might that have been different?*
- *What concerns about trying this approach should we talk about now?*
- *Sometimes a quick huddle with another teacher can give new insights and inspire you to try something different. What do you think about that?*
- *So, you said the most recent approach didn't work as well as you thought it might. What do you want to try next?*
- *What if ____?*

PURPOSE: Pursue Rationales

The more you know about your colleagues' thinking or their rationales for instructional decisions, the better able you will be to tailor coaching experiences to their individual strengths and needs. Your healthy pursuit of information immediately demonstrates respect for their knowledge and understandings, while offering you invaluable insights into their thinking, instructional practices, challenges, mindset, beliefs about teaching and learning, and more. Consider statements or questions that enable you to get behind your colleagues' thinking so you have a context for teaching decisions. Pursue each teacher's rationales, or the "why" behind instructional decisions.

Prompts

- *Talk me through your thinking about that.*
- *What did you learn about this child as a reader (writer) that informed your goals?*
- *You noticed ____. How did that influence your planning for instruction?*
- *How does that fit with your understanding of the child's challenge?*
- *What would you like me to know about the child (group) I will be observing? Because . . . ?*
- *Talk about your goals for the child as a reader and writer. How did you determine those goals?*
- *What different approaches could you make to help your students use flexible decoding skills?*
- *What's in the way of ____'s ability to express her ideas in writing?*
- *What was your thinking about ____ when you decided to ____?*
- *Talk about your reasons for that decision.*
- *You decided to ____. That was because . . . ?*
- *What might you do differently? Because . . . ?*
- *Is there another way to think about that? Talk about why you say that.*

PURPOSE: Help Teachers Generalize New Learning

Specific language is narrow and focused on concrete information, actions, or facts, which is in itself useful in certain situations. It often relies on closed-ended questions and statements that require precise answers. Generative learning is promoted through using language that influences the teacher to consider how the new thinking can be applied more broadly. As a coach, use language that leads the conversation to have an impact that goes beyond that particular lesson or student or instructional context.

Prompts

- *How will that knowledge (understanding, insight) help you with ____?*
- *What knowledge (understanding, insight) can you take from that to help you with your other groups?*
- *How will that help you with other readers (writers)?*
- *I noticed how you switched your approach to ____, which we discussed in our last session. How do you think that went? What was the impact on your students?*
- *How do you see this new learning fitting into your current repertoire of teaching moves?*

- *How will our talk today about these students influence your work with other students?*
- *How will this discussion about your students as readers (writers) influence your teaching of reading (writing) in general?*
- *How will your work with these students as writers inform your work with them in reading?*
- *What new insights do you have that will help you with other students?*
- *What are your most useful insights from today's teaching?*
- *What new thinking from our session do you want to try out?*
- *How will you apply today's teaching to future teaching?*
- *How did the article help you think about literacy in other content areas?*

PURPOSE: Support Analysis and Reflection on Instructional Practices

Every time you observe a teacher in action—whether during the conversation in a professional book club, while leading a learning walk, when observing a lesson, or when noticing how a teacher works with students individually or in small groups—you have a fresh opportunity to learn more about the person's beliefs, understandings, strengths, and goals for further learning. Your purposeful use of facilitative language can promote the teacher's self-reflection and honest analysis.

It's important that your language not convey judgment or an evaluative stance. Instead, communicate your belief that the teacher's knowledge, experiences, and unique perspectives are assets that the two of you will work together to build on. Instead of dead-end phrases that discourage self-reflection and growth, such as "Good lesson" or "You should have," invite deeper, nonjudgmental thinking with language such as the prompts that follow.

Prompts

- *During yesterday's meeting with the other third-grade teachers, you seemed very excited about a few of the instructional approaches that were shared. Which one would you like to try first with your own students? Let's plan how you'll use it and when.*
- *Let's talk about your pacing during today's lesson. I noticed that you were able to keep the lesson moving and the children engaged without sacrificing their understanding of important concepts. What takeaways do you have for future lessons?*
- *Let's look at some of the students' performance data from their work in reading. Maybe we will get a sense of which of your instructional approaches are working and which students might need a boost.*

- *I wonder if you'd like to try journaling about the new instructional practices you are trying and how they are going.*
- *Have you ever considered having a colleague record one of your lessons? Many teachers have found that reviewing the video later helps them analyze their instructional moves from a different perspective.*
- *If you had ____, what do you think the students would have done?*
- *It seemed helpful to the children when ____.*
- *Talk about what you think went well in the lesson. Were there aspects you are now thinking about differently?*
- *Were there any times when you felt things weren't going as you wanted? What are your insights about that?*

Up **Next**

This chapter closes out Part 1. In Part 2, we turn to what every coach needs most: a reliable playbook. In it you'll find a variety of coaching structures (beginning with one-on-one coaching in classrooms), so that you can choose the right one at the right time to lift the expertise of your colleagues.

PART

2

The **Playbook**

Learn to coach

In every context

With fourteen winning plays

Chapter 8

The Play: **One-on-One Coaching**

Here is where the rubber meets the road. It's just you and a single teacher now, in a classroom filled with exuberant and expectant children. There is so much promise in the space between you and the teacher, and some apprehension as well about how this most important interaction will go. Will the teacher come away from the experience feeling like something meaningful has happened? Will your coaching be received positively, and will it have a positive impact on the teacher's instruction and attitudes about coaching? It's natural for you to feel a little anxious, especially if one or both of you is new to one-on-one coaching. After all, one look at the faces of the students in that room tells you the stakes are high. Before you begin, it's important to know what one-on-one coaching is and what it is not (Figure 8–1).

What Coaching Is	What Coaching is Not
▪ An opportunity for the teacher to have more than one set of eyes on the students to observe learning behaviors ▪ A chance to have a partner for thinking about solutions to a problem or about shifts in teaching ▪ A way to help teachers focus on their use of language and its impact on learning ▪ A way to closely observe students and the impact of teaching decisions on their learning outcomes	▪ A time to check on whether a teacher is implementing new initiatives ▪ A way to fix a colleague's teaching ▪ An attempt to change a teacher's style to conform with the way others teach or the way you think the teacher should teach ▪ An evaluative observation

Figure 8–1

We've both been where you are now, so we know exactly how charged one-on-one coaching can be. On the pages that follow, you'll find a dependable framework for one-on-one coaching as well as essential information you'll need to plan, execute, and debrief your one-on-one coaching sessions with confidence and ease.

BENEFITS OF ONE-ON-ONE COACHING

- Helps teachers try out different teaching moves and focus on the effects of their teaching decisions
- Supports teachers in establishing classroom routines and procedures
- Supports the classroom application of new learning
- Focuses on specific areas of teaching (e.g., observing reading and writing behaviors, using student data, planning, pacing, language)
- Builds teacher agency as you help teachers reflect on the impact of their teaching decisions on student learning

Coach One Teacher at a Time

While working in small groups has its benefits, one-on-one coaching can truly be transformative. The reason this form of coaching is so effective is clear: it is embedded in the authentic act of teaching and the close observation of learning that is specific to one teacher at one point in time.

One-on-one coaching allows you to build on individual strengths and differentiate your approach according to each teacher's unique needs. It develops a sense of agency in teachers because they see the direct link between their own teaching decisions and student learning outcomes. It also provides a safe space in which teachers can ask for help in specific areas and benefit from having you as a partner to strategize and try out new approaches in a practical, hands-on way.

One-on-one coaching is beneficial for new teachers and veteran teachers alike. With new teachers, you can work on foundations like classroom management routines and instructional procedures. With more experienced teachers, you can build on their knowledge by helping them make small shifts in their teaching to maximize time, use student data more effectively, or hone their language for clarity. Most important, one-on-one coaching provides time for you to listen to teachers, understand what they know and are wrestling with, and together find ways to lift the level of expertise.

A Framework for Coaching

We have found it helpful to use the same basic framework for coaching individual teachers and small groups. Everyone finds comfort in a routine, and establishing one that works for you and your colleagues not only makes planning easier but also helps everyone know what to expect from the coaching experience (Figure 8-2).

FRAMEWORK FOR A COACHING SESSION

PRE-OBSERVATION CONVERSATION

Meet for a pre-observation conversation: Look at data, learn what your colleague has planned for the observation, and identify how you can be most supportive.

10-15 min

OBSERVATION

Observe a lesson: You (occasionally with colleagues) observe a lesson and record significant teacher and student language and note the time at particular points.

15-60 min

POST-OBSERVATION CONVERSATION

Meet for a post-observation conversation: You and your colleague(s) analyze the teaching and learning, reflect on new understandings, and evaluate the coaching process and how it might be improved.

20-30 min

Figure 8-2

Plan and Prepare for Coaching

You know the drill. If you want to do something well, you need to be prepared. Coaching–whether on the playing field or in the classroom–is rarely predictable, and you never know when you'll need to change your plan based on the teacher's shifting needs and priorities and what you notice in the moment. That's what responsive coaching is all about, and it requires you to be nimble enough to change direction as seamlessly as possible. One-on-one coaching is effective (Figure 8–3) when you are prepared. Here's what you'll need to know about planning for the expected and the unexpected.

Plan your timing, space, and coverage. Start with a plan for logistics. Schedule times with the teacher for a pre-observation conversation, an in-classroom observation, and a post-observation conversation. In some cases, this might require you to work with your administrator to provide classroom coverage (so that your colleague is free to meet without having to manage the classroom at the same time) and to reserve a meeting space. When coverage is not possible, be creative in using planning times, lunches, recess times, or before-school and afterschool times. (Be sure the time doesn't conflict with teachers' contracts.) It is better to meet in a less perfect scenario before and after the observation than not at all. Some coaches meet with teachers in a corner of the classroom while students are engaged in independent work. Other coaches enlist the teacher's grade-level colleague to read aloud to both groups. While it is ideal for the pre-observation conversation to take place right before the observation and the post-observation conversation shortly after, you may need to plan for another time

A Word About Timing

A typical coaching observation can take from fifteen minutes to an hour depending on the type of lesson. For example, observing an interactive read-aloud might take only fifteen minutes, while observing a full writing block might take an hour. Add on ten to fifteen minutes for the pre-observation conversation and about twenty to thirty minutes for the post-observation conversation. You will find much more on time management in Chapter 22, but do note the importance of staying flexible in your use of time to keep coaching sessions as responsive as possible.

WHAT MAKES ONE-ON-ONE COACHING SO EFFECTIVE?

It is a **collaborative process.**

You and the teacher are in it together as you think, problem-solve, and brainstorm as partners.

It is **authentic.**

One-on-one coaching mostly takes place in classrooms, firmly rooting the experience in real teaching of real students. Coaching can't work if the teacher is just putting on a show.

It is **nonevaluative.**

This one is easy to remember: no judging, no fixing.

It is **productive.**

Busy teachers need to know that their time with you will pay off. That means working efficiently and always leaving something helpful and insightful behind.

It is **responsive.**

You respond to the teacher's current understandings and goals for improving their practice. Come prepared with ideas for the agenda, and also invite the teacher to contribute to it.

Figure 8-3

of day or even another day. Be proactive in working with the teacher to carve out this valuable time.

Finding a space where your colleague can talk openly can be challenging. Authentic coaching requires vulnerability and confidentiality, so whenever possible, consider reserving a place in the school that allows for privacy. Because coaching also may involve taking a deep dive into student data, you need to find space where you can openly discuss students without their classmates overhearing.

QUICK TIP

Consider creating a coaching notebook to organize your coaching resources all in one place. See Chapter 23 for information on assembling a physical or digital notebook.

Read notes from the last coaching session. Teachers feel valued when you respect the work you have done together previously and can pick up where you left off without wasting time. Knowing your colleague's current goals will help you think more meaningfully about the ways you can offer support throughout the coaching session.

Reflect on your previous work. Your goal is to build teacher expertise over time, and your notes should enable you to remind teachers of their progress. Think about areas in which teachers can continue to grow, and celebrate the progress with your colleagues.

Let the teacher set the agenda. Always work with teachers to determine the type of support they want at a particular time. You and the teacher should be on the same page about the focus of the observation before the pre-observation conversation. Figure 8-4 shows the types of literacy lessons you might observe.

COMMON TYPES OF LESSONS FOR LITERACY TEACHING AND LEARNING

Reading	Writing	Phonics and Word Study
Interactive read-aloud	Shared and interactive writing	Phonological awareness lessons (includes phonemic awareness)
Shared reading	Differentiated writing groups	Phonics lessons
Reading comprehension lessons	Writing lessons	Word study lessons (includes syllabication and morphology)
Strategies and skills lessons	Craft lessons	Vocabulary lessons
Book clubs	Grammar/conventions lessons	
Differentiated reading groups	Independent writing	
Independent choice reading	Writing conferences	
Reading conferences		

Figure 8-4

Examine student work. Though you often look at student work with teachers during a pre-observation conversation, there may occasionally be times when a teacher asks you to review student work before the coaching session to give you a deeper perspective of the learners in the class.

Review professional resources to ground your thinking. Just a quick refresh about a particular teaching move or type of instruction can help you be a stronger thought partner for the teacher. Reviewing resources and placing a few sticky notes also allows you to more quickly call to mind a helpful passage to support the conversation. If possible, make the resource a "leave-behind"; or better yet, refer to a resource the teacher already has.

Jot down language you might find helpful. As part of preparing for a coaching session, select a few language prompts that you think may be helpful in focusing the conversation in productive ways.

The Pre-observation Conversation

The one-on-one coaching session begins with a pre-observation conversation that sets the tone for thinking together, clarifying, and extending thinking. Without a pre-observation conversation, teamwork may not be established. Coaches may set themselves up for failure and be seen as evaluators rather than as thought partners. Most important, the conversation gives your colleague the opportunity to share data and information about the students that will ground your conversation. The teacher explains plans and rationales for the materials selected, sets priorities, and identifies aspects of the teaching that would be helpful to notice. You and your colleague set goals, and you have an opportunity to listen for your colleague's concerns.

Coaching Moves for the Pre-observation Conversation

Consider using some of the following coaching moves during your pre-observation conversation along with the sample language to help you make these moves. However, no two pre-observation conversations are ever the same. The language provided should by no means be used to create a script, nor should you feel an obligation to use all the moves listed here. Try to keep the pre-observation conversation to no more than fifteen minutes. We offer these suggestions as options for working one on one with teachers to meet their individual needs.

A Reflection Journal for Teachers

Encourage teachers to bring a notebook (hard copy or digital) to take notes and write their reflections during the coaching session. Like your coaching notebook, a reflection journal gives teachers a place to capture their thinking so they can contemplate their own growth over time.

Discuss the impact of the prior coaching session. When you start by talking about the last session, you send the message that there is continuity to the work and that you care about how the thinking you do together impacts teaching decisions. You also set the expectation that you will work together to build on previous experiences.

Sample Language

- *Talk about how our last coaching session has influenced your teaching.*
- *We worked together on ____ last time. What are you thinking about the impact on your teaching?*
- *Last time, you expressed concern about ____. Now what are you thinking?*
- *Talk about any changes you've made to your teaching from our last session together.*
- *In the last coaching session, you set the goal of ____. How is that going for you?*
- *What have you learned since our last coaching session about ____?*

Follow the teacher's lead. Enter the conversation as a listener, ready to follow your colleague's lead in determining priorities for coaching. When you start with an open-ended question, you set the tone that you are there as a collaborative partner. You are not there to fix the teaching or to enact your own preset agenda, though you do bring some goals based on the previous sessions, the focus of recent professional learning sessions, and insights from school data. Figure 8-5 lists some of the areas teachers might ask you to focus on. As you listen, take notes so you will remember important points while observing.

Sample Language

- *What would you like to think about together today?*
- *How can I be helpful to you today?*
- *What do you hope to learn from today's coaching session?*
- *What parts of your literacy teaching are going well?*
- *Where do you want to focus your attention?*

- *What do you want to accomplish today in your teaching?*
- *What are you working on in your teaching of reading (writing, phonics)? How can I support you?*
- *What's important to you right now?*

Determine a Focus Together

Teachers sometimes ask you to focus on a particular area of their teaching during the observation. They might ask you to look at any of the following:

- Lesson pacing
- Clarity/brevity of language
- Balance of teacher and student talk
- Recordkeeping
- Use of wait time
- Organization of materials and supplies
- Evidence of responsive teaching
- Use of language that prompts students to think and problem-solve
- Identification of individual goals for students

Figure 8-5

Build your colleagues' trust in you and in themselves. The more your colleagues are asked to consider these questions, the better they will get at answering them. As they grow in trust, they begin to understand that you are there to support them, and they will be more open to asking for help. In the beginning, you might encounter colleagues who routinely say, "I don't know what I want support with. Just tell me if I'm doing it right." Of course, that is your opportunity to say, "I can't do that, but we can be two sets of eyes on your students so we can talk together about how your teaching is supporting them."

Sample Language

- *Let's think together about what you've been working on in your teaching.*
- *What is going well in your teaching?*
- *What have you found challenging?*
- *In what ways have you been taking risks lately in your teaching?*
- *Here are some things I'm always trying to improve in my own teaching.* (List some options from Figure 8-5.) *Would it be helpful for me to support you in any of these areas?*

Seek to understand. The more insight you can gain about how your colleague is thinking, the more effective your coaching will be. The pre-observation conversation is the perfect time to learn about the lesson your colleague has planned and the rationales for it. We have found that a shift in teacher understanding can happen even before the teaching begins when you ask your colleague to articulate the thought process behind the plan.

Sample Language

- *What are your goals for the lesson today?*
- *What do you want your students to understand and be able to do as readers (writers) based on your teaching today?*
- *Can you share your thinking about _____?*
- *What new thinking do you plan to try out today?*
- *How did you prepare for today's lesson?*
- *What concerns about trying this approach do you want to talk about now?*
- *How are you thinking of going about that?*

Ground the conversation in the three cornerstones of literacy as a complex process. Be sure to inquire about the students' strengths and needs and how the materials and teaching decisions will support them. You will be able to look for evidence in the lesson and come back to discuss these in the post-observation conversation. As coach, keep these three important elements in mind because they are integrally connected (Figure 8-6):

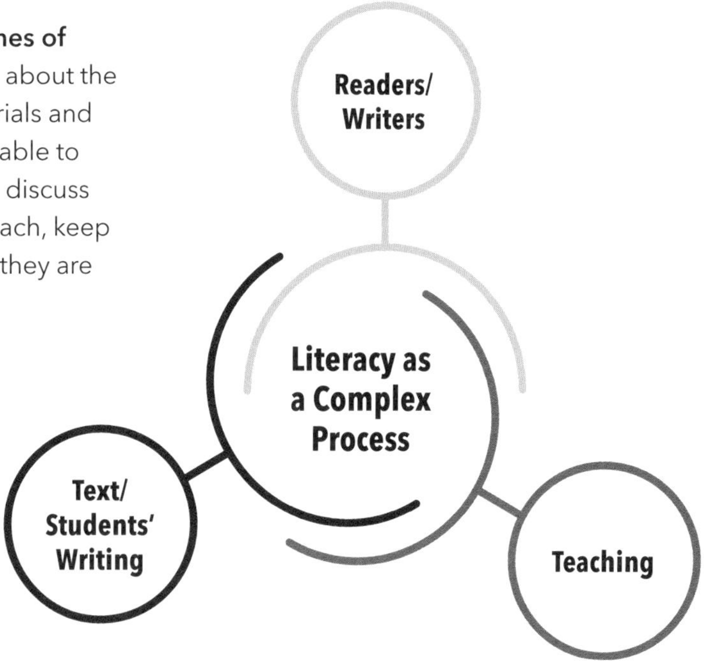

Figure 8-6

Sample Language

- *What do the readers (writers) understand?*
- *How does the text (student's writing) support students in building an effective reading (writing) process?*
- *How does the teaching support the students in building an effective reading (writing) process?*
- *How does the text provide opportunities for the readers to apply flexible decoding skills?*
- *What are the important learning opportunities this text will offer?*
- *What are your teaching priorities for your readers (writers) today? And that's because . . .?*
- *What is this text really about? How are you thinking your students will get to that level of understanding?*

Look together at student work. Looking at student work with a colleague can be eye opening for both of you because both of you will notice things that might give different information. In addition, teachers often feel more comfortable discussing their students than themselves, so it's a good entry point for

Pre-observation Conversation: What You Might Bring

- Reading records
- Writing samples
- Anecdotal notes
- Reader's notebook
- Writer's notebook
- Short video clip of a student's oral reading or talk about reading (writing)
- Benchmark assessment data
- Data from phonics assessments
- State test scores

teachers who are not yet comfortable with coaching. Taking time in the pre-observation conversation to talk about how student work can influence planning emphasizes the importance of using data to make teaching decisions.

When you analyze student work together, you also help your colleague learn a generative process to use in all aspects of planning. The goal is for your colleague to think in this way when you are not there. Besides analyzing student work together, help your colleague think about what evidence to look for during the lesson to determine whether the teaching decisions are successful. Figure 8-7 offers a few prompts to help your colleagues link assessment of student work to planning.

If You Want to...	You Might Say...
Invite the teacher to consider what they know about the students and how that information impacts planning. These prompts also send the powerful message that you can't plan lessons without having the students in mind.	▪ *Talk about the students you will be teaching today.* ▪ *How have you used information about the students as readers (writers) to plan for your teaching today?* ▪ *Given what you know about the students as readers (writers), why did you decide to teach this lesson to your students today?*
Prompt the teacher to consider the types of data that are useful for planning.	▪ *What information about the students could help you think about that?* ▪ *Talk about the data you used to plan for today's lesson.*
Support the teacher in analyzing the data and linking it to instructional planning.	▪ *What can you infer the student understandsfrom _____?* ▪ *What are you thinking might be a goal for this student based on _____?* ▪ *Let's look at our district's literacy goals (e.g., standards, curriculum frameworks) to think about what the student understands.* ▪ *Let's look at some of the students' performance data in reading. Maybe we'll get a sense of what's working well and what areas may need attention.* ▪ *Based on this information, where do you think the children may have some difficulty processing the text (applying the principle to their writing, etc.)?* ▪ *What is getting in the way of the students' fluency (e.g., efficient word analysis, knowledge of high frequency words)?*
Help you and the teacher consider what evidence to look for across the lesson.	▪ *Where do you anticipate finding evidence of _____ during the lesson?* ▪ *How will you know if _____?* ▪ *Would you like me to observe particular students for evidence of their active participation (understanding, engagement)?* ▪ *How will you assess their learning?* ▪ *How will you know your students processed the text well?*

Figure 8-7

Discuss plans for honoring all students' experiences and perspectives. The pre-observation conversation provides the opportunity for thinking about how to consider students' unique identities when planning lessons. For example, you might ask teachers to think about representation in classroom materials (whose voices and/or images are missing), develop plans for seeking a variety of student voices across the lesson, and make specific adjustments to support multilingual learners. Invite teachers to think about how their own background and experience has shaped their planning and teaching, and prompt them to expand their perspective.

Coaching for Culturally Responsive Teaching

As coach, you play a central role in fostering an inclusive environment and supporting culturally appropriate instructional practices by

- creating equitable and inclusive learning environments for both students and teachers,
- helping teachers select curriculum materials that support critical thinking,
- designing professional learning opportunities that enable the community to respect every person's unique identity,
- helping adapt teaching methods to ensure that each person's strengths and unique identities are recognized, and
- reflecting on your own biases, challenging stereotypes, and confronting injustices—and helping others do the same.

Sample Language

- *Talk about how you considered the students' unique experiences and perspectives in the resources (texts, materials) you selected. How are your students' identities represented?*
- *How can you make sure no biases are reflected in your use of data?*
- *How will your lesson promote the sharing of varied perspectives?*
- *How will you support the multilingual learners in the group?*
- *What patterns in the data or evidence might indicate inequity?*
- *What did you notice about students' interests in books (activities, topics)?*
- *What are some ways you've thought about being more inclusive of the range of students?*

Offer to co-plan a lesson as an alternative way to support teachers. At times, you may decide to schedule a longer pre-observation conversation to co-plan a lesson. Co-planning can establish a generative process for teachers to use in the future as well as introduce them to helpful planning tools, so the extra time is well spent. The goal is to co-construct a lesson in a way that will be helpful to the teacher in the short run and boost confidence and independence in the long run.

Sample Language

- *What information will we need to make a plan?*
- *You know your students best. What information can you share about them to help with our planning?*
- *What is essential for the students to be able to process this text well (write in this genre, etc.)?*
- *What examples do you think will be helpful for the students to take on the new learning?*
- *How will you know your teaching was successful?*

Show a brief video clip to demonstrate an aspect of teaching. You might find it helpful to show a short video clip (two to three minutes) during the pre-observation conversation to demonstrate an aspect of teaching. Watching the video clip together is a way to engage your colleague in a discussion of a common teaching example by noting teaching decisions and specific language. A brief discussion of the impact of the teaching decisions in the video might inspire the teacher you are coaching to reflect on planning decisions, or it might help you co-plan a lesson.

Sample Language

- *Take a look at this video clip to notice ____ (e.g., the students' interest level, the balance of talk between the teacher and the student, the way the teacher introduces the text).*
- *How might what you saw in this video help you think about your own plan?*

The Observation

You and your colleague both need to know what to expect during the lesson observation, so be clear about what you will be doing while your colleague is teaching. Clarify from the beginning that you will serve as the memory of the lesson, so you plan to take notes to use during the post-observation conversation. Reassure teachers that the notes are only for use during the coaching sessions and will not be shared with anybody in the school.

Teachers may ask if they can have a copy of your notes after the session. We have found that it is not useful to share them because the way we take notes is often not legible to others. You likely have your own shorthand that is tricky for others to understand. Simply explain to teachers that you think the notes will be challenging for them to read. However, there is no reason you can't share them if you want to or if the teacher insists. The notes are not anything more than a record of the lesson, but they set the stage for an effective post-observation conversation.

Spot Modeling

It's not generally a good idea to interrupt the flow of a lesson, but you and your colleague may have decided in the pre-observation conversation that there is a particular spot in the lesson where it would be helpful for you to model with the students. Make sure students know what you'll be doing beforehand so they will expect it. In the debriefing, be sure to discuss the notes or questions the teacher jotted down while observing your teaching.

Observe silently and generally avoid interacting with students. While there are some exceptions (see Spot Modeling), most of your time will be spent observing silently and avoiding any student interactions. If you talk or interact with students, you will disrupt the teacher's lesson. Observing in silence also reinforces the idea that you are not there to fix the lesson or the teaching but to be a second set of eyes and ears for thinking together.

You might on occasion engage in what we call *whisper* or *nonverbal coaching*. It is critical that you and your colleague agree that you might do this, and be sure any whisper coaching is related to whatever the teacher wants supported. This could include catching the coach's eye and nodding at a student who has been quiet for the entire lesson to suggest inviting the child into the conversation. Or, you might spontaneously whisper an idea you've had for a very brief teaching interaction. While this can be helpful, be cautious about interrupting the lesson or making your colleague feel like you are trying to fix something that is going wrong. Only whisper or give nonverbal cues when you think it will really make a difference for your discussion of the lesson later and will be generative for your colleague in future lessons. Constant interrupting to insert your own ideas not only steals your colleague's sense of agency but also interrupts the flow of the lesson and hinders your ability to collect evidence of teaching and learning.

Transcribe any significant language you heard from your colleague and students during the lesson. We recommend creating two columns on a sheet of paper, one for what your colleague says and one for what the students say. Of course, you will make your own abbreviations, but be sure you can read them later! By recording what the teacher says, you hold up a mirror for your colleague's self-reflection about the language used, the clarity of the instruction, the responsiveness of the teaching, the amount of teacher talk and student discourse, and the usefulness of the prompts in getting students to think deeply. You can also record important time transitions throughout the lesson, which can be useful when talking about pacing. Figure 8–8 shows notes recorded by a coach during a book club discussion with first graders and their teacher. (You will find a blank, full-size version of Note-Taking Tool: Coaching Notes as **OR 8.1** in the Online Resources.)

ONLINE RESOURCE 8.1

Having a record of your colleague's and the students' specific language allows for a post-observation conversation based on what you heard and saw. And, when you can analyze their exact language, you and your colleague will be better able to infer how students are processing the text or thinking about their writing. You can also reflect together on the direct impact of your colleague's instructional decisions on student learning. We find it helpful while observing to quickly check or star specific places that may be useful to discuss after the lesson.

Focus on teacher-identified priorities while taking in the entire lesson. It's easy to get lost in a lesson and lose sight of what your colleague identified as priorities for the observation, especially when other issues pop up during the lesson. Validate your colleague's request for support by capturing notes that directly address the stated priorities, but also note your own genuine questions about the teaching and learning across the lesson by writing your wonderings in the margins.

Reflect on what you have observed. Before meeting with your colleague, carve out a few minutes right after the lesson (if possible) to reflect on the observation. This will also give the teacher time to think about the lesson before you meet to debrief. When you take the time to review the transcript and collect your thoughts, you can more efficiently guide the post-observation conversation and approach it with one or two big ideas. Identify teaching strengths and evidence of student learning—not for the purpose of evaluating or complimenting the teaching but so you can build understandings from the parts of the lesson that led to student learning. As you review the transcript, look for patterns in teaching and identify and prioritize a few major coaching points.

NOTE-TAKING TOOL

INSTRUCTIONAL CONTEXT	TEACHER'S NAME	DATE
Book Club Discussion	Mrs. Frasier	10/14

TEACHER	STUDENT
1:30 p.m. What are you thinking about the book?	K— I liked how the elephant played in the mud. M— The mouse got muddy too. J— I thought it was funny that the elephant sprayed water on the mouse at the end. M— Yeah to clean him.
What else are you thinking about? *John, can you take us to the place that shows they are sad? How could you tell they are sad?	J— They were sad because they were too muddy. (J—turns to page; students follow) A— Look—he has tears. M— He washes his face. The mouse got soap and water. A— Between his toes, eyes and face.

Your Literacy Coaching Playbook **Online Resource 8.1 | Note-Taking Tool:** Coaching Notes, **Version 01**

Figure 8-8

Be sure to plan how you will address the specific areas the teacher asked you to think about. Use this time also to find relevant pages in any professional books, resources, or curriculum that you may want to share. We always write our first words at the end of the transcript so that we can open the conversation in a productive way that links to the specific lesson.

Following are some questions you can ask yourself to prepare for the post-observation conversation:

- *What are the two or three big ideas that will be helpful to talk about?*
- *How will I move from one big idea to another?*
- *How will I use the resources I have chosen?*
- *What language will I use to promote inquiry and address my coaching points?*
- *How will I address the concerns of the teacher?*

Taking this brief time for both you and your colleague to collect your thoughts independently will make for a more fruitful discussion after the observation because you have been sure to prioritize the important points.

The Post-observation Conversation

As with the pre-observation conversation, it is essential to schedule a time to debrief after the observation. Not only does this time allow you to address your coaching points and any specific areas the teacher asked you to focus on, but it also provides the opportunity to look at resources and/or student work to identify future goals for both teaching and learning. Without this collaborative time after the teaching, the observation can easily be misconstrued as an evaluative check on whether the teacher is implementing new ideas in the classroom. The post-observation conversation allows you to wonder alongside your colleague about the impact of teaching decisions and to further brainstorm ways to meet the needs of the students in the classroom.

Below you'll find brief discussions of ways to promote reflection and generative thinking in the post-observation conversation. The most important goal of the debriefing is to develop understandings from the teaching and learning that will transfer to future instruction. It's all about moving forward, not about "fixing" the lesson. You will notice echoes of the pre-observation conversation throughout the post-observation conversation, particularly in the use of evidence of student learning.

First, set the tone. Your first words might be something like the following: "You were concerned about scaffolding the readers with a short introduction. What did you notice about how your introduction supported the students?" The way you open the discussion sets the tone for the whole conversation, so invite specific reflection from the start.

Use an open-ended approach, but be ready to guide the conversation away from becoming evaluative. We advise against asking, "How do you think it went?" because your colleague will likely respond, "I think it went well" or "It didn't really go as planned." Of course, you could respond with "Talk about what you think went well," but it's better to avoid this evaluative talk from the beginning with a different opening. Figure 8–9 shows other suggestions for starting the conversation:

If You Want to...	You Might Say...
Allow the teacher to guide the discussion from the beginning. Though they are very open-ended, these prompts keep the conversation grounded in the teaching.	▪ *What are some important ideas that surfaced for you today in the way your students took on the writing?* ▪ *Based on today's lesson, what aspects of your teaching are you now thinking about differently?*
Start the conversation on a positive note without falling into an evaluative mode. These prompts set the stage for the teacher to think about when and why the students were engaged and/or what caused shifts in the students' learning.	▪ *Your students really seemed to enjoy _____, didn't they?* ▪ *You must be feeling like you got a shift in processing today. What did you notice?* ▪ *Talk about where you felt you made the biggest shifts in your students' reading (writing, phonics skills) today.*
Help further the discussion and elicit more response when the conversation dwindles.	▪ *Were there any surprises for you today?* ▪ *What else do you want to talk about?*

Figure 8-9

Encourage careful noticing and naming of students' learning behaviors. Responsive teaching rests on your colleague's ability to closely observe individual students and notice and name (Ray 2002, 18, 21) their learning behaviors, strengths, and needs. Teachers who recognize the value of systematic observation and rely on it regularly develop the ability to make moment-to-moment teaching decisions based on students' precise strengths and needs. In short, they are able to recognize evidence of learning—or evidence of challenge—and act on it.

Some teachers are natural observers of children, and others may need practice. The post-observation conversation is an opportunity to help teachers get better at identifying specific observations and their implications. The transcription you created during the observation along with any work the students produced will be helpful references during these conversations. Try using some of the language in Figure 8–10 to encourage your colleague to notice precise student responses and name learning behaviors:

If You Want to...	You Might Say...
Ground the conversation in evidence of student learning.	▪ *What did the children learn to do today as readers? writers?* ▪ *What did the child do to make you think that?* ▪ *What did you see (hear) the children do (say) that made you think that?*
Reinforce and support the teacher's ability to observe and analyze learning behaviors.	▪ *What did you think when you saw _____?* ▪ *You seemed pleased when you noticed _____.* ▪ *You're noticing that _____.* ▪ *You seemed surprised by _____. Why?*
Help the teacher hone the ability to observe and name learning behaviors.	▪ *Here's what I saw: _____. Talk about what you saw.* ▪ *I noticed that _____. (Refer to transcript.)* ▪ *This is what I saw _____. (Refer to transcript.)* ▪ *I have found that children often _____. What did you notice about your students?* ▪ *_____ said _____. What are you thinking about that?*
Encourage the teacher to notice patterns in evidence across the classroom.	▪ *What patterns did you notice in the students' responses? in their learning?* ▪ *What evidence made you realize that children were struggling in this area?* ▪ *What patterns do you notice from looking at these work samples?*
Support the teacher in evaluating evidence that validates teaching decisions.	▪ *What information did you find most useful?* ▪ *What information or data might you try to capture in your next lesson?* ▪ *What ongoing data or information might you collect that will help you inform your teaching?*

Figure 8-10

Use specific examples of teacher and student language to analyze the impact of teaching decisions. The most important aspect of individual coaching is building a teacher's understanding of effective instructional practices. Use the lesson you observed to reflect on the teaching decisions, but don't fall prey to trying to fix this lesson. Instead, think about what would be helpful for your colleague to learn for future lessons. The art of coaching lies in this delicate balance between addressing the specifics of the lesson while keeping the bigger takeaways at the center of the conversation (Figure 8–11).

If You Want to...	You Might Say...
Encourage the teacher to identify places in the lesson where the teaching decision was effective or did not result in the intended outcome.	▪ *Talk about teaching decisions that you felt were effective with your students today.* ▪ *Where did you feel your teaching was the most effective? When was it the least effective?* ▪ *When were you thinking the students were the most engaged? When were they the least engaged?* ▪ *Where did you feel things weren't going as well as you wanted? What are your insights about that?* ▪ *Where in your teaching today were you feeling challenged to make the best decision?* ▪ *What did you notice about how the student responded to your question?* ▪ *Why do you think the children were able to figure that out?* ▪ *I noticed that _____. How effective was that for your students?* ▪ *I noticed that you _____. It seemed to support _____.* ▪ *Let's talk about your decision _____.*
Help the teacher develop flexibility in decision-making. When you help the teacher consider alternative decisions and outcomes, you develop the teacher's agency and ability to think flexibly, which allows for more responsive teaching.	▪ *That was your plan, but what changed your thinking?* ▪ *If you had decided _____, how might that have been different?* ▪ *What else could you try?* ▪ *What were you thinking you might have done differently in your teaching today?* ▪ *When you saw _____, what choices did you have?* ▪ *What were you hoping would happen?* ▪ *If you had _____, what do you think the children would have done?*

Figure 8-11

Address the teacher's agenda. One way to build trust in your coaching relationships is to make sure teachers feel heard. If a teacher identifies an area for you to focus on during the pre-observation conversation, make sure to circle back to it during the debriefing. You can open this part of the conversation by saying, "You asked me to look at _____" or "You asked me to focus on _____ during the lesson. What are you thinking about that?"

Figure 8–12 shows a few examples of language you might use to prompt your colleague to think with you about a variety of important areas or a particular aspect of the teaching. Use the generative prompts to help teachers transfer new understandings to future lessons:

Area of Focus	Thinking Together	Generative Prompts
Pacing	▪ *Where did the lesson seem long?* ▪ *Where do you think you could have shortened the lesson?* ▪ *Where might you have tightened the lesson?* ▪ *I can tell you the time on that.* (Refer to your recorded times.)	▪ *From what you noticed, what are some ways you might work on pacing going forward?* ▪ *What have you learned about your pacing that will be helpful in your next lessons?*
Clarity of Language	▪ *About five minutes into the lesson, you noticed that your directions were not clear. What did you see (hear) the children do (say) that made you think that?* ▪ *Where in the lesson did you feel your instructions were the clearest?*	▪ *What will you do to make your language clearer going forward?*
Equity and Access	▪ *Whose voices were missing during the lesson?* ▪ *What do you think helped support your multilingual learners in the lesson?* ▪ *Let's think about what else you could have done to engage the multilingual learners in the discussion.*	▪ *Let's talk about some ways to include more voices during future discussions.* ▪ *What are you thinking you will do in your future planning to get more students involved in your lesson?*

Figure 8-12

Direct your colleague to professional resources and reading. It is not enough to simply tell your colleague where to find information. If you want a teacher to really read and use a resource, look at it (or part of it) together and have sticky notes ready so your colleague can mark it. Ask your colleague to read a few lines or a paragraph and share thoughts about it. Keep it short and brief. This allows your colleague to build knowledge and reflect on the lesson with the new thinking in mind.

Sample Language

- *Skim the bullets on page x , and think about which ones might be helpful to you.*
- *Read paragraph ____ in column ____. What does this make you think about your lesson?*
- *Look at this section. What might be helpful to use from here in planning your next lesson?*

Use Video as a Resource

Select a one- or two-minute video clip of teaching to help the teacher reflect on an aspect of the lesson. Just as reading a passage can help the teacher see something new, a short video clip can help the teacher reflect on the lesson and construct new understandings about teaching and learning.

Help your colleague reflect on new understandings and set future goals. Carve out time at the end of the coaching session for your colleague to reflect on what has been learned and how the new thinking will be used. Help your colleague identify goals and priorities with your support. Your colleague needs to own the goals that will emerge from the thinking you do together. You, of course, should note their goals so you have them for reference in future sessions. We recommend having teachers write down their own reflections and goals in their reflection journal.

Sample Language

- *What are your next goals (priorities) for your readers and writers?*
- *What do you want to focus on next in your teaching of reading and writing?*
- *How will you apply your new thinking to future lessons?*
- *What are your most useful insights from today's teaching?*
- *What are your priorities for helping the children become more effective at ____?*

On occasion, co-plan the next lesson. After briefly discussing the lesson, you and the teacher might decide to co-plan the next lesson to apply the new understandings from the observed lesson. This co-planning can be simple and informal. Talking through just a few major points of the next lesson can be enough to get the teacher started.

Sample Language

- *Let's think about this book together. Based on what you know now about the students, how are you thinking you would introduce it to the class tomorrow?*
- *Knowing the students' level of engagement went up when you did ____, what could you plan for tomorrow's writing lesson to get them engaged from the beginning?*

- *Thinking about your pacing: What parts of this reading lesson seem most important for your students? What parts might you cut in the future?*

Invite feedback. Constructive feedback helps all learners. Solicit honest feedback from the colleagues you coach. Consistent with your commitment to ongoing improvement of your craft, invite feedback at the end of your coaching session to make shifts in your coaching. Your colleagues will be willing to share their feedback when they know you are sincere about making thoughtful changes based on their constructive comments.

Sample Language

- *How did our time together help you think about your teaching?*
- *What was not helpful to you in our time today? What would you change in our time together?*
- *What was most useful for you in our time together?*
- *What did you learn today that you want to share with your colleagues?*
- *What is it that we talked about today that you found helpful?*
- *Can you suggest what else would be helpful for us to talk about the next time?*
- *Can you suggest anything that you would have changed in the way we worked together today?*

A Protocol Tool for One-on-One Coaching

We have summarized the process for one-on-one coaching in a protocol as shown in Figure 8-13. (You will find a full-size version of Protocol Tool: One-on-One Coaching as **OR 8.2** in the Online Resources.) There is no need to think about the process as rigid. You can use items selectively. The description in the protocol illustrates how a one-on-one coaching session might go. We recommend printing it out and keeping it handy in your coaching notebook (Chapter 23).

Extend Learning with Video

Video clips provide the opportunity to freeze a few minutes of active teaching for further reflection and discussion. They are also useful for reaching more teachers or supplementing individual coaching. Figure 8-14 is a simple protocol you can follow to make the most of

ONLINE RESOURCE 8.2

PROTOCOL TOOL

ONE-ON-ONE COACHING

PARTICIPANTS	TIMING
TEACHER, COACH	45-105 min

PRE-OBSERVATION CONVERSATION (10-15 min)

- Meet with the teacher one-on-one.
- Have a brief interaction about your last coaching session and invite your colleague to share the impact.
- Examine recent data and think together about students' strengths and needs.
- Talk with the teacher about the specific goals, rationales, plans, and expected outcomes of the lesson.
- Gather evidence of teacher's understandings.
- Make note of specific areas the teacher would like you to notice or think about.

OBSERVATION (15-60 min)

- Create two columns on your paper, one for what teacher says and the other for what students say.
- Observe silently and avoid student interactions.
- Transcribe the significant language from the lesson (teacher and students).
- Record time transitions.
- Identify teaching strengths and evidence of student learning.
- Note genuine questions about teaching and learning.
- Look for patterns in teaching.
- Identify and prioritize a few major coaching points for possible discussion.
- Maintain a focus on teacher-identified priorities while taking in the entire lesson.
- Provide time for the teacher and you to think about the lesson before debriefing.
- Identify brief excerpts in professional resources that might support the discussion.
- Write down the words you will use to open the post-observation conversation.

POST-OBSERVATION CONVERSATION (20-30 min)

- Discuss and analyze the lesson.
- Use specific examples of teacher and student language.
- Share and discuss coaching points/priorities using professional resources and student artifacts to support the discussion.
- Respond to the teacher's questions posed in the pre-observation conversation.
- Summarize and set goals for teaching and further learning.
- Ask for feedback on the session.
- Invite the teacher to share what was helpful/less helpful about the coaching experience.

Your Literacy Coaching Playbook — **Online Resource 8.2 | Protocol Tool:** One-on-One Coaching, **Version 01**

Figure 8-13

ONLINE RESOURCE 8.3

using video for coaching. (You will find a full-size version of Protocol Tool: Using Video in One-on-One Coaching as **OR 8.3** in the Online Resources.)

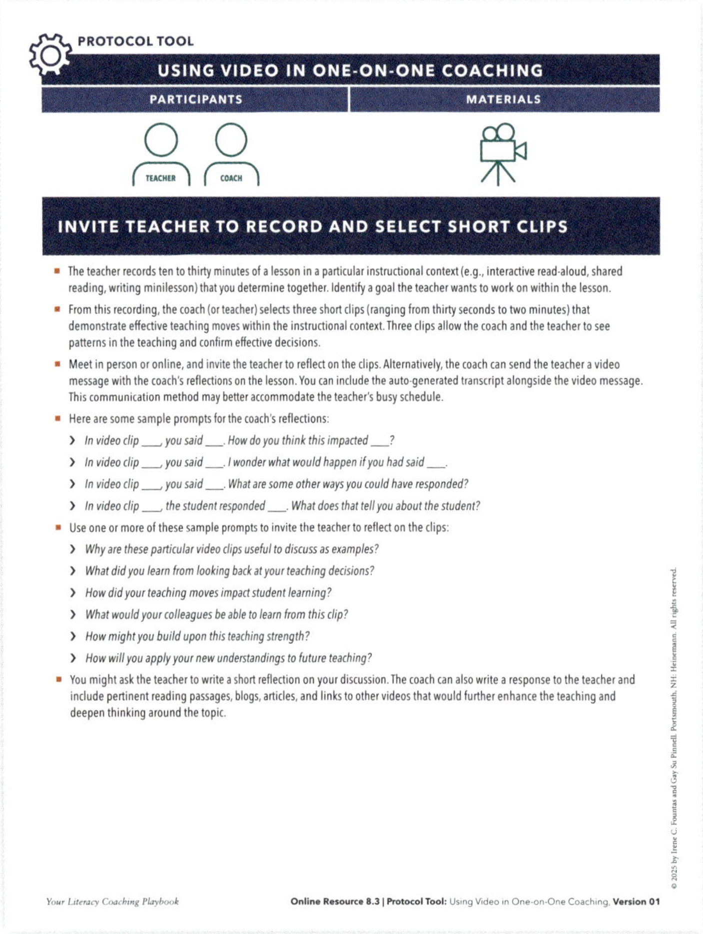
PROTOCOL TOOL

USING VIDEO IN ONE-ON-ONE COACHING

PARTICIPANTS	MATERIALS
TEACHER, COACH	

INVITE TEACHER TO RECORD AND SELECT SHORT CLIPS

- The teacher records ten to thirty minutes of a lesson in a particular instructional context (e.g., interactive read-aloud, shared reading, writing minilesson) that you determine together. Identify a goal the teacher wants to work on within the lesson.
- From this recording, the coach (or teacher) selects three short clips (ranging from thirty seconds to two minutes) that demonstrate effective teaching moves within the instructional context. Three clips allow the coach and the teacher to see patterns in the teaching and confirm effective decisions.
- Meet in person or online, and invite the teacher to reflect on the clips. Alternatively, the coach can send the teacher a video message with the coach's reflections on the lesson. You can include the auto-generated transcript alongside the video message. This communication method may better accommodate the teacher's busy schedule.
- Here are some sample prompts for the coach's reflections:
  - *In video clip ___, you said ___. How do you think this impacted ___?*
  - *In video clip ___, you said ___. I wonder what would happen if you had said ___.*
  - *In video clip ___, you said ___. What are some other ways you could have responded?*
  - *In video clip ___, the student responded ___. What does that tell you about the student?*
- Use one or more of these sample prompts to invite the teacher to reflect on the clips:
  - *Why are these particular video clips useful to discuss as examples?*
  - *What did you learn from looking back at your teaching decisions?*
  - *How did your teaching moves impact student learning?*
  - *What would your colleagues be able to learn from this clip?*
  - *How might you build upon this teaching strength?*
  - *How will you apply your new understandings to future teaching?*
- You might ask the teacher to write a short reflection on your discussion. The coach can also write a response to the teacher and include pertinent reading passages, blogs, articles, and links to other videos that would further enhance the teaching and deepen thinking around the topic.

Your Literacy Coaching Playbook **Online Resource 8.3 | Protocol Tool:** Using Video in One-on-One Coaching, **Version 01**

Figure 8-14

Though nothing compares to meeting one on one with your colleagues in person, video offers its own benefits. Your colleagues have the opportunity to observe for themselves their own language and its impact on their students' behaviors. They can replay the video, slow it down, or rewatch selected portions to gain insight into which teaching moves had an impact, which is in the end what coaching is all about. The important conversations you have in one-on-one coaching cannot really be replicated or replaced through video coaching, but using it to supplement individual coaching is yet another way to offer your colleagues an opportunity to lift their level of expertise.

Up **Next**

In Chapter 9, we present a potentially time-saving format for coaching: cluster coaching. Instead of coaching a single teacher, several teachers gather to observe each other's teaching.

Chapter 9

The Play: Cluster Coaching

Something special happens when teachers gather to observe one another's teaching. Maybe it's safety in numbers or the power of the group, but inhibitions tend to fall away, a sense of shared purpose and collaborative inquiry fills the room, and both the host teacher and the observers are more willing to take risks, share insights, and support one another. Perhaps the biggest advantage of cluster coaching is that you can facilitate the learning of multiple teachers in one session, which can be quite helpful if you're often strapped for time.

What Is Cluster Coaching?

Cluster coaching is collaborative inquiry that results in new insights for a host teacher and two or three observing teachers. The framework for cluster coaching is similar to that of one-on-one coaching: pre-observation conversation, observation, and post-observation conversation. All participating teachers take part in the pre-observation and post-observation conversations. During the observation, the observing teachers watch the host teacher teach a lesson. The group setting of cluster coaching calls for some unique considerations in planning and in the coaching moves you'll want to know about.

BENEFITS OF CLUSTER COACHING

- Maximizes time by meeting in a group instead of with an individual teacher
- Allows for all to hear several voices and perspectives
- Provides opportunities for teachers to develop common understandings, language, and goals
- Hones teachers' ability to closely observe students' behaviors

A Framework for Cluster Coaching

Use the same basic framework for cluster coaching as you do for one-on-one coaching (Figure 9–1). Your role within the framework changes slightly because you guide the group to build understandings collectively. Ask clarifying questions and think alongside the teachers as you do in one-on-one coaching, but now you have the added role of facilitating the conversation so that your colleagues productively build on one another's contributions.

FRAMEWORK FOR A CLUSTER COACHING SESSION

PRE-OBSERVATION CONVERSATION

Meet for a pre-observation conversation: The coach facilitates the host teacher's sharing of the plan, rationales, and goals for the lesson. The coach may pose one or two questions to focus the conversation.

10-15 min

OBSERVATION

Observe a lesson: The group observes their colleague teach a lesson and records their noticings and wonderings and any important, specific teacher and student language.

15-60 min

POST-OBSERVATION CONVERSATION

Meet for a post-observation conversation: The group thinks about the teaching and learning together, shares their noticings (including those identified as a focus), asks genuine questions about the teacher's decisions, and reflects on what they will take back to their own teaching from the observation.

20-30 min

Figure 9-1

Plan and Prepare for Cluster Coaching

The biggest challenge for cluster coaching is the fact that you have to accommodate and coordinate more than one person's schedule. After you have identified the observers (usually two or three participants to minimize traffic in the classroom and scheduling challenges), work with your administrator to arrange coverage for teachers to participate in all three parts of the cluster coaching session—the pre-observation conversation, the lesson observation, and the post-observation conversation. This might mean the pre- and post-observation conversations have to take place on different days from the lesson observation. Do what you can to keep them as close together as possible.

You will also need to invite a specific teacher (if you have a reason to do so) or seek a volunteer to be the host teacher and teach the lesson. In the role-play on pages 84–86, notice how one literacy coach introduces the idea of cluster coaching and invites teachers into the process. Communicate that host teachers are not invited to serve as models for everyone else; they are simply generous colleagues who are willing to share their practice. Depending on the variety of professional learning opportunities, you might schedule cluster coaching a few times a year (as staffing for coverage allows), varying the host teacher each time.

Establish Common Understandings

If you are meeting with a group for the first time, take a few minutes to establish some common guidelines for observing in a classroom with a group of people. For example, whenever a group of adults enters a classroom, it can change the dynamic for the students and teacher. Talk about how to minimize distractions so the teacher and students can stay focused. The more the lesson resembles what happens when you are not there, the more authentic it will feel and the more helpful it will be for everyone.

You'll want to establish norms for cluster coaching before the first session. Figure 9-2 shows what one coach shared with her colleagues. After sharing the chart, she asked for questions and additional suggestions, and updated the chart. Because your colleagues know they all will likely be in the role of the host teacher at some point, they are usually grateful for these guidelines and happy to provide feedback. If time allows, you might construct the norms with your colleagues.

The most important thing you can ask of your colleagues is that they be fully present during the observation. If they are fully present, they are not as likely to chat with colleagues, interact with students, or be distracted by a device. Even well-intentioned interactions like redirecting students can change the lesson dynamic and cause distraction. This quick conversation prior to the observation ensures that the host teacher feels respected and that the students' learning experience is prioritized.

Keep Conversations Positive

Stress the importance of keeping the conversations positive and nonevaluative through thoughtful word choices. In addition to establishing expectations for the lesson observation, set the stage for positive and productive conversations before and after the observation. Offer examples of negative or evaluative language so teachers can recognize and stay away from it in their own talk. One idea is to ask people to avoid making negative comparisons like, "That went great, but it would never work in my room with my group of students" or "I don't have other adults in the room like you, so that wouldn't work." Help the group discuss how negative comparisons erode productivity. Instead, provide alternatives to evaluative language. Instead of comments like "I liked how you . . ." or "I loved . . . ," encourage your colleagues to use phrases like, "When you did this, I noticed . . ." or "Based on what I saw, I was thinking . . . ."

Sample Norms for Observing During Cluster Coaching

- Turn off all devices before entering the classroom.
- Sit or stand in a place where you can clearly see the lesson but not obstruct the students.
- Be fully present and attentive.
- Avoid interacting with students.
- Avoid side conversations with colleagues.

Figure 9-2

The Pre-observation Conversation

Many of the coaching moves you make in a one-on-one pre-observation conversation are the same in cluster coaching, but here you manage the input of a group. For example, you look at student data; listen to the host teacher's plans, rationales, and goals for the lesson; ask genuine questions; and discuss any areas of teaching the host teacher would like to focus on. The difference is that you invite the group to think along with them, encouraging the group to ask questions to understand the host teacher's thinking. You may need a little more time for the pre-observation conversation than you do for for one-on-one coaching.

A Coaching Role-Play

Once again, we turn to a brief role-play to illustrate how a pre-observation conversation for cluster coaching might prepare your colleagues to observe the lesson and think about its implications for their own teaching.

Coach: *Thank you, Mr. G., for sharing your teaching with us today so that we can think together about how to build strong decoding skills in our small-group lessons. Mr. G. has generously volunteered to allow us to observe a lesson so that we have a shared example to use in thinking about our own teaching of decoding while students are reading connected text.*

What to Notice: The coach quickly thanks the host teacher, emphasizes that he has volunteered to be the host teacher, and communicates the focus of the lesson.

Coach: *Tell us a little about your students and about your plans for this lesson. (Pauses as he shares, and observes teachers jotting down a few notes.) Mr. G., would you tell us a little about what you have taught this group about decoding new words? What are their strengths, and what do you see as challenges? Teachers, take a look at page 27 in your curriculum guide to see a range of goals for word analysis at this level.*

What to Notice: The coach invites the teacher to share information about his students with the group and to talk about the lesson he has planned. She also asks him to share the students' strengths and needs. Then she invites them into the curriculum resource to expand their understanding of the competencies students need to demonstrate at this grade level. By bringing the teachers into the resource, the coach gives them a tool to think about their own instruction while also providing more context for understanding their colleague's teaching decisions.

Coach: *In our last professional learning session on using morphology to decode new words, we explored language that confirms students' efficient use of word parts to solve new words while reading connected text. We talked about the importance of students noticing word parts like syllables, word roots, prefixes, and suffixes. Jot down one or two examples of language prompts that you think help students confirm their use of word parts or notice word parts to solve new words. (Pauses here for a minute or two.)*

Let's have a quick share. Will each of you share one of the prompts you wrote down? As you observe the lesson today, notice language that Mr. G. uses to prompt his students to work through new words and to confirm their attempts or successful use of decoding skills to read new words.

What to Notice: The coach links to a recent professional learning session and gives a one-sentence summary of what was discussed there. Then she provides another opportunity for engagement by having each teacher jot down and share examples of language that prompts students to notice word parts when solving new words. This quick interaction also primes the teachers to pay attention to the language Mr. G. uses throughout the lesson.

Other ways to engage the group include the following:

- Revisit a pertinent quote from a professional resource.
- Invite the group to review a curriculum document with descriptions of goals for students at the grade level.
- Invite them to share specific teaching moves they have found helpful when teaching students to use word parts.
- Ask them to turn and talk about what they would want to know from student data prior to teaching a lesson on word-solving skills.
- Examine some reading or writing data on the students.

Coach: *Mr. G., is there anything the group has shared that you think might be helpful to you today? Is there anything special you'd like us to look for and notice in your lesson?*

What to Notice: The coach made it clear to the host teacher that the group is there to observe but also to help by taking good notes during the observation. They will share their noticings on how the teacher's decisions appeared to be helpful to the students. They will also share their wonderings.

Coach: *As you are aware, we'll sit in the back of the group so we can see and hear, but we won't talk with the students. While Mr. G. is teaching, we'll be the memory of the lesson. Everyone, make a line down the middle of your paper. On the left side, note what Mr. G. says to the students after they make an error or when they have difficulty, and on the right side, note the students' attempts at new words. We'll use these notes to talk about language after the lesson. Also, put a star by the things you wonder about so you can ask any questions that arise for you.*

What to Notice: The coach engages the group by having each of them create a very simple two-column chart, which they will fill in during the observation and discuss afterward. This sets the expectation that they will be active contributors to the discussion and that their thinking matters. The coach also reminds the group of some of the considerations they have previously discussed for observing, such as avoiding interactions with students.

The Observation

Part of the benefit of cluster coaching is that the group has the opportunity to practice careful observation. Because everyone is observing the same lesson, they will be able to share what they noticed, compare notes, and become more careful observers. The more specific everyone can be in their note-taking, the more productive the post-observation conversation can be.

Before you begin the observation, ask teachers to split a piece of paper in half so they can make notes on the interactions. We often ask the observers to record teacher language on one side and student language on the other side. Depending on the type of lesson, you might choose to have each observer focus on one or two students. Choose one or two of the following questions for teachers to keep in mind as they observe.

Sample Language

- *What evidence shows the strengths of the students?*
- *What are the students learning how to do as readers (writers, word solvers)? How do you know?*
- *What language did the teacher use that was helpful to the students in solving their own problems?*
- *What are your wonderings?*
- *How is the teacher making the learning generative so the children can apply their new understanding to future reading?*
- *What is new learning that you can use in your own teaching?*

The Post-observation Conversation

The difference between a post-observation conversation for individual coaching and one for cluster coaching is that in cluster coaching you guide the conversation of the whole group so that all participating teachers can share what they noticed and build on one another's ideas. The group observation has the advantage of several perspectives. Following are a few of the moves you might use to make the most of working with a small group.

Incorporate a variety of facilitating techniques. One such technique is to take a minute to ask each observing teacher to jot down two or three noticings or wonderings that would be interesting to discuss. Instead of broader prompts, you might first select a category such as strengths you observed in the students or teaching moves that were helpful. Consider having pairs share their thinking together first and then share with the group. Be sure to prompt the teachers to address the goals the host teacher identified in the pre-observation conversation.

Help teachers build on one another's ideas. Cluster coaching is most effective when you are able to start with one of the teacher's noticings and build to a bigger idea through the sharing of multiple voices. Consider using some of the following language to facilitate this process.

Sample Language

- *What do you think about that idea?*
- *How is your thinking different from ____?*
- *What can you add to that?*
- *Thank you for sharing your thinking. Who would like to add to that?*
- *What else are you thinking?*
- *Do you agree with that? Why or why not?*
- *If you agree that ____, what does it mean for your teaching?*
- *What other way is there to think about that?*

Listen more, talk less. Your most important coaching move is effective listening. Be extra cautious about inserting yourself into the conversation. Allow teachers the space to hear and learn from one another. Enter the conversation when you can add a comment or question that will lift the thinking of the group or will move the conversation to a more productive place. This will also allow you to listen for comments that you might want to restate to make them generative for everyone's learning.

Provide time for reflection. Save time at the end of the conversation for teachers to reflect on and share what they will bring back to their own teaching. Invite teachers to write down their takeaways and share at least one with the group. People take away different things from a discussion, so having the chance to listen to their colleagues might remind them of something else they learned. Use the following language to support this process.

Sample Language

- *What did you learn from this experience that you will take back to your own teaching?*
- *What do you plan to try with your students after observing today's lesson?*

- *What new understanding(s) are you walking away with after today's session?*
- *What does this all mean for your own teaching?*

Ask for feedback. As with any coaching session, end cluster coaching with a request for honest feedback. Ask each member of the group to quickly share what was helpful for them and what might be improved for the next cluster coaching session.

A Protocol Tool for Cluster Coaching

ONLINE RESOURCE 9.1

We summarize the process for cluster coaching in Figure 9-3. (You will find a full-size version of Protocol Tool: Cluster Coaching as **OR 9.1** in the Online Resources.) We recommend printing out the protocol tool and keeping it handy in your coaching notebook (Chapter 23).

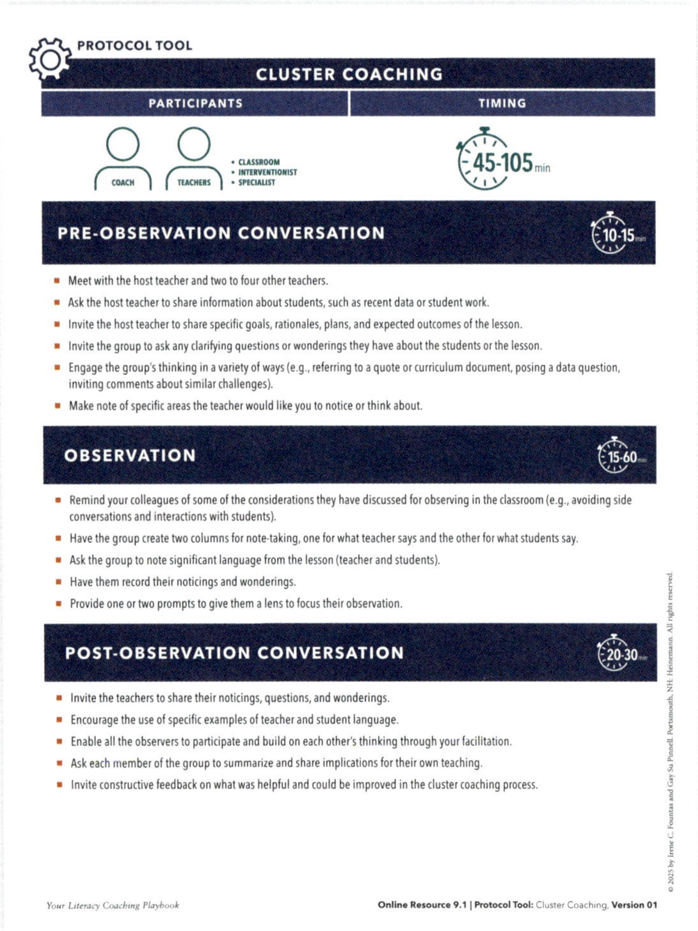

PROTOCOL TOOL

CLUSTER COACHING

PARTICIPANTS	TIMING
COACH; TEACHERS (• CLASSROOM • INTERVENTIONIST • SPECIALIST)	45-105 min

PRE-OBSERVATION CONVERSATION 10-15 min

- Meet with the host teacher and two to four other teachers.
- Ask the host teacher to share information about students, such as recent data or student work.
- Invite the host teacher to share specific goals, rationales, plans, and expected outcomes of the lesson.
- Invite the group to ask any clarifying questions or wonderings they have about the students or the lesson.
- Engage the group's thinking in a variety of ways (e.g., referring to a quote or curriculum document, posing a data question, inviting comments about similar challenges).
- Make note of specific areas the teacher would like you to notice or think about.

OBSERVATION 15-60 min

- Remind your colleagues of some of the considerations they have discussed for observing in the classroom (e.g., avoiding side conversations and interactions with students).
- Have the group create two columns for note-taking, one for what teacher says and the other for what students say.
- Ask the group to note significant language from the lesson (teacher and students).
- Have them record their noticings and wonderings.
- Provide one or two prompts to give them a lens to focus their observation.

POST-OBSERVATION CONVERSATION 20-30 min

- Invite the teachers to share their noticings, questions, and wonderings.
- Encourage the use of specific examples of teacher and student language.
- Enable all the observers to participate and build on each other's thinking through your facilitation.
- Ask each member of the group to summarize and share implications for their own teaching.
- Invite constructive feedback on what was helpful and could be improved in the cluster coaching process.

Your Literacy Coaching Playbook **Online Resource 9.1 | Protocol Tool:** Cluster Coaching, **Version 01**

Figure 9-3

Extend the Learning

You can extend what your colleagues have learned in cluster coaching by following up with other plays in your playbook. Here are some ideas:

- Offer to follow up with one-on-one coaching (Chapter 8) with teachers who would like continued support on the topic.
- Coordinate learning partners for peer coaching (Chapter 10) so teachers have an opportunity to explore their new learning in their own classrooms with a colleague's support.
- Use a professional learning session (Chapter 11) to delve deeper into a challenge, issue, or interest that surfaced during the group's discussion.
- Consider planning a series of bite-size professional learning sessions (Chapter 12) to address smaller topics or challenges that need attention.
- After teachers have had an opportunity to apply what they learned, consider organizing a learning walk (Chapter 14) to gain an understanding of how teachers throughout the school are applying the ideas explored.

- Lesson study (Chapter 15) can be a helpful way to revisit the ideas explored during the coaching session so the study group members have the opportunity to plan, try out, and revise a lesson related to the topic.

The power of cluster coaching is that it accomplishes so many things at once. It gives colleagues the opportunity to build their professional relationships and to share their expertise with one another. It provides teachers the collective experience of observing teaching and learning. The teachers practice becoming better observers of students' reading and writing behaviors as they listen to their colleagues share their thinking. They develop trust and continue to grow as a community of learners. Most important, cluster coaching gives your colleagues the opportunity to gain new understandings and insights into their own teaching so they can have a greater impact on student learning.

Following Up

- Vary the composition of the group to allow for greater diversity in thinking. You might even want to form a group based on particular needs (e.g., focus on managing independence).
- Invite the group to reflect on their experience with cluster coaching and share insights with you or each other at another common meeting time.
- Follow up with other professional learning opportunities.

Up **Next**

In Chapter 10, we turn to peer coaching, a highly effective structure that pairs two teachers with common interests or needs in a round of collaborative inquiry. The payoff? A reciprocal learning loop that builds the expertise of both teachers and improves their observation and teaching skills.

Chapter 10

The Play: **Peer Coaching**

Imagine a school in which classroom doors are always open, teachers talk publicly with one another about their triumphs and challenges, and everyone learns how to think like a coach to help a colleague explore new ideas, adopt more effective teaching methods, and gain important insights about students that only another teacher can provide.

Peer coaching—when two teachers observe each other's teaching in order to learn from one another—offers a way to encourage openness, sharing, and collaboration among individual teachers that will benefit them and their students.

BENEFITS OF PEER COACHING

- Builds trust among members of the school community
- Develops collaborative relationships between teachers
- Supports mutual problem-solving
- Extends learning from other professional learning experiences
- Builds professional capacity in the school as you teach your colleagues how to support each other's learning
- Elevates teachers' identity as capable team members

What Is Peer Coaching?

Although it can be fun and rewarding, peer coaching is much more than a social time with peers. As you will learn in this chapter, peer coaching is a carefully scaffolded yet simple process in which two teachers follow a basic protocol and use designated resources to make the work productive. Note, though, that it would be best for the teachers to have experienced one-on-one coaching and possibly cluster coaching before trying to take on peer coaching.

This type of professional learning is designed for both the host teacher, who teaches a lesson, and the visiting teacher, who observes, to develop new understandings. The host teacher does not provide a "model lesson" with the purpose of teaching a colleague; nor does the visiting teacher evaluate the lesson for the purpose of offering advice. Instead, it is a process of collaborative inquiry with the host teacher providing data for analysis.

The visiting teacher is expected to be another set of eyes, sharing significant noticings and posing genuine questions. The host teacher is expected to respond to those inquiries while offering their own noticings and wonderings. Together, they build a deeper understanding of a particular aspect of teaching and discuss the power of teaching decisions in responding to students. Sometimes, learning partners plan follow-up lessons or develop support materials together and meet again to observe how their co-planned lessons impact student learning. Each teacher gets the chance to teach and observe.

Through collaborative inquiry, both teachers walk away with a greater understanding of teaching and learning. Your role as a coach is to get them to this point—to facilitate learning partnerships and teach them how to have the kind of conversations that lift each other's thinking.

> *"Many believe that the essence of the coaching transaction is to offer advice to teachers following observations. Rather, teachers learn from one another while planning instruction, developing support materials, watching one another work with students, and thinking together about the impact of their behavior on their students' learning."*
>
> —**BEVERLY SHOWERS AND BRUCE JOYCE** (1996, 16)

A Framework for Peer Coaching

Learning partners can use the basic framework from one-on-one and cluster coaching to structure peer coaching. Figure 10–1 describes how peer coaching looks within this framework. As we discuss later in the chapter, you may initially join the two learning partners for each part of the peer coaching session to get it started, but later they will meet on their own while you support them in other ways.

Plan and Prepare for Peer Coaching

Before peer coaching begins, meet with teachers to introduce the process and allow your colleagues to ask questions. Consider starting one peer coaching partnership earlier than the others so you can record a session. For teachers unfamiliar with peer coaching, watching a few short video clips will demystify the process.

FRAMEWORK FOR A PEER COACHING SESSION

PRE-OBSERVATION CONVERSATION

Meet for a pre-observation conversation: The visiting teacher listens to the host teacher's plans, goals, and rationales for the lesson and asks questions to understand the teacher's thinking. Partners look together at student data and any resources or student work relevant to the lessont.

10-15 min

OBSERVATION OF TEACHING

Observe/teach the lesson: The host teacher teaches the lesson while the visiting teacher observes, taking notes and recording significant teacher and student language, as well as noticings and wonderings.

15-60 min

POST-OBSERVATION CONVERSATION

Meet for a post-observation conversation: The learning partners think about the teaching and learning together and consult any relevant resources to think more about the lesson. Both teachers reflect on their new understandings and set goals for their own teaching.

20-30 min

Figure 10-1

Whether you show a video clip or not, be sure to communicate the collaborative nature of the partnership and emphasize that peer coaching is not evaluative; rather, it is an opportunity to build understandings together.

The scaffolding you provide does not end with this opening conversation, but a short, explanatory introduction does make a difference. It establishes expectations and lays the foundation for collaborative work. Let's explore some of the important points made in this introduction.

Sample Introduction: *Peer coaching is an opportunity for you and a colleague to collaborate and build deeper understandings about a particular instructional context or area of teaching. So, I am excited that we will be starting peer coaching this month! I will coordinate learning partnerships so that you and a colleague will be able to observe each other teach and then have time to think and learn together. This will provide a practical way to follow up on what you learn during professional learning sessions and our one-on-one coaching sessions. To help you learn the framework we'll use for peer coaching, I will guide your first sessions.*

Your time is valuable, so I will work with you and Principal Hernandez to schedule peer coaching in a way that minimizes your time out of the classroom. But please be as flexible as you can as we do our best to accommodate everyone.

Your goal will not be to give each other advice or evaluate one another's teaching. Instead, you will focus together on observing the students' reading and writing behaviors and discussing how students respond to the teaching decisions. The look-for tools developed during our professional learning sessions will help focus the observations and discussion during your sessions. I look forward to working with you to get peer coaching up and running. What questions do you have?

Select Learning Partners

Notice in the introduction that the coach will coordinate the partnerships. We recommend that you play a role in matching learning partners, at least initially. Since you have the unique vantage point of seeing many of your colleagues teach, you will be able to offer suggestions for partnerships that will help teachers grow. When you coordinate partnerships, you avoid the natural temptation for teachers to choose partners simply based on friendship, which from our experience, does not always lead to the most growth. We are not saying that friends can't make great learning partners, but there is more to consider in matching colleagues for peer coaching

We list some of the ways you might pair your colleagues (Figure 10–2). For example, you might suggest a partnership between peers who have the same instructional goals (e.g., differentiation in small-group teaching, improving word recognition skills, teaching for phonological awareness). Or, you might choose to pair colleagues who bring different strengths to the table—for example, a new teacher and an experienced teacher or a teacher experienced with teaching multilingual learners and one less experienced can lift each other in unexpected ways. Learning partnerships are dynamic. They should change to best fit your colleagues' needs. However you decide to pair your colleagues, scaffolding the peer coaching process will support them in becoming productive learning partners.

A FEW WAYS TO PAIR PEERS

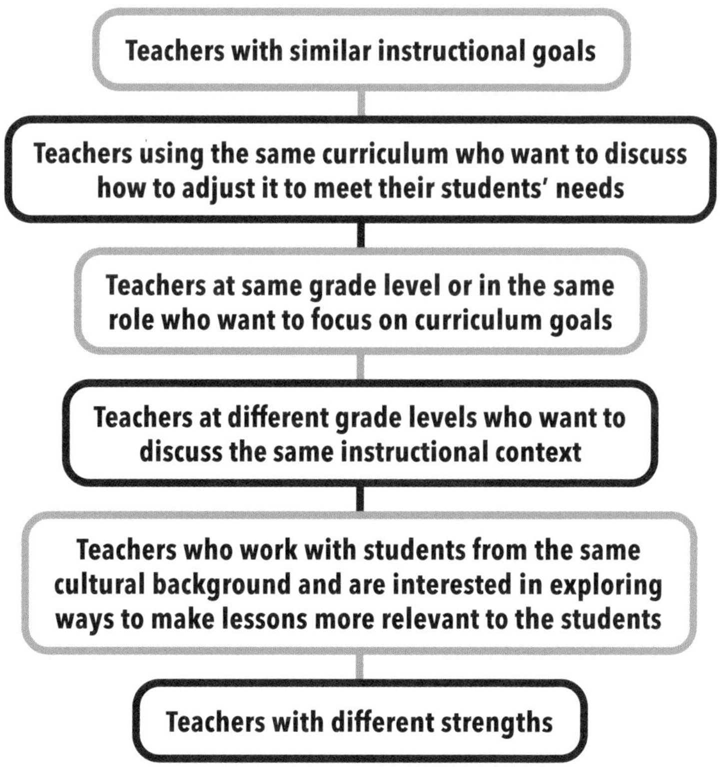

Figure 10-2

Connect the Learning

One way to scaffold peer coaching is to link the sessions to other professional learning opportunities you have provided or plan to provide soon. For example, if shared reading is a topic of a professional learning session, you might follow up by having two teachers come together to observe one another's shared reading lessons. Or, you might suggest pairs meet to coach one another in an instructional context you have been working on in one-on-one or cluster coaching. When you connect peer coaching to other professional learning, conversations deepen because each of your colleagues brings a foundation of common knowledge to the process. You can also support peer coaching with observational look-for tools (Chapter 13) developed in your professional learning sessions (Chapter 11). These tools help your colleagues focus on the elements of high-quality instruction.

Of course, you won't always want to connect peer coaching to other professional learning experiences. Sometimes, peer coaching will arise from a common interest in a specific topic between two colleagues. However, when there is synergy between the types of professional learning you offer, you create opportunities for deeper dives and exciting growth.

Stay on the Same Page with Look-for Tools

To create look-for tools, your colleagues need to be able to identify the markers of high-quality instruction and come to common understandings about different instructional contexts. Through the process of creating these observational tools of what to look for in different instructional contexts, they develop deeper understandings because they generate the tools. In Chapter 13, we provide a process for developing look-for tools. These tools are very useful in peer coaching because your colleagues can refer to them to identify specific areas in their teaching they want to explore together.

Video—An Alternative to Live Teaching

Video does not completely replace the experience of live teaching. Live teaching allows you to really get a sense of the atmosphere–what is happening everywhere in the classroom. It allows you to pick up on nuances video sometimes doesn't. That being said, if you are having difficulty scheduling time for your colleagues to be out of their classrooms, video is a convenient alternative.

Use the structure of the peer coaching lesson to support the video watching; simply replace the live teaching observation with the video clip. Using video as an alternative might mean learning partners have to meet over a few days to accommodate time for recording the lesson, but they will still have the opportunity to think together about teaching and learning. They can watch the clip together or separately–whatever time allows. An added bonus of using video is that the host teacher has the opportunity to observe the lesson as well.

Schedule Time for Peer Coaching

In the sample introduction, the coach makes a point of acknowledging the value of colleagues' time, particularly in the classroom. Just as with one-on-one and cluster coaching, find time for peers to have a short conversation (ten to fifteen minutes) before the lesson observation, time for the lesson observation, and time for a post-observation conversation (twenty to thirty minutes). You may need to ask your administrator for help finding coverage for your colleagues to leave the classroom. If teachers have common planning time, take advantage of it for the pre- or post-observation conversation. Ask partners to be flexible, possibly changing the time they normally teach literacy, to accommodate their colleague's schedule so both peers can be in the classroom during the literacy block.

A Protocol Tool for Peer Coaching

The best way to support your colleagues in peer coaching is to offer them a protocol they can follow to make the most out of their time together, so in Figure 10–3 we provide a simple procedure to follow. (You will find a full-size version of Protocol Tool: Peer Coaching as **OR 10.1** in the Online Resources.) Review it with your colleagues to support their peer coaching sessions.

ONLINE RESOURCE 10.1

Two Ways to Scaffold Peer Coaching: What to Say and Do

We recommend a few options for getting peer coaching up and running. Select the options that fit within your time frame. Use just one of these options, or layer them to offer more support for your colleagues.

Option 1: Join teachers in their first peer coaching session.

To help introduce the concept of peer coaching, you might join your colleagues for their first coaching session. In this situation, you might take on any of the following roles.

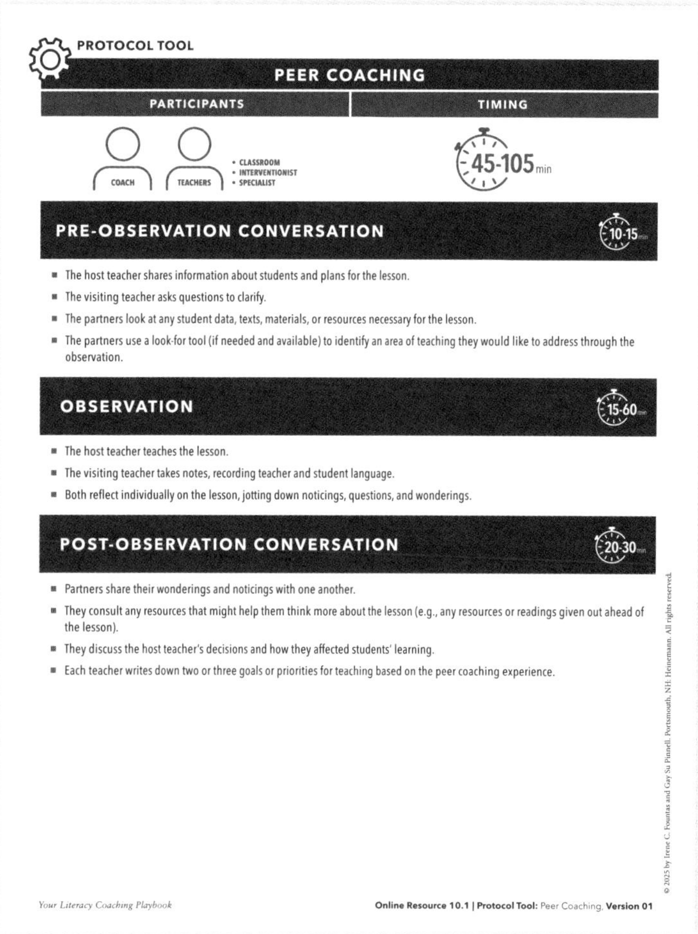
PROTOCOL TOOL

PEER COACHING

PARTICIPANTS	TIMING
COACH; TEACHERS (• CLASSROOM • INTERVENTIONIST • SPECIALIST)	45-105 min

PRE-OBSERVATION CONVERSATION (10-15 min)

- The host teacher shares information about students and plans for the lesson.
- The visiting teacher asks questions to clarify.
- The partners look at any student data, texts, materials, or resources necessary for the lesson.
- The partners use a look-for tool (if needed and available) to identify an area of teaching they would like to address through the observation.

OBSERVATION (15-60 min)

- The host teacher teaches the lesson.
- The visiting teacher takes notes, recording teacher and student language.
- Both reflect individually on the lesson, jotting down noticings, questions, and wonderings.

POST-OBSERVATION CONVERSATION (20-30 min)

- Partners share their wonderings and noticings with one another.
- They consult any resources that might help them think more about the lesson (e.g., any resources or readings given out ahead of the lesson).
- They discuss the host teacher's decisions and how they affected students' learning.
- Each teacher writes down two or three goals or priorities for teaching based on the peer coaching experience.

Your Literacy Coaching Playbook **Online Resource 10.1 | Protocol Tool:** Peer Coaching, **Version 01**

Figure 10-3

1. **Model peer coaching.** In this case, one colleague teaches while you and the visiting teacher observe. In the role of visiting teacher, you and the host teacher conduct the pre- and post-observation conversations while the actual visiting teacher observes the interaction. Demonstrate using a look-for tool to ground the talk in a specific aspect of teaching and/or looking at a section of an article to deepen the discussion. Leave time at the end to debrief what the visiting teacher noticed about the interactions between you and the host teacher.

   Sample Language

   - *Talk about what you noticed or wondered about our conversation.*
   - *What did you notice about how we kept the discussion productive and grounded in teaching and learning?*
   - *Talk about the role of evidence in our discussion. When did it help to ground the conversation?*
   - *How did our use of resources and/or readings impact our discussion?*
   - *What did you learn about peer coaching that you will take to your next peer coaching session?*

2. **Participate as a third learning partner.** In this case, simply add your own noticings and wonderings alongside your two colleagues, redirecting the conversation as needed away from evaluative or unproductive conversation. Keep the conversation focused on the teacher's decisions and their effect on students' learning. You might direct your colleagues to an

Keep the conversation focused on the **teacher's decisions and their effect** on students' learning.

excerpt of relevant reading to show them how to use resources during the pre- or post-observation conversation. Leave time at the end to ask what they noticed about the conversation.

Sample Language

- *What do you think was helpful today in our conversation?*
- *Talk about the parts of our discussion that you found the most powerful or important.*
- *When did you feel we got off track? How did we redirect the conversation to be more productive?*
- *Talk about how the brief reading may have impacted our learning.*
- *What is something you learned about peer coaching that you will bring to your next session?*

3. **Observe the partners as they engage in peer coaching.** Record their language so you can refer to it afterward. Once they complete the post-observation conversation, offer brief feedback, sharing your noticings and wonderings about the session.

Sample Language

- *When did you feel your conversation was the most energized? When was it the most productive?*
- *Talk about what you learned about teaching from the discussion with your peer.*
- *How did the resources you used help you?*
- *What resources might have led to a deeper discussion?*
- *I wonder if you did ____, how that might have changed your conversation.*
- *Talk about how your notes on the lesson helped you stay grounded in evidence of student learning.*
- *Describe anything that surprised you.*
- *What are your goals for your next peer coaching session?*
- *Talk about what you would change for your next coaching session.*

Option 2: Demonstrate peer coaching in a fishbowl.

We recommend using a one-hour professional learning session to kick off peer coaching. Invite your colleagues to sit in a circle. Ahead of time, prepare two of your colleagues to demonstrate a post-observation conversation. Have the pair sit in chairs in the center of the group. For context, ask the two demonstrating colleagues to explain what they talked about in their pre-observation conversation and to briefly share the lesson one of them taught and the other observed (see Figure 11-7 on page 113).

After they have provided sufficient context and answered any questions posed by the group, invite the two teachers to conduct their post-observation conversation. If they used a look-for tool to focus their conversation, ask them to share it. If you prepared your two colleagues with readings that they might refer to during their conversation to develop deeper understandings, have them share those also. Observers in the outer circle should jot down what they notice about the interaction. To help the observers focus, ask part of the group to concentrate on the role of the visiting teacher while the rest of the group concentrates on the role of the host teacher. At the end of a brief conversation, invite teachers in the outer circle to share their noticings. Figure 10-4 shows an example of the noticings of one group. Here is some language you might use to debrief the fishbowl experience.

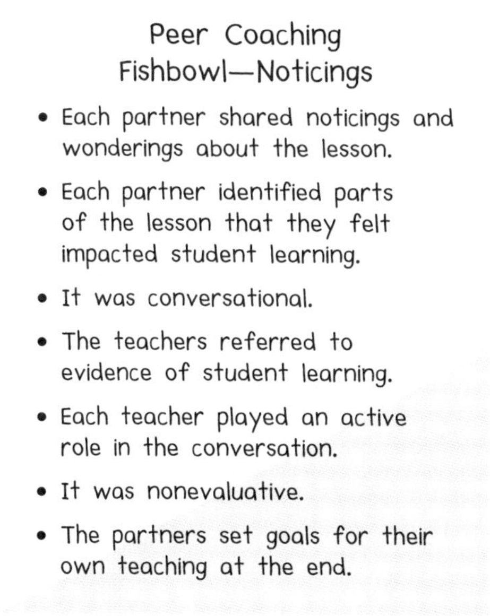

Figure 10-4

Sample Language

- *What did you notice about the roles of the two teachers?*
- *What did you notice about the structure of the conversation?*
- *What did you notice about the tone of the discussion?*
- *Talk about how the teachers connected teaching and learning.*
- *What was something that surprised you about this exchange?*

Ten Ways to Support Ongoing Peer Coaching

Once you've established peer coaching, continue to provide support as needed. Here are ten ways you can support your colleagues in continuing to learn from one another:

1. Continue to coordinate learning partners as needed to best suit the needs of your colleagues. Change partners occasionally, work with teachers to identify their needs, and pair them accordingly.
2. Schedule peer coaching when you think it would be helpful to teachers. Peer coaching doesn't have to be something that you have going on all the time. Maybe make a goal for everyone to be involved at least two or three times a year.
3. Provide relevant resources or readings to learning partners before their peer coaching sessions to support their work.
4. Make sure look-for tools (Chapter 13) are readily available for learning partners to use during peer coaching.
5. Encourage teachers to write a five-minute reflection in their journals right after their peer coaching sessions. These reflections on their experiences can be valuable throughout the year. Ask them to share reflections at your next gathering.
6. Invite teachers to share two or three goals and takeaways from their peer coaching session.
7. Provide time during a professional learning session for learning partners to share their experiences with peer coaching so colleagues can learn tips from one another.
8. If needed, offer your colleagues language prompts to deepen their conversation. Keep them simple. Offer three or four prompts to help them in their pre- or post-observation conversation.
9. Provide suggestions for the type of student work or data they might want to look at together before or after a lesson. Offer some ways for them to think about the data.
10. Ask for feedback from your colleagues about how you can improve their experience in peer coaching.

Up **Next**

In Chapter 11, you'll learn how to write a new chapter in your school's history of professional learning by providing a variety of active, highly collaborative professional learning sessions for busy teachers.

Chapter 11

The Play: **Professional Learning Sessions**

Think about the professional learning sessions or workshops that you have attended. What do you remember about them? Were there some that made you think, "Well, that was a waste of time!" Were there others that made you think, "Wow, I can't wait to get back to my classroom to try out what I learned!"? This chapter will help you design professional learning sessions like the latter. Certainly, you want your colleagues to leave saying, "Wow!"

BENEFITS OF PROFESSIONAL LEARNING SESSIONS

- Cultivate an environment of collaboration and teamwork
- Allow for sharing updates on implementation of instruction, curriculum, or data
- Encourage deeper thinking on a topic or school initiative for both new and experienced teachers
- Strengthen the link between assessment, data analysis, and teaching
- Provide an opportunity for development of rubrics and observational tools to support the implementation of a common vision for literacy learning
- Engage teachers in collaborative inquiry

What Are Professional Learning Sessions?

Professional learning sessions (PLS) are planned, organized opportunities designed to engage teams of teachers in exploring new content, examining resources, analyzing data, and reflecting on their practice for the purpose of building common understandings about a topic that can be directly applied in the classroom. These sessions are efficient, productive, and connected to the instructional contexts teachers are using in the classroom (Figure 11–1). They also should link directly to what teachers are exploring in the other contexts for professional learning we describe in this book. A professional learning session on interactive read-aloud, for example, might be followed up with coaching sessions or a lesson study on interactive read-aloud.

Having observed your colleagues in action in classrooms, talked with them as individual teachers, and learned about the students they teach, you have a deep knowledge of the individuals in your school and what they need from you. Draw on that knowledge to structure learning sessions that are productive for a specific

Figure 11-1

group of adults. Involve your colleagues from the beginning in determining topics, goals, and desired outcomes for the time they will spend together. When teachers have a voice in this process, they have a vested interest in applying what they learn, which can result in real change. And by providing opportunities for the teachers to evaluate the sessions and give feedback for future professional learning, you develop their agency in determining the course of their own learning.

A Framework for Professional Learning Sessions

Using a consistent framework for your sessions will help you be efficient in your planning and to set up routines that allow for a productive and fast-paced session. The framework involves three parts (Figure 11-2). We recommend allotting approximately sixty to ninety minutes per session to give participants time to engage in collaboration and inquiry.

FRAMEWORK FOR A PROFESSIONAL LEARNING SESSION

INTRODUCTION

Make connections to previous learning, share goals for the session, and invite questions and comments.

10-15 min

ACTIVE LEARNING EXPERIENCE

Actively engage participants in thinking, talking, and applying content:

- Analyze student data.
- Watch and discuss video clips of teaching.
- Engage in modeled lessons and role-play.
- Plan lessons.
- Read and discuss segments of a professional text or article.

35-55 min

REFLECTION AND EVALUATION

Ask teachers to reflect on their new learning and their goals for applying it to their teaching. Invite teachers to evaluate the session, provide feedback, and offer suggestions for future learning.

15-20 min

Figure 11-2

Plan and Prepare for Professional Learning Sessions

Your time together with colleagues is limited, so it is important to plan well and prepare in advance of the event. First, consider how much time you have allotted for this specific type of professional learning across the year, and then set realistic goals for what can be accomplished.

The amount of time your district or administration provides for teachers to be out of their classrooms is an important consideration. From contractual agreements to coverage challenges to competing initiatives in the school for out-of-classroom time, there are many factors to consider. You won't necessarily be able to change these factors, but you can certainly advocate for more time for professional learning.

QUICK TIP

When longer blocks of time are not possible for more in-depth PLS, think about creating opportunities for bite-size learning, or *micro learning* as it is sometimes called (see Chapter 12).

> ### Working with Teacher Cohorts
>
> You might consider working with different cohorts of teachers so that you can differentiate content based on their needs. For example, you might have a cohort of new teachers and a cohort of experienced teachers who are looking for ongoing support. Some literacy coaches find it helpful to meet every other week with an initial cohort and monthly with a more experienced cohort. Another way to divide teachers into cohorts is by grade levels or grade-level bands including the specialists that support the grade level if it is appropriate to the session focus.
>
> We encourage you to consider the many advantages of mixed cohorts. Usually, experienced teachers have a lot to offer the newer teachers, and the newer teachers offer fresh thinking for the group. Meeting with teachers in grade-level bands (e.g., K–2, 3–5) can also be powerful. Each year, the cohorts can go deeper in their explorations of literacy instruction. After all, children need year after year of excellent teaching.

Schedule Time for PLS

Although it may not always be possible, we recommend that you schedule PLS once a month. They can be of varying duration. That adds up to nine or more regular sessions, which will require strategic and creative planning on your part. The earlier you meet and plan with administrators, the easier it will be to make the schedule work. Here are some ways some coaches have scheduled time:

- Meet with cohorts of teachers after school once a month or biweekly.
- Meet with groups of teachers (usually at the same grade level) during common planning time.
- Use regularly scheduled release time (e.g., curriculum/professional learning days).

Establish Goals for PLS

Work together with your colleagues to determine topics you'll want to address across the year based on school-wide initiatives and goals, analysis of student data, and the teachers' needs and interests. This kind of long-view planning allows you to address a series of connected topics over time to build common understandings. In addition to soliciting your colleagues' input on topics and goals for the sessions, ask for their feedback at the end of every session so you can adjust your approach for the next session as needed. Here are some ways to gather that feedback:

- At the last part of a session, form a circle and invite each teacher to jot down something that worked well and something that they would improve. Then have a quick share around the circle.
- Provide a survey at the end of a session or via email afterward to probe what teachers would like to focus on next.
- Use "exit slips" at the end of a session. Ask teachers to respond to one or two questions on a notecard to gauge their understandings of the session goals. Plan your next session goals based on their responses.
- Take notes during coaching sessions. Identify common patterns in teachers' stated goals that you might be able to address through a professional learning session.
- As you engage with your colleagues in informal conversations in the hallways, classrooms, and lunchrooms, note topics that will be supportive.

As you write the goals for the next session, review the feedback you receive, along with your school's curriculum goals, and the relevant student data that should drive the plan for professional learning.

Ten Keys to Planning and Facilitating a Successful Session

1. **Keep authentic inquiry at the foundation.**
   The teachers need to do the thinking. They need to construct their own understandings (engage in the thinking rather than being told what to think) to develop ownership and agency. Choose from a range of inquiry-based activities, described later in this chapter, to give them the opportunity to explore new ideas and take them on as their own.
2. **Use slide presentations judiciously.**
   Teachers learn more from interacting with and reading resources themselves rather than listening to you summarize what the resources are about. They need group discussion to deeply understand the concepts. Be flexible with your slide deck, skipping around as necessary, to address needs. Use as few slides as possible and avoid reading them to participants.
3. **Choose readings thoughtfully.**
   Keep readings brief. Divide longer readings among participants and have them share what they have read with one another. Select readings from resources teachers own so they can get to know them, revisit them, and value their contents. Provide sticky notes, highlighters, etc., so teachers can interact with the text and make notes about their thinking.
4. **Show brief video clips with a particular purpose.**
   If you choose to use video to show an example of teaching, try to keep it under five minutes to keep teachers' attention or break longer videos into segments and discuss them before showing more. Provide time for partners or triads to talk between parts of longer clips. Plan the prompt you want to give observers before they begin to watch a video. The prompt provides a lens that influences the way they watch the teaching and learning. We offer some suggestions later in this chapter.
5. **Invite lots of conversation.**
   Vary the way participants talk—with partners, in small groups, or with the whole group. Sometimes, you might have participants jot down a few notes before sharing to give them time to process their thoughts.
6. **Don't make the session handout heavy.**
   If you provide too many handouts, chances are they will be put aside unread. Provide only the most relevant and practical information on a very small number of handouts. Maybe even just one.

A Word About Virtual Sessions

Sometimes it just makes sense to conduct a session virtually. For example, if you are a coach who is spread across several schools, videoconferencing will allow you to maximize time and minimize travel. However, when at all possible, we recommend meeting in person for the social benefits it affords and to maximize engagement.

If you do find yourself in need of a virtual session, keep teachers actively engaged with tools like chat, polling, video, interactive whiteboards, and breakout rooms for small-group discussions. Provide lots of time for reflection and talk, and encourage your colleagues to keep their cameras on, if they feel comfortable, so the group can develop a sense of community.

7. **Provide plenty of wait time and use techniques that ensure all voices are heard.**
   As with children, there are some adult learners who process their thoughts before they talk and others who process their thinking aloud. To give everyone a chance to be heard, make sure you pause, and don't always call on the first people to raise their hand. Consider techniques such as turn and talk, or give teachers a short time to write before sharing out.
8. **Start on time, end on time, and keep things moving.**
   Show that you respect your colleagues' time by keeping to the time as advertised. If you have good reasons to extend time, do it consciously and limit or omit other activities. Assign timekeepers as needed.
9. **Observe participants' body language to assess how they are taking on the learning.**
   Notice if participants appear overwhelmed, stressed, comfortable, or fully engaged. Shift your facilitation moves based on what you notice. Don't be afraid to cut content if participants seem overwhelmed. You will get to it when they are ready.
10. **Build in time for reflection.**
   Ask teachers to bring a reflection journal so they can make notes to see how their thinking changes over time. Vary the prompts you use for reflection, and offer opportunities throughout the session for teachers to process their thinking in writing and through sharing with one another (see pp. 114–115).

A Key Tool: The Reflection Journal

If the budget allows, consider giving every teacher a bound journal at the beginning of the school year. Ask them to bring it with them to all professional learning opportunities. This way, teachers can keep all their thinking about professional learning in one place.

An Easy-to Use-Planning Template

ONLINE RESOURCE 11.1

Use the template we provide to plan a professional learning session. (You will find a blank, full-size Template Tool: Plan for a Professional Learning Session as **OR 11.1** in the Online Resources.) Using the template will help keep your sessions structured and focused yet varied in the ways you engage teachers. Figure 11-3 shows an example of how a coach might use this template. We provide a more detailed plan than you would probably write so that you can envision a session while you become familiar with the template. Nonetheless, we recommend jotting down some of the language you will use during the learning session because it will enhance the clarity of your instructions, prompt deeper thinking, and increase overall efficiency. Keep in mind that there are many ways to engage teachers in active learning. In this example, colleagues read, plan, and role-play. Later in this chapter, you will find other options for the active learning experience (see pp. 107-114).

TEMPLATE TOOL

PLAN FOR A PROFESSIONAL LEARNING SESSION

Session topic: teaching phonics/word study in shared reading	**Session length:** 1 hour	**Materials:** copies of printed article/blog, slides; teachers bring a big book, poem, or chart, and their reflection journal

INTRODUCTION

Link to Previous Learning 5 min	Sit in a circle for easy sharing: *We have been thinking together about using shared reading to develop all aspects of effective reading. Last time we talked about specific teaching moves to support fluent reading in the lesson. Turn and talk for three minutes about how you have taught for fluency through shared reading over the last two weeks and what you learned about the impact on your students.*
Goals 5 min	Teachers move to tables. Show slides with goals: *Today we are going to explore how to teach for specific phonics and word study skills when you revisit a text. Notice the three specific goals for the day on the slide. Any questions?*

ACTIVE LEARNING EXPERIENCE

Timing 35 min	**Reading:** *See the list of partners. You have two readings on your table–an article and a blog on ways to revisit a text to develop understandings about phonics. Each of you read one of them and share with your partner what you found important and helpful. Then a few of you will share with the whole group. (15 minutes)* **Planning:** *Using your big book or chart, plan how to revisit the text to teach for phonics and word study skills that you are currently teaching in your classroom. You can work alone or with your partner. Assume the students have read the text several times and are fluent readers. (10 minutes)* **Sharing:** *Combine your pair with a second pair to make a group of four. Take turns taking the role of the teacher and students with one of the texts. The teacher will engage the students in revisiting the text for three to five minutes to notice and think about phonics or word study. (10 minutes)*

REFLECTION AND EVALUATION

Reflection 5 min	Join the circle again to share: *What did you take from the reading and role-play that will affect your teaching of phonics over the next two weeks? Turn and talk.* Have participants share with the whole group after pairs share.
Goal Setting 5 min	*For the next two weeks, as you revisit shared reading texts, try out explicit ways to develop strong phonics skills. Write down two goals you have for this work. Bring your experiences to our next meeting.*
Evaluation 5 min	Provide time for completion of a survey (or send an online survey via email later) to gather feedback for the next session.

Your Literacy Coaching Playbook **Online Resource 11.1 | Template Tool:** Plan for a Professional Learning Session, **Version 01**

Figure 11-3

Key Elements of Collaborative Inquiry

- Teachers think together about relevant issues related to student learning.
- Topics are meaningful, timely, and important to the team.
- Teachers ask for and seek actual data to provide information.
- Conversations are rooted in concrete evidence of student learning (e.g., observations, patterns in data, student work).
- Opportunities are provided to build and expand knowledge of content and instructional practices to inform discussion and decision-making.
- Teachers are the driving force in actions that result in the improvement of student outcomes.
- Teachers work together to identify common challenges, analyze and interpret relevant data, and test out instructional practices.

Professional Learning Sessions: What to Say and Do

As you can see from the planning template (Figure 11–3), the framework supports active learning and links to classroom practice. The coaching moves you make within this framework should engage your colleagues, deepen their conversations, and lift their understandings. Following are suggestions for what to say and do in each part of the framework to ensure your sessions are fresh and engaging.

Introduction

The energy you bring to the very beginning of a professional learning session sets the tone for what comes next. Following are some coaching moves that can help you engage participants right from the start.

Connect to prior learning from previous sessions. Connections provide a sense of continuity and give teachers time to share successes or, in some cases, challenges they've encountered. Use prompts that invite teachers to share what they have done in their teaching that's specifically related to the topic of the previous session.

Sample Language

- *Talk about something you learned in our last session and tried in your classroom this week.*
- *Last week we talked about how to keep minilessons brief. If you've been working on that, how did it go?*
- *What moves from our last session have you used to amplify students' diverse voices, backgrounds, and experiences?*
- *Engaging students in interactive read-alouds was a big topic last week. Is there a particular book that really engaged your students this week? What did you do differently?*
- *Talk about a way you were responsive to a student's needs this week. How did you apply what you learned from our last session?*
- *Share something that was effective in your teaching of phonics this week. How did that relate to our last session?*
- *What evidence did you collect this week that showed that your teaching of ____ was successful? Relate that to last week's discussion of how important it is to use and understand data and evidence.*
- *Share a change you saw in your students' writing since our last session. What led to that change?*

Use open-ended prompts to give teachers a chance to share both the successes and the challenges they've encountered since the last session. After teachers have had a chance to share for one or two minutes about their teaching, discuss how the previous session's topic links to the new topic.

Create a "parking lot" on chart paper to save issues or challenges that your colleagues would like to address at another time (Figure 11-4). Make sure you circle back to parking lot topics at the end of the session, during one-on-one coaching, or as part of the next session to show that you are listening to your colleagues' concerns.

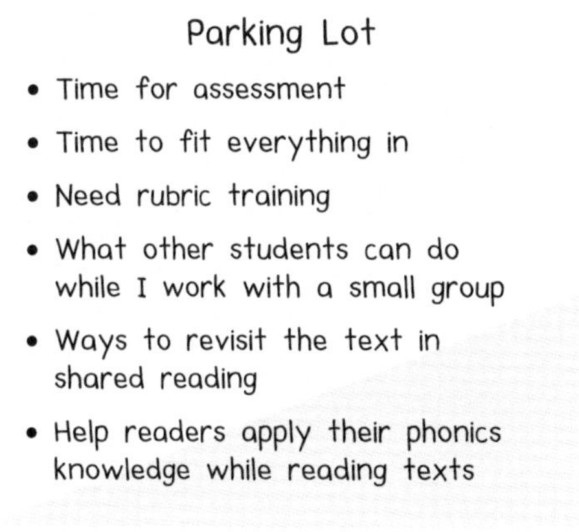

Figure 11-4

Share the agenda, goals, and intended outcomes for the session. Your clear identification of goals and outcomes sets expectations for your colleagues and keeps the session focused. Make sure to connect the goals to the teachers' previous feedback, noticings, and/or interests. Be transparent about how you used the feedback to plan the goals of the session. And keep the list of goals short.

Sample Language

- *Read the goals for today's session, and turn and talk about what you are most interested in discussing.*
- *Based on your feedback from the last session, our goals for today's session are ____. Any questions or comments?*
- *We decided together that today we would focus on ____. What are you thinking about that?*

Once you've shared the session goals, invite questions or comments and add to the parking lot any topics that are not on the day's agenda.

Active Learning Experience: Engaging Teachers in Inquiry

After the introduction, waste no time jumping into an inquiry-based activity to build foundational knowledge. Spend most of the time on activities that engage teachers in meaningful discussion and inquiry. We offer some ideas here to inspire your thinking along with coaching moves that can enhance the inquiry. Depending on your timing, you might plan for just one activity, or you might combine any of the following options to give your colleagues opportunities to lift their expertise and build common understandings:

Option 1: Read and discuss brief excerpts from a professional resource, article, blog, or handout. Learning multiplies when teachers read and talk together about a topic. And reading brief passages provides a safe way to dip into sometimes uncomfortable waters, try on new ideas, and discuss thinking with others. Build a collection of articles, blogs, and passages that lifted your own expertise and understanding. Engage teachers in reading and discussing them in a variety of ways—with a partner, in small groups, or with the whole group.

Notice how the prompts below break the reading into smaller, digestible chunks while also asking colleagues to engage in a particular way with the text. When you ask your colleagues to summarize the most important idea, pull out the big ideas, or paraphrase important points, you begin to build common understandings and spark authentic discussion. Ask the group to give a real-life example of the reading—how the ideas described actually look and sound in teaching. That simple question can make the reading practical and meaningful.

Sample Language

- *Read the title of the chapter (or the heading of a section). What are you thinking right away?*
- *Read paragraph ____ in column ____ and think about the most important idea.*
- *Skim the section (page, chapter). What are the big ideas?*
- *Skim the five bullets. Which one is the most important for you? What stands out for you?*
- *Read the paragraph that begins ____. What is most challenging for teachers?*
- *Read the paragraph that begins ____. Give an example of that from your classroom.*

Although it will take more time, try asking teachers to talk about their reading in pairs or triads to invite more voices into the conversation. Vary these configurations often to keep discussions dynamic and fluid. If you have teachers turn and talk too many times in a row, it gets old. It starts feeling formulaic and partners who don't have as much to say miss out on deeper conversations. At the same time, if you're always asking your colleagues to share with the entire group, you might routinely hear from the same people. Changing it up keeps the inquiry fresh and discussions more interesting.

Sample Language

- *Decide with your partner who will read the first three paragraphs and who will read the next two paragraphs. Summarize what you learned for your partner.*
- *Skim the first column. What is the most important word (phrase, sentence)? Jot it down. As we go around the circle, share what you wrote.*
- *Skim the first three paragraphs. What would that look like in your teaching? Share your thinking in pairs.*
- *Skim the first three paragraphs and think about what is a new understanding or a good reminder for you. Share in threes.*
- *Read paragraph ____. Do you agree? Share your thoughts with a partner.*
- *Read (or skim) the first column. Think about one of your students. Talk to the person next to you about how that would apply.*

Option 2: Write about readings. Another way to keep your colleagues engaged is to ask them to write about their reading. Give them a quick one or two minutes to jot questions, wonderings, or reflections after reading a brief excerpt and before sharing.

You can also teach your colleagues how to sketch-note—a more visual and creative way to take notes. Figure 11-5 shows how one teacher used sketch-noting to capture thoughts about an article.

Invite small groups of colleagues to write about their reading by charting their thinking after reading. This process can result in deeper thinking and collaborative conversations as teachers work together to decide what goes on the chart. Charting also allows you to include more reading. You can divide readings among smaller groups and have your colleagues use their charts to teach one another about what they read.

Sample Language

- *Think about chapter ____. Jot down three new insights to share with your colleagues.*
- *Read the ____ section of chapter ____. Think about the critical elements in an instructional context. Discuss and chart what is in the way of accomplishing the goals as described. Then discuss and chart ideas for how to resolve the issues.*

Become a Fan of Sketch-Noting

Sketch-noting is a way to make thinking visual by using drawings, borders, boxes, and arrows to brainstorm and connect ideas. Consider inviting your colleagues to sketch-note their ideas to reflect on their reading either in their own reflection journals or on chart paper to share with others. Sketch-noting is not only fun but also invites more visual learners into the process. And it creates engaging visuals that will be memorable for your colleagues as they apply new ideas to their teaching.

EXAMPLE OF SKETCH-NOTING

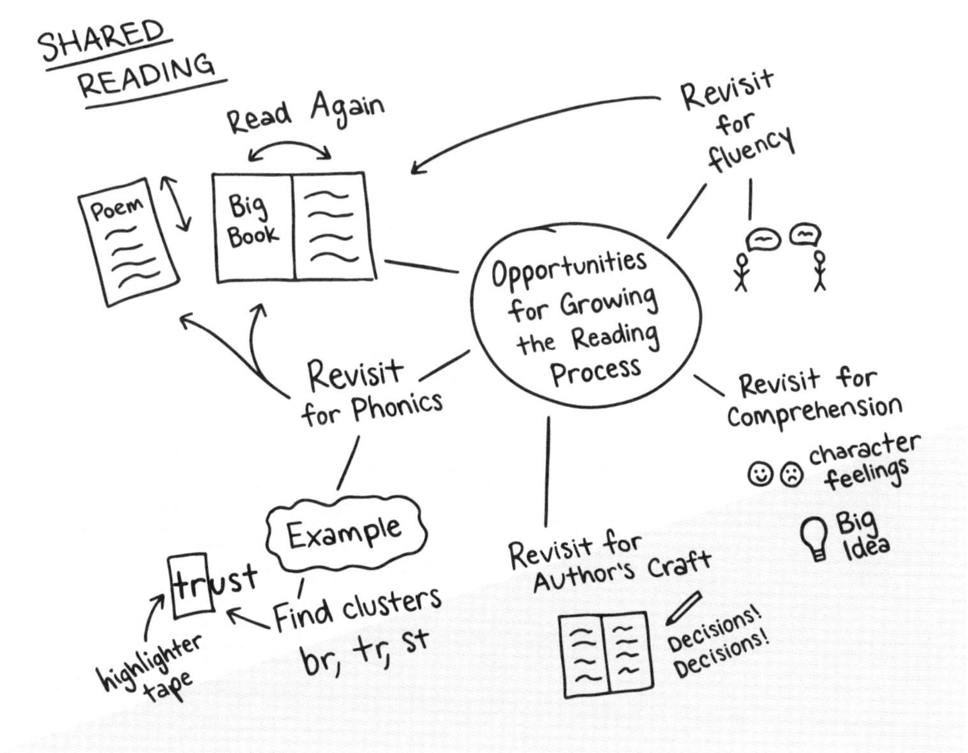

Figure 11-5

- *Skim the section on ____. Use sketch-noting to illustrate the big ideas on chart paper. Or write a summary.*
- *Skim the first ____ sections of chapter ____. Chart the big ideas and give three examples to illustrate these ideas.*
- *Read the first ____ paragraphs. Make a visual representation of what stood out to you.*

Option 3: Discuss short video clips. Watch and discuss short video clips of teachers in action to help your colleagues hone their ability to observe students' reading and writing behaviors, discuss the implications of different teaching decisions, and build common understandings of different instructional contexts.

The way you introduce a video clip affects the way people view it. Decide if you want to use an open-ended prompt so that participants experience the teaching without a particular lens or a specific prompt to help them concentrate on a particular aspect of teaching. Each type of prompt serves a purpose, so choose your prompts thoughtfully. We have found that less specific prompts are helpful when you first introduce a new type of teaching because teachers have the opportunity to take it all in and walk away with general noticings. But more focused prompts will tune the teachers in to critical aspects of the teaching and learning. Whatever you choose, encourage your colleagues to avoid evaluative language such as "I liked when . . ." or "I don't like how he . . ." when discussing the video clip. Guide them to use descriptive language instead, for example, "When the teacher said . . . , I noticed that the students . . . ."

Create a Digital Library

Build a collection of video clips for different instructional contexts. Select professional video clips you think are useful, but also collect videos of your teaching and that of others in the school. Your colleagues will appreciate watching video clips that show the students in their own school. As with all forms of observation, emphasize the fact that no lesson is perfect. Video clips of teaching are not models but opportunities to discuss teaching and learning.

Sample Language (General/Open Prompts)

- *Write down anything that stands out to you.*
- *Write down your noticings/wonderings.*
- *What do you notice about the teacher's language?*
- *What are surprises for you?*
- *What teaching decisions are most helpful to the students?*
- *What strengths do you see in the students as readers (as writers)?*
- *What evidence of student learning do you see?*
- *Record what you notice about the role of the teacher (students).*
- *Record the students' talk. What does it tell you about their understandings?*
- *How does the video clip help you think about your own teaching?*

Sample Language (Content-Specific Prompts)

- *How does the teacher's language promote independence or give students agency?*
- *How does the teacher support the students' comprehension of the text?*
- *How does the teacher support the students in using phonics to decode while reading continuous text?*
- *How does the teacher use mentor texts to support the students' writing?*
- *What might be in the way of the students' successful processing of the text?*

Occasionally, you might ask each of your colleagues to bring a short video clip, about two or three minutes long, of their own teaching related to something you have been working on as a group, for example, helping children read fluently. Depending on the number of participants, watch the videos as a whole group or in small groups, pairs, or triads. Before watching, work together to create a simple look-for tool to guide the discussion, including questions or key elements to look for in the video clips (see Chapter 13).

Option 4: Analyze student work. Professional learning sessions are an ideal setting for colleagues to develop a common way of looking at student work. As they work together, colleagues calibrate the way they are assessing students, which leads to more consistent expectations across classrooms and grades. Here is one way you might scaffold this collaborative inquiry:

1. Introduce the activity by inviting the whole group to look at the same piece of student work. Use a document camera or provide photocopies of whatever you are reviewing (e.g., phonics assessment, writing about reading, reading record, original writing).
2. Provide teachers with a resource to evaluate the work (e.g., district or curriculum standards, *The Fountas & Pinnell Literacy Continuum*, a relevant rubric). Ask teachers to divide a paper into thirds, labeling the columns as shown in Figure 11-6.
3. Guide the group to identify the student's strengths and to provide evidence for their thinking. Then ask them to identify possible next steps for the student, building from the student's strengths.
4. After you have analyzed a sample as an entire group, ask your colleagues to work with a partner to analyze their own student's work.

Make Your Own Rubrics

Consider asking teachers to develop their own rubrics to engage them in collaborative inquiry around assessment. For example, you might have teachers create a rubric for writing personal narratives at each grade level and then compare them across the grades. After teachers have developed the rubrics, use them together to ensure everyone is using them in a similar (and reliable) way. As an alternative, use an artificial intelligence platform to develop a rubric. Then have teachers evaluate the rubric.

Strengths	Evidence	Next Steps
• Understands how to choose interesting verbs to express meaning	• "he muttered under his breath" • "she sprinted to the bus" • "Henry glanced around"	• Expand understanding of word choice by looking at adjectives and use of specific nouns

Figure 11-6

Option 5: Model a lesson with teachers as the learners. In our experiences, teachers generally love opportunities to participate in modeled lessons, but it's essential that they participate as themselves, rather than pretending to be students.

Tell them they will have the chance to talk about how they might use this lesson with students after the experience, but for now they are to take off their teacher hat for the duration of the lesson and immerse themselves as a reader or writer, not as a teacher. After they have participated in the lesson, ask them to resume their teaching role to debrief the lesson.

Sample Language

- *What did you notice about the ways you engaged in thinking?*
- *How did the questions and prompts affect the way you thought about the text?*
- *What did you notice about the writing process?*
- *What did you find supportive as a learner? What was challenging?*
- *How did the introduction to the text affect the way you experienced it?*
- *What did you notice about the ways you turned and talked?*
- *What did you notice about the text selection?*
- *How did sharing at the end of the writing lesson affect your learning?*

Option 6: Role-play with transcripts. Asking teachers to each take an assigned role in a transcript brings a lesson on a page to life. Make sure to give each participant a copy of the transcript to follow along, even those who may be observing the role-play. Though it has similarities to the experience of watching a video clip, using a transcript in a role-play is unique because your colleagues have the chance to really study the language of the teacher and students. With a transcript, teachers can look back to find even more specific evidence for their thinking. Notice how the sample language directs them to zero in on the language as they read the transcript aloud for the group.

Sample Language

- *What evidence do you see in the students' talk that they are able to think beyond the text?*

- *What does the teacher say to help the students find text evidence for their thinking?*
- *What teaching moves does the teacher make that lead to deeper discussion?*
- *How does the students' talk show that they are listening to one another?*
- *Talk about how the teacher's language choices promote independence.*

After the role-play, support teachers in debriefing with some of the same language we suggest for video clip observations (pp. 110–111). Of course, there are numerous other questions you might ask related to the teacher's and students' language. The big idea is that the transcript and role-play offer opportunities for you and your colleagues to take a deeper dive into language choices and what they reveal about student thinking and teacher decision-making.

Option 7: Engage teachers in a fishbowl observation. The fishbowl method of observation (Figure 11–7) involves inner and outer circles. The participants in the inner circle (the fishbowl) typically engage in a discussion of some sort while members of the outer circle observe and take notes.

We have used this method for multiple purposes, such as teaching our colleagues about starting book clubs with students. In that case, we typically ask a group of teachers to read a book (or short story) and mark a few places in the text they want to discuss. We invite them into the inner circle to have a brief discussion (five to ten minutes). The rest of the participants form an outer circle to take notes about what they observe in the discussion. The coach then charts the observations made by the outer circle and asks participants what they noticed about the experience. Through the participation of both the inner and outer circles, the group develops a common understanding of the important elements of book clubs while also learning a method for introducing them to their students.

You can also use the fishbowl method for observing a role-play. Some coaches have used it to help teachers gain an understanding of the types of conversations that happen in one-on-one coaching. Ask a colleague you have coached for a while to have a pre-observation conversation in a fishbowl to demystify what happens during a coaching session. In other words, fishbowls are yet another way to engage your teachers in collaborative, inquiry-based learning during PLS.

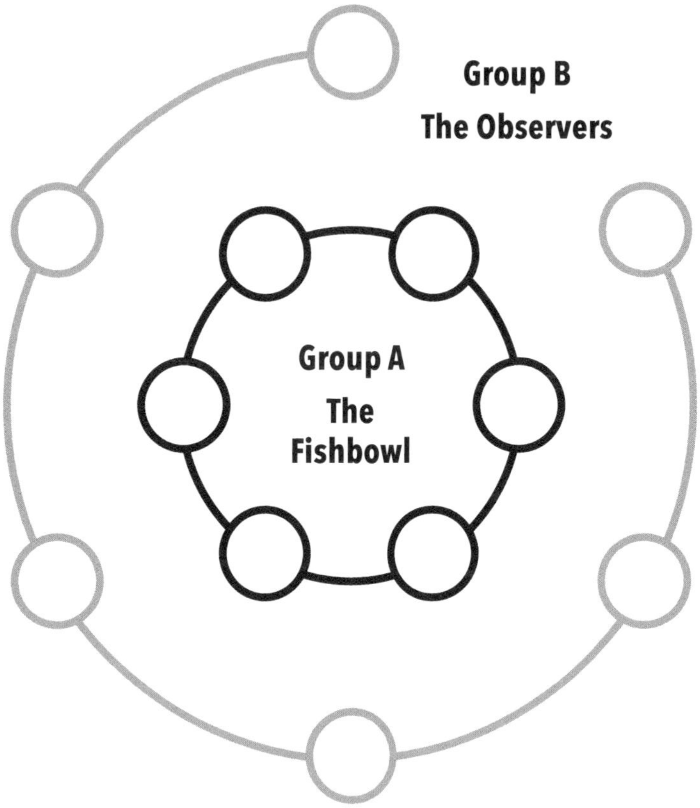

Figure 11-7

Option 8: Plan lessons together. In the sample plan for a professional learning session (see Figure 11–3 on p. 105), you'll find an example of how to integrate planning into a learning session. In that example, the coach asks teachers to use a big book, poem, or chart to plan part of a shared reading lesson. Make sure to provide materials or ask your colleagues to bring the materials they will need to plan, and offer clear instructions for the planning process on a slide or handout. Your colleagues learn so much when they have time to talk together about how to apply new learning to lesson planning. And they come out of the session with the bonus of a ready-made lesson to use the next day!

Reflection and Evaluation: Making the Link to Practice

The important next step is guiding your colleagues to link the new learning gained from these experiences to their teaching. How will they apply the new learning? What are the implications for logistics (e.g., timing, scheduling, recordkeeping)? How will they build in assessment to evaluate these new practices? And what are their personal goals for implementing the new learning? There are several coaching moves you can make to invite reflection and forward thinking.

Write personal journal reflections. A very brief written reflection serves two purposes. First, it gives teachers time to process what they have experienced over the course of the session so they can integrate the new ideas into their current teaching framework. Second, it gives them a written record of their new thinking which makes it more likely for them to transfer the learning to practice. Select prompts that invite your colleagues to reflect in different ways:

> ***Video Reflections***
>
> If time is short, ask teachers to record a brief video or audio reflection after they leave the session and send it to you and/or their colleagues.

Sample Language (Reflect on Learning)

- *What three big ideas did you take from today's session?*
- *Write one thing you learned from your colleagues today.*
- *Write about something that was confirmed for you, something new you plan to try, something you are still wondering about.*

Sample Language (Reflect on the Impact of Teaching)

- *Write three ways in which today's work will impact your teaching.*
- *What changes do you plan to make to your teaching based on today's work?*
- *Identify one specific action you will take this week to apply your new learning.*

Sample Language (Reflect on Setting Goals)

- *What are you excited to try? Make that a goal. What is something you are still thinking about?*
- *Write three goals you have for your teaching from today's work. Which one will you implement first?*
- *Write two short-term goals and one long-term goal you have for your teaching based on today's session.*

Sample Language (Reflect on Challenges)

- *What challenges do you anticipate as you try to apply your new learning? What are you thinking you might do to overcome these challenges?*
- *Name three things you are worried about in applying this new learning. Brainstorm a few possible solutions.*

Sample Language (Reflect on Needs)

- *What resources do you need to apply your new learning?*
- *What other professional learning opportunities do you need to apply your new learning?*
- *How can I help support your efforts in applying this new learning?*
- *What administrative support would help you apply your new learning?*
- *What technology support would you need to support this implementation?*

Share reflections. After teachers have had quiet time to write their reflections, invite them to share at least one of them in pairs or with the whole group. Consider asking everyone to share a reflection on something different from the contribution of the previous person so they hear different ideas from one another. If you are short on time, simply pose some of the reflection questions we have listed and open the floor for everyone to share orally in pairs or with the whole group.

Reflect on learning as a group. There are numerous ways you can have teachers reflect on their learning collaboratively. Here are two ideas to spark your thinking:

1. *Go on a gallery walk*. Ask small groups of two or three teachers to create charts listing their takeaways. Encourage them to use writing and/or drawing to express their ideas. Have groups post their charts around the room and invite your colleagues to do a gallery walk—that is, move clockwise around the room to read each other's ideas. If there is time at the end, ask everyone to share something they read on a chart that they plan to apply to their teaching immediately.
2. *Use carousel charting.* Post charts around the classroom with headings covering the major ideas or subtopics explored in the session. For example, if the session addressed writing lessons, you might title each chart with a different part of the writing lesson structure. Working in small groups, your colleagues "carousel" around the room by reading what is on each chart and adding a few bulleted understandings relevant to the content of each chart. Each group's additions build on the previous group's contributions.

Change up how you ask teachers to reflect. Vary the ways you ask your colleagues to reflect to keep this part of the session fresh and engaging. Think about asking teachers to sketch-note their reflections (see Figure 11-5 on p. 109) or use mind mapping. Mind mapping involves creating a diagram that shows connections between new concepts, insights, and possible action plans. Figure 11-8 shows how a teacher used mind mapping to put together ideas and reflect on new learning about shared reading. You might also invite teachers to add their reflections to a virtual whiteboard or to a physical whiteboard or bulletin board.

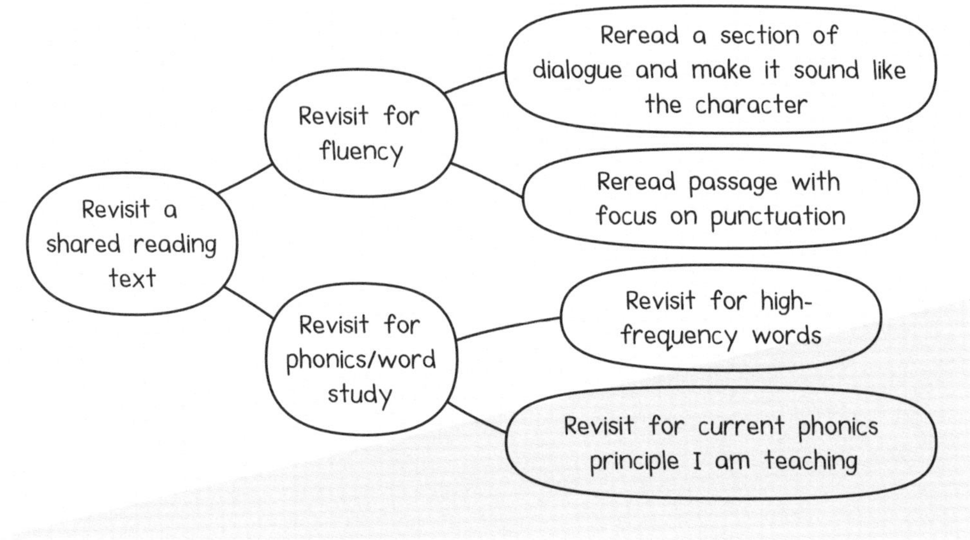

Figure 11-8

Take Time Yourself to Reflect

It is equally important that you take time to reflect on each session and your own goals for moving forward. Here are some things to think about:

- *How did the teachers take on the new learning? What did their talk and body language convey?*
- *How will you follow up with this learning (e.g., individual coaching, cluster coaching, lesson study, peer coaching)?*
- *How will the teachers' feedback inform the next session?*

Ask for Feedback

We've already discussed in this chapter the importance of soliciting feedback at the end of a professional learning session, so be sure to save time to gather this important information (see p. 102). Express your appreciation for how much you value the group's feedback and be sure to use it in your planning.

Sample Language

- *What things worked best for your learning in today's session?*
- *What did you find challenging but useful?*
- *What did you not find helpful?*
- *What are your goals for our next session?*
- *What are other ways you would like support? Ideas might include peer coaching, feedback on video clips, or a professional book club to further explore a topic.*

A Protocol Tool for Professional Learning Sessions

The process for planning PLS is summarized in Figure 11-9. (You will find a full-size version of Protocol Tool: Professional Learning Sessions as **OR 11.2** in the Online Resources.) Though the process is not rigid, the protocol illustrates how you might facilitate your PLS. We recommend printing out the protocol tool and keeping it handy in your coaching notebook (Chapter 23).

ONLINE RESOURCE 11.2

Extend the Learning

Extend and build on the learning from PLS by following up with opportunities for teachers to apply their learning in different contexts as described here.

Coaching Teachers: One-on-one and cluster coaching (Chapters 8 and 9) provide your colleagues with the highest level of support for applying new learning directly to their teaching. We recommend scheduling your colleagues for one-on-one or cluster coaching in the weeks following a session. At the end of a session, circulate a sign-up sheet with the times you are available for coaching so teachers can choose slots that work for them. This will not completely eliminate the need to follow up with individuals for scheduling, but it will cut down on the time you spend coordinating coaching sessions. Another way to extend learning is through peer coaching (Chapter 10). Though less scaffolded than one-on-one or cluster coaching, peer coaching gives your colleagues the opportunity to learn from one another and the freedom to explore ideas related to new learning with a trusted partner.

Look-for Tools: Create observational tools to look for the characteristics of high-quality instruction in specific instructional contexts. In the process of creating these helpful tools, you'll generate discussion about the key ideas and elements that would be most helpful to include (Chapter 13).

Learning Walks: After you've built strong understandings around a particular instructional context in a series of learning sessions, consider organizing a learning walk (Chapter 14) to notice how these understandings are being implemented across classrooms, grade levels, and so forth.

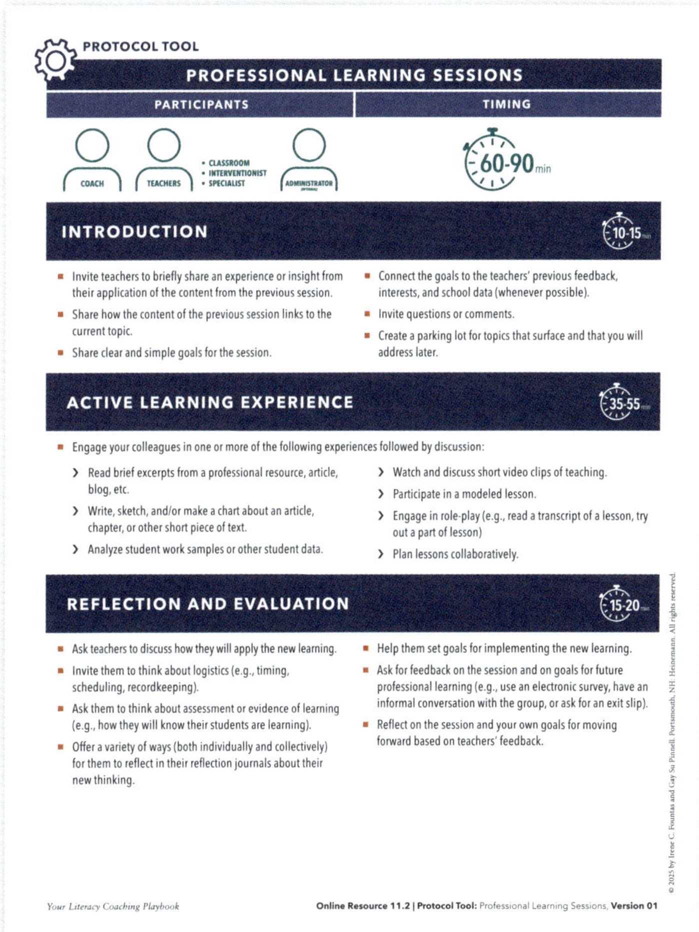
PROTOCOL TOOL

PROFESSIONAL LEARNING SESSIONS

PARTICIPANTS	TIMING
COACH; TEACHERS (• CLASSROOM • INTERVENTIONIST • SPECIALIST); ADMINISTRATOR (OPTIONAL)	60-90 min

INTRODUCTION 10-15 min

- Invite teachers to briefly share an experience or insight from their application of the content from the previous session.
- Share how the content of the previous session links to the current topic.
- Share clear and simple goals for the session.
- Connect the goals to the teachers' previous feedback, interests, and school data (whenever possible).
- Invite questions or comments.
- Create a parking lot for topics that surface and that you will address later.

ACTIVE LEARNING EXPERIENCE 35-55 min

- Engage your colleagues in one or more of the following experiences followed by discussion:
  - Read brief excerpts from a professional resource, article, blog, etc.
  - Write, sketch, and/or make a chart about an article, chapter, or other short piece of text.
  - Analyze student work samples or other student data.
  - Watch and discuss short video clips of teaching.
  - Participate in a modeled lesson.
  - Engage in role-play (e.g., read a transcript of a lesson, try out a part of lesson)
  - Plan lessons collaboratively.

REFLECTION AND EVALUATION 15-20 min

- Ask teachers to discuss how they will apply the new learning.
- Invite them to think about logistics (e.g., timing, scheduling, recordkeeping).
- Ask them to think about assessment or evidence of learning (e.g., how they will know their students are learning).
- Offer a variety of ways (both individually and collectively) for them to reflect in their reflection journals about their new thinking.
- Help them set goals for implementing the new learning.
- Ask for feedback on the session and on goals for future professional learning (e.g., use an electronic survey, have an informal conversation with the group, or ask for an exit slip).
- Reflect on the session and your own goals for moving forward based on teachers' feedback.

Your Literacy Coaching Playbook — **Online Resource 11.2 | Protocol Tool:** Professional Learning Sessions, **Version 01**

Figure 11-9

Lesson Studies: In a lesson study (Chapter 15), teachers plan, teach, and revise a lesson together using their new learning from PLS as a foundation.

Professional Book Clubs: Select a professional book or text related to the content you have been studying in your PLS and invite your colleagues to participate in an informal book club (Chapter 17) to delve deeper into the topic.

Through active learning experiences and collegial discussions, professional learning sessions provide a context in which teachers can share what they know, build their expertise, and reflect on their goals for continued growth in their teaching with the ultimate goal of improving student learning outcomes.

Up **Next**

In Chapter 12, we introduce a structure we call "bite-size professional learning" because it is designed for short bursts of professional learning that are usually no more than thirty minutes long and frequently much shorter. Turn the page to take a bite out of this uniquely efficient structure.

Chapter 12

The Play: **Bite-Size Professional Learning**

We know. There's too much to do and too little time. But if you've got ten minutes, you've got all the time you'll need to impact your colleagues' teaching using bite-size professional learning sessions (PLS)—a very effective little power play for maximizing the time you have to support continuous teacher growth. In today's ever-changing, fast-paced world, bite-size professional learning is an essential component of modern professional learning that addresses teacher challenges in a practical way.

As a coach, you chart new territory and problem-solve to accomplish great things in your school. Yet, time is likely a constant challenge as you work to provide a suite of high-quality learning experiences for every teacher. So, let's think outside the box about how to use small slices of time to shape the growing expertise of every teacher in the school.

BENEFITS OF BITE-SIZE PROFESSIONAL LEARNING

- Maximizes the time you have
- Engages learners with more limited attention spans
- Addresses timely issues quickly because of easy scheduling
- Gives quick access to the most pertinent information on a topic
- Breaks bigger concepts into digestible chunks
- Makes concepts easy to retain because of the narrow focus

What Is Bite-Size Professional Learning?

Bite-size professional learning sessions, sometimes called "micro sessions" or "micro learning," are short bursts of simple, highly focused, and active professional learning experiences that are usually ten, fifteen, twenty, or at most thirty minutes long. Though time is short, quality is not sacrificed because the narrow focus still allows you to plan experiences that engage teachers in collective inquiry. As with longer PLS, teachers might read and discuss a short text, watch video clips of teaching, analyze student work, or even do a role-play. The differences are that the topic is smaller, participants engage in only one activity for a very brief time, and the content is focused on only one or two tightly defined learning goals. In this chapter, we will help you understand the benefits of bite-size PLS, when to use them, and a process for planning them.

A Framework for Bite-Size Professional Learning

We recommend scheduling anywhere from ten to thirty minutes for bite-size professional learning. Anything longer will require more strategic planning and scheduling, and the whole idea behind this play is that it is quick, accessible, and easy to schedule. Bite-size professional learning is informal by design and doesn't necessarily require a structured routine. However, we have found it helpful to use a modified version of the framework for longer PLS to keep our planning focused (Figure 12-1). The more consistent you are with routines, the more efficient and effective you will be in facilitating these short bursts of professional learning.

FRAMEWORK FOR A BITE-SIZE PROFESSIONAL LEARNING SESSION

INTRODUCTION — 1-2 min

Introduce the goal of the micro session and its relevance to current work.

ACTIVE LEARNING EXPERIENCE — 6-20 min

Actively engage participants in one short learning experience. For example, they might

- analyze student data,
- watch and discuss a video clip of teaching,
- engage in a modeled lesson or role-play,
- plan a lesson,
- read and discuss a short excerpt from a professional text or article, or
- look at and discuss an infographic.

REFLECTION — 3-8 min

Ask teachers to reflect on the new learning and identify their goals for applying it to their teaching.

Figure 12-1

Plan and Prepare for Bite-Size Professional Learning Sessions

Thoughtful planning ensures that your brief time with colleagues is packed with a punch. To make the most of this time, you need to be prepared and well provisioned. Here are some helpful hints to ensure teachers will benefit from every second:

- Be ready to start on time.
- Prepare clear and concise directions for the active learning experience.
- Remind colleagues to bring any needed materials.
- Make sure you have any necessary materials organized and ready for distribution.
- Be realistic about how long things will take, establish time limits, and cut where necessary.
- Things always take longer than you think, so remember that less is often more.
- Time for talk is essential, so when planning, err on the side of less content and more talk.
- Use memorable images and pictures in your slides to represent ideas. Visuals make a difference especially when you have only a short time to develop understandings.
- Capture ideas on charts you can photograph and send to colleagues.

Multimedia Tip

You might record bite-size sessions and put them in your video library for replay.

Schedule Time for Bite-Size Professional Learning

Because teachers are often more available for shorter periods of time, you will likely find it easy to schedule bite-size professional learning. You can set up micro sessions quickly for just-in-time learning on a topic that recently emerged as a need. Here are some ways you might invite and gather your colleagues for this work:

- Advertise a quick after-school or before-school session in an inviting email.
- Visit a grade-level meeting, and spend a few minutes working with the team of teachers on a topic.
- Offer ideas for a few short sessions, and ask teachers to sign up for the ones that spark their interest.
- Use part of regularly scheduled meetings (e.g., faculty meetings, data meetings, literacy team meetings) to offer these short bursts of professional learning.

NEW TEACHER

Short bursts of professional learning are easily digestible for the new teacher, who might become overwhelmed by longer sessions.

Don't Bite Off (Pun Intended) More Than You Can Chew

Busy teachers often find it helpful to focus on and consume smaller, digestible parts of more complex concepts and tasks. The challenge for you in planning bite-size PLS is choosing a topic that's small enough to explore in the time you have. Figure 12–2 lists some examples of topics coaches have addressed through micro sessions. In just ten minutes, you can offer teachers a few ideas that they can turn around and immediately apply to their teaching. More importantly, this quick

What Is a Digestible Chunk?

- An exploration of nonfiction books to read aloud
- A book share of mentor texts for writing
- Planning strong text introductions
- Ways to make words or sort words to support phonics and word study
- Reading the punctuation to support fluency
- Teaching phrasing to support fluency
- Supporting students in understanding the author's message
- Efficient reading and writing conferences
- How to give a good book talk
- How to apply grammar rules to writing
- Quick writes for the writer's notebook

Figure 12-2

interaction generates an idea exchange. It energizes teachers to think about new ways to work with their students. It inspires conversations that spark interest into larger topics that you might later address in longer PLS (Chapter 11). The most important move you can make in your planning is to be realistic about what you can address in a short period of time to maximize the impact.

Think about how you might build on a series of bite-size sessions to develop a larger concept over time. One coach we know designed a series of sessions based on teachers' request for support in learning how to help students deepen their comprehension of texts during interactive read-aloud and independent reading. The coach decided to focus on language moves that deepen comprehension but knew there would not be enough time to explore this topic in a longer session. So, she decided to break the umbrella topic into five bite-size or micro sessions, as shown in Figure 12-3.

During each twenty-minute micro session, the group focused on just one language move. This very narrow focus gave the coach and her colleagues the opportunity to delve deeply into each type of language move and apply it right away. The narrow focus in small bursts may be retained better because the learning is applied immediately. Bite-size sessions are also ideal for learners with limited attention spans who need quick access to pertinent information. As you are selecting and planning topics for bite-size professional learning, don't worry about the fact that there might be more to learn about a topic. You will get there!

LANGUAGE MOVES TO SUPPORT DEEPER COMPREHENSION OF TEXTS

Micro Session 1
Provide Evidence from the Text
Language move to teach students how to provide evidence for their thinking

Micro Session 2
Identify the Author's Message
Language move to teach students how to think about the author's message

Micro Session 3
Notice Author's Choice of Language
Language move to teach students how to consider the author's choice of words and phrases

Micro Session 4
Consider Author's Choice of Genre
Language move to teach students how to think about the author's choice of genre

Micro Session 5
Connect Texts
Language move to teach students to connect the text to other texts

Figure 12-3

Taking advantage of the small pockets of time in your colleagues' day to bring them timely professional learning will accumulate over time and ultimately impact student learning.

Bite-Size Professional Learning: What to Say and Do

The bite-size sessions you plan will be more impactful if you keep active learning at the heart of your planning. Engage your colleagues from the start with brief, hands-on experiences:

- Work with manipulatives, such as magnetic letters for building words or word cards for word sorts.
- Ask participants to prepare and give a book talk (a one- to two-minute advertisement of the book) for their favorite read-aloud book. Share with the whole group or meet in small groups of three or four.
- Use carousel charting (p. 115) to build charts about the topic being explored.
- Engage in role-play of introductions to texts.
- Talk in triads about a handout, a short article, or an infographic.
- Provide several quotes about a topic and invite your colleagues to discuss.
- Complete a quick analysis of student writing papers in pairs.
- Engage in small peer discussion circles about a short video clip.
- Have partners share two or three minutes of video that they recorded (on phones) of their teaching.
- Analyze a short video clip of a student reading.

This bulleted list is just a sampling of the ways you might engage teachers in exploring a topic through very brief, hands-on interactions. Be sure each session fits an actual need, is very focused, and targets key nuggets of information. And remember to make it fun!

QUICK TIP

Use bite-size learning to revisit an aspect of a topic that was presented previously to go deeper or to clarify any common challenges across the team of teachers.

Your Recipe for Success

- Start with one or two clear goals.
- Invite your colleagues to suggest topics of need.
- Be flexible enough to arrange for bite-size sessions quickly to respond to current teacher needs.
- Break down complex concepts or topics into smaller chunks that are easily understood.
- Build in time for discussion to promote collaborative thinking.
- Stick to the important nuggets. You can always refer the teachers to further resources if they want them.
- Use headings, bullet points, and visuals, such as sketch-notes, to make your topic appealing.
- Use a variety of relevant media to engage the learners (e.g., audio clips, videos, photos).

A Sample Plan for a Bite-Size Professional Learning Session

Let's take a look at a coach's plan (Figure 12–4) for how to engage teachers in active learning for one of the micro sessions shown in Figure 12–2. Note that we've included the coach's detailed language for each part of the plan. Although you might not use scripted language to the degree we do here for the purpose of this example, we do encourage you to think about and jot down some of the language you plan to use in the session. (You will find a blank, full-size Template Tool: Plan for Bite-Size Professional Learning as **OR 12.1** in the Online Resources.) The more you know about what you are going to say, the tighter you will be able to keep the session. There is no time to waste on extraneous words!

ONLINE RESOURCE 12.1

TEMPLATE TOOL

PLAN FOR BITE-SIZE PROFESSIONAL LEARNING

Session topic: identify the author's message	**Session length:** 20 minutes	**Materials:** *Prompting Guide, Part 2, for Comprehension* (Fountas and Pinnell 2009) or other resource on language prompts, video clip, chart paper; teachers bring reflection journals

INTRODUCTION

Link to Previous Learning 1 min	*Over the past two weeks, you have had opportunities to support your students' deeper thinking about texts. At our last session, we worked on using a language move to teach students how to provide evidence for their thinking.*
Goals 1 min	*Today we are going to think together about another type of language move that fosters deep thinking about a text.*

ACTIVE LEARNING EXPERIENCE

Timing 5-15 min	**Watch a video clip:** *Let's look at a three-minute video clip of a teacher and students talking about an expository nonfiction book. As you watch, notice the language the teacher uses and its effect on the students' thinking.* **Invite discussion:** *Turn and talk with your partner about the language the teacher used and how it influenced the readers' thinking and talking about the book. Where did you notice a shift in the students' thinking from a summary to a deeper understanding of the author's real message?* **Share:** Invite partners to share their thinking about how the teacher prompted the students to think beyond the literal message to the deeper message. Create a chart as an example for the group: Literal message: *You have to train and practice to be a star dancer.* Deeper message: *Follow your passion and be willing to work at it. When you succeed, you can help others develop expertise.*

REFLECTION AND EVALUATION

Reflection 1 min	Have teachers look at a resource, such as *Prompting Guide, Part 2, for Comprehension: Turn to page 68, "Focus on Big Ideas."* To expand their thinking, have them skim the series of prompts and think about how they might use them with their students: *How can you envision using these with texts you plan to use in your classroom this week?*
Goal Setting 1 min	*This week, look for opportunities to talk about what the author is really trying to say in both fiction and nonfiction texts. Write down two specific prompts you plan to use to engage your students in thinking about the author's message. When we meet next, be prepared to share how both prompts are contributing to your students' deeper comprehension of texts.*

Your Literacy Coaching Playbook **Online Resource 12.1 | Template Tool:** Plan for Bite-Size Professional Learning, **Version 01**

Figure 12-4

A Protocol Tool for Bite-Size Professional Learning

We have summarized the process for a bite-size professional learning session in Figure 12-5. (You will find a full-size version of Protocol Tool: Bite-Size Professional Learning as **OR 12.2** in the Online Resources.) Though the process is flexible according to your needs, the description in the protocol does provide some helpful reminders. You can use this in conjunction with the planning template (Figure 12-4). We recommend printing out both the protocol tool and planning template and keeping them handy in your coaching notebook for quick and easy planning.

ONLINE RESOURCE 12.2

The scope of this bite-size session is very limited—the exploration of just *one* language move to get students thinking deeper with just *one* short video clip and a quick skim of a resource. Most of the time is spent on talk. No matter how short the burst of professional learning, collegial talk is the key to developing common understandings and raising the level of teacher expertise. Time for reflection and goal setting is equally important so that there is the immediate connection back to the classroom.

Bite-size professional learning can be a game-changer for you, particularly if you are a coach who has limited time to introduce and explore topics with your colleagues. Add bite-size learning sessions to your playbook and think about how they might open opportunities for ongoing, collaborative learning within your district or school. Just ten minutes can create lasting change.

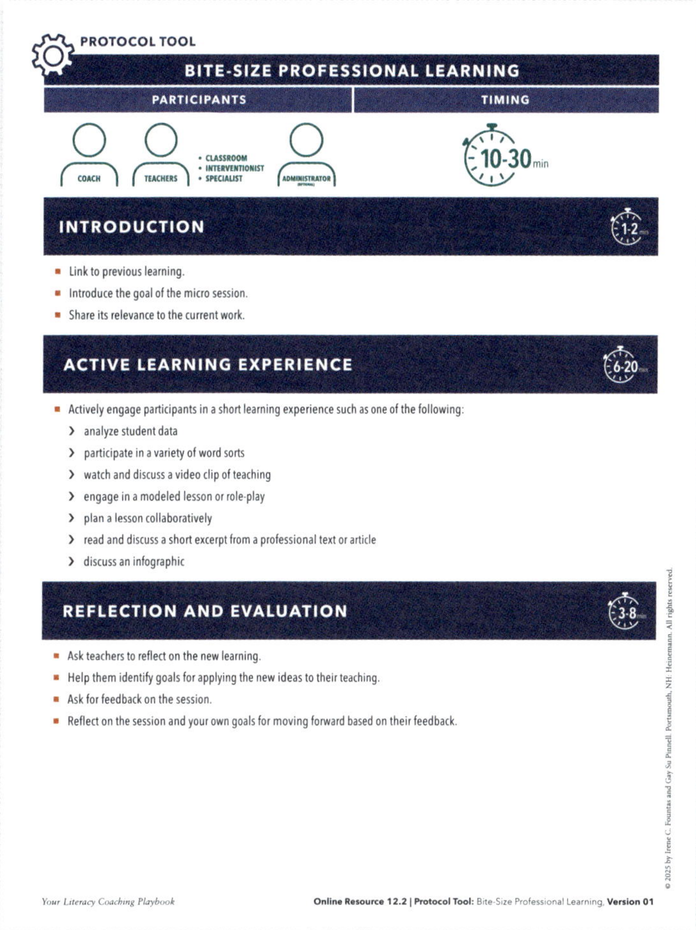
PROTOCOL TOOL

BITE-SIZE PROFESSIONAL LEARNING

PARTICIPANTS	TIMING
COACH; TEACHERS (• CLASSROOM • INTERVENTIONIST • SPECIALIST); ADMINISTRATOR (optional)	10-30 min

INTRODUCTION 1-2 min

- Link to previous learning.
- Introduce the goal of the micro session.
- Share its relevance to the current work.

ACTIVE LEARNING EXPERIENCE 6-20 min

- Actively engage participants in a short learning experience such as one of the following:
  - analyze student data
  - participate in a variety of word sorts
  - watch and discuss a video clip of teaching
  - engage in a modeled lesson or role-play
  - plan a lesson collaboratively
  - read and discuss a short excerpt from a professional text or article
  - discuss an infographic

REFLECTION AND EVALUATION 3-8 min

- Ask teachers to reflect on the new learning.
- Help them identify goals for applying the new ideas to their teaching.
- Ask for feedback on the session.
- Reflect on the session and your own goals for moving forward based on their feedback.

Your Literacy Coaching Playbook — **Online Resource 12.2 | Protocol Tool:** Bite-Size Professional Learning, **Version 01**

Figure 12-5

Up **Next**

In Chapter 13, we discuss how to develop well-crafted observation tools and why it's so important that teachers co-create them with you.

Chapter 13

The Play: **Look-for Tools**

It's important to have the right tools for the job. Careful observation requires a lot, which is why you need the right tools to provide a lens through which you and your colleagues can spot what makes instruction productive, coherent, and consistent with your school's instructional goals. We call these observational tools "look-for tools" because the name so accurately describes what they are: a list of the elements of high-quality instruction you would want to "look for" during an observation. The tools are meant to be flexible and can always be revised, but they focus the thinking in an agreed-upon direction and provide cohesion in instructional goals. For example, think about watching a writing conference. What important parts should you see the teacher and student working through? What instructional moves? In other words, what would you *look for*?

BENEFITS OF DEVELOPING LOOK-FOR TOOLS

- Allows teachers to communicate their understanding of the elements of high-quality instruction within a particular instructional context
- Gets everyone on the same page about the characteristics of high-quality instruction
- Gives teachers a lens with which to focus their observation and reflection of teaching and learning
- Provides a tool to use in multiple coaching scenarios (e.g., one-on-one coaching, cluster coaching, peer coaching, learning walks) to support the professional learning
- Provides an agreed-upon, grass-roots tool for administrators to use in their evaluation process
- Allows teachers to develop a common language with which to talk about their teaching

But here's the thing: Teachers benefit enormously from co-developing look-for tools with you. When teachers are involved in developing these tools, they determine what is essential in each instructional context, develop common language, and have meaningful conversations about what constitutes high-quality instruction. These characteristics then become a different kind of lens through which they can reflect on their own teaching and teaching by colleagues.

Think from Inside

We have found that when you engage teachers in thinking, talking about, and constructing a look-for tool, they understand it from the inside instead of simply looking at a top-down list of expectations or directives from the school or district. When teachers engage in this collaborative work, they contribute to building the school's common vision for literacy learning while concretely translating the vision into practice one element at a time.

When you work with your colleagues to develop observational tools, you capture the characteristics of high-quality instruction in different contexts. For teachers, the tools help solidify their common understandings. For you, they become reliable ways to navigate your observations so you don't miss important indicators that tell you and your colleagues to focus on a particular aspect of instruction.

In this chapter, we'll help you and the teachers in your school work together to develop look-for tools through a process that will benefit all.

Plan and Prepare for Developing Look-for Tools

First, spend time building knowledge and developing a common understanding of the instructional context (Figure 13–1) or focus of the tool. During professional learning sessions (PLS), described in Chapter 11, you might engage teachers in reading about the context, watching video clips of lessons, role-playing transcripts of teaching and learning, and planning lessons. PLS offer time to build these deep understandings. You might also consider using a series of bite-size PLS (Chapter 12) to focus on a series of the smaller elements of an instructional context, such as individual lesson components, and build the understandings over time. You might follow up with one-on-one or cluster coaching to further develop teachers' knowledge. Through PLS, bite-size PLS, and coaching, teachers become active participants in identifying the specific criteria for high-quality instruction. From these common understandings, engage your colleagues in building observational tools to support and further their professional growth.

Instructional Contexts

You might develop look-for tools for any of these or other instructional contexts:

- Whole-group reading and writing lessons
- Small-group reading, writing, and phonics instruction
- Reading and writing conferences
- Independent reading
- Book clubs
- Interactive read-aloud
- Shared reading
- Phonics and word study lessons
- Interactive writing
- Guided writing
- Project-based learning
- Cooperative learning
- Reading and writing in content areas

Figure 13-1

Schedule Time to Develop Look-for Tools

You may be thinking, "Sounds great, but when do we do this work?" We recommend allocating about an hour to the thoughtful development of a look-for tool for each instructional context. This work can be done anytime you have a group of teachers together who have experienced previous professional learning related to the instructional context. We have seen coaches create look-for tools during PLS, faculty meetings, and grade-level meetings. If you choose to do this work during grade-level meetings, eventually you will need a time for all teachers to meet and discuss the results so you can combine their thinking into one tool. If necessary, you could even use a series of bite-size PLS to develop each part of the tool.

In addition to scheduling a time to build the tool together, we recommend you schedule another hour for your colleagues to try out the tool by applying it to a recorded lesson. An hour will also give them time to suggest any necessary revisions to the tool.

NEW TEACHER

Colleagues new to teaching especially will benefit from developing look-for tools because it gives them the opportunity to put together everything they have learned about a context. They will benefit from using look-for tools to focus in specific ways on aspects of their own teaching. Encourage them to focus on one aspect at a time so they don't become overwhelmed by the whole process.

Develop Look-for Tools: What to Say and Do

Let's look at a possible process for engaging teachers in constructing and refining a look-for tool for the instructional context of interactive read-aloud. Note that there can be many variations of this process that will achieve the same goal.

Before you meet with the teachers, be sure they've had the time they need to develop their understanding of interactive read-aloud. As we described, you might spend two or three PLS engaging your colleagues in a series of active learning experiences such as reading about interactive read-aloud, watching video clips of interactive read-aloud lessons, and planning lessons.

Once teachers have a strong common understanding of the instructional context, begin the process of developing the look-for tools (Figure 13–2). As you read through this example, jot down tips and big ideas such as those that follow:

- Teachers are at the center of this work. Their words and understandings are the foundation for the look-for tools, but don't worry if they don't use technical terms yet.
- The work is inquiry based. Teachers construct the look-fors together through conversation and discussion and gain new insights.
- By breaking the lesson framework into parts or categories (e.g., planning, introducing the text, reading the text, discussing the text) and listing them on a chart, teachers are invited to think more specifically and add more detailed bullets about each part of the instructional context.
- Collaboration is at the heart of the process as teachers read, discuss, and identify common understandings that they agree should be a part of the tool.

- The coach acts as the facilitator of this process and takes the role of summarizing the charting into a workable document.
- The group has the opportunity to revise the tool after trying it out.
- Teachers develop ownership over the tool because they developed it, tried it, refined it, and discussed ways to use it.

DEVELOPING A LOOK-FOR TOOL FOR OBSERVING INTERACTIVE READ-ALOUD

Collect thinking.

Have small groups (or pairs) refer to their professional resources and use their knowledge of a high-quality interactive read-aloud lesson to create bullets for each of five categories pertinent to the instructional context. Select a recorder to make a chart of the points for each category. Use a prompt similar to the following:

- For each category what are the most important things you would look for in an effective lesson?
  - Planning and Preparation
  - Introducing the Text
  - Reading the Text
  - Discussing the Text
  - Revisiting the Text

Share thinking.

Have the groups post their charts around the room organized by category. For example, all the charts on planning and preparation would be posted in the same area. Have the teachers do a gallery walk (teachers walk slowly clockwise around the room, reading each other's charts). Ask them to jot down their noticings. You might say something like the following:

- *Jot down whatever stands out to you.*
- *Jot down similarities or differences you notice.*

Identify commonalities.

Reconvene and discuss teachers' noticings. Facilitate the conversation so that all participate. Most likely, the teachers will have noticed that most of what they listed was similar, although there may have been some variations in word choices. Some might express that they felt their group missed something important or listed items that are less important. Here is some language you might use:

- *What patterns did you notice across the charts?*
- *Talk about what you are thinking now that you've reviewed the other charts.*
- *Were there important parts that you felt were missing?*

Explain next steps.

Summarize by letting your colleagues know that you will use the charts to create a draft chart that closely reflects what they specified. Explain that you will list only the most important points to keep it short and that you will create a column on the right side of the tool for some quick notes.

Create the draft look-for tool.

Develop a document (see Figure 13-3 on p. 131 for an example) that explicitly describes the most important points and is consistent with the rationales of high-quality instruction. You may need to shape the language a bit or add something important that was omitted.

Figure 13-2 continues

Share and try out the draft look-for tool.

At your next meeting, share the document you created. Explain anything you added. Also explain that the group can continue to revise the tool after they've used it. Ideally, you will distribute the document and try it out together by showing a video and asking them to use the look-for tool to make notes in the right-hand column. If time is a challenge, break the tool into sections and view only one or two parts of the lesson. You might use this sample language:

- *I've tried my best to capture your thinking on this look-for tool. Please take a moment to read through and note any questions or wonderings you have.*
- *We will take a few minutes to try out the tool by watching a few parts of an interactive read-aloud lesson. Use the tool to look for the characteristics of high-quality instruction that you determined were most important.*
- *Make note of any revisions you suggest after you use the tool to watch this lesson.*

Revise the draft look-for tool.

Engage your colleagues in a discussion of how the tool helped them look at the lesson and what new insights they have about interactive read-aloud after trying the tool. Explain that you will make revisions and note the version of the tool in the bottom corner.

- *How did the tool influence your learning?*
- *Are there any revisions you want to suggest?*
- *This tool can change as our understandings continue to develop. We can revisit the tool in the future and refine it as needed.*

Identify ways to use the tool.

Invite teachers to think about ways they might use the tool to reflect on their own practice and during one-on-one, cluster, or peer coaching.

- *How can you use this tool to reflect on your teaching of interactive read-aloud?*
- *How might we use this tool in our coaching sessions?*
- *How might you use this tool with peers?*
- *How might you and the principal use this tool to reflect together on your goals and document your growth?*

Figure 13-2 continued

ONLINE RESOURCE 13.1

Look-for Tools for School-Wide Projects

Consider developing look-for tools to support school-wide projects. For example, if your school is looking to expand representation in text collections, you might work with your colleagues to develop a tool for what to look for in classroom library collections.

Figure 13-3 shows an example of a look-for tool we have developed using this process. (You will find a blank, full-size Look-for Tool: Interactive Read-Aloud Lesson as **OR 13.1** in the Online Resources.) Notice how the look-for tool succinctly captures the most important elements of interactive read-aloud. It is purposely concise so that teachers, coaches, and administrators can use it quickly and easily to identify areas to target for improved teaching and learning. You can find a wide variety of similar observation tools in our book *Leading for Literacy* (Fountas and Pinnell 2022).

We cannot emphasize enough the power of constructing these tools with your colleagues. The development of the tool itself serves as deep professional learning because teachers must engage in meaningful discussions and identify key understandings to produce effective look-for tools.

LOOK-FOR TOOL

INTERACTIVE READ-ALOUD LESSON

PLANNING AND PREPARATION	Notes:
The teacher: ▪ Selects a text that is engaging, enjoyable, and worthwhile ✓ ▪ Selects a text that is age/grade appropriate and culturally relevant ✓ ▪ Selects a text that can serve as a mentor text in reading and writing minilessons ▪ Understands the opportunities in the text to expand students' vocabulary, language, background, and literacy knowledge ▪ Selects appropriate goals from instructional goals	• How did Michael select goals? How did he know they were appropriate for group?
INTRODUCING THE TEXT	
The teacher: ▪ Provides a very brief introduction prior to reading the text ▪ Engages students' genuine interest prior to reading the text ✓ ▪ Engages students' thinking about the topic, genre, series, author, illustrator and/or makes a link to another text ✓	• Intro relevant, maybe too long (5 mins)? • Kids seem engaged.
READING THE TEXT	
The teacher: ▪ Reads at a comfortable pace with expression ✓ ▪ Invites spontaneous personal responses and multiple perspectives ▪ Pauses at a few carefully selected points for students to talk about their thinking with each other ▪ Uses a variety of talk structures (e.g., pairs, triads, whole group) ▪ Prompts, comments, or questions to promote thinking within, beyond, about the text (see *The Fountas & Pinnell Literacy Continuum*) ✓	• Too long for antsy K students? • Lots of individual response to teacher prompting-more turn and talk? • Too many stopping points? How selected?
DISCUSSING THE TEXT	
The teacher: ▪ Facilitates a meaningful conversation by inviting personal response and critical thinking, encouraging students to build on each other's ideas ▪ Facilitates a discussion that builds vocabulary, language, knowledge, and deeper understanding of the text–its message and relevance to their lives and the world → ▪ Encourages attention to the writer's/illustrator's craft ▪ Promotes the use of evidence from personal experience and/or the text to support thinking	• Ran out of time. • Very little discussion after reading text. • Ended by telling lesson of story. • No kid input.
REVISITING THE TEXT	
The teacher: ▪ Rereads selected parts for close analysis if appropriate ▪ Is selective and brief in returning to the text ▪ Helps students notice aspects of the writer's or illustrator's craft to build deeper understanding	

Your Literacy Coaching Playbook **Online Resource 13.1 | Look-for Tool:** Interactive Read-Aloud Lesson, **Version 01**

Figure 13-3

A Protocol Tool for Developing Look-for Tools

ONLINE RESOURCE 13.2

We have summarized the process for developing look-for tools in Figure 13-4. (You will find a full-size version of Protocol Tool: Developing Look-for Tools as **OR 13.2** in the Online Resources.) The description in the protocol summarizes the steps found in Figure 13-2. Adjust and tweak the process based on the size of your group, the time you have, and the type of instructional context. We recommend printing out the protocol and keeping it handy in your coaching notebook (Chapter 23).

Extend the Learning

Once developed, the look-for tools give your colleagues a lens through which to focus their observation of teaching and learning in a variety of professional learning settings.

Use Look-for Tools in Coaching

In one-on-one or cluster coaching, center the discussion and reflection on a common set of criteria with teacher-developed look-for tools. During the pre-observation coaching conversation, ask teachers to skim the bullets on the look-for tool to identify areas of strength and any areas of potential focus. Use the tool in the post-observation conversation in the same way to reflect on different elements of the lesson. The look-for tool criteria serve as a scaffold for setting specific goals for teaching within a particular instructional context. When the same tool is used over time, teachers can see their progress in concrete terms.

The tool can be particularly useful for learning partners to use during peer coaching (Chapter 10) because it gives them an accessible way to discuss the lesson and keep it focused on the characteristics of high-quality instruction.

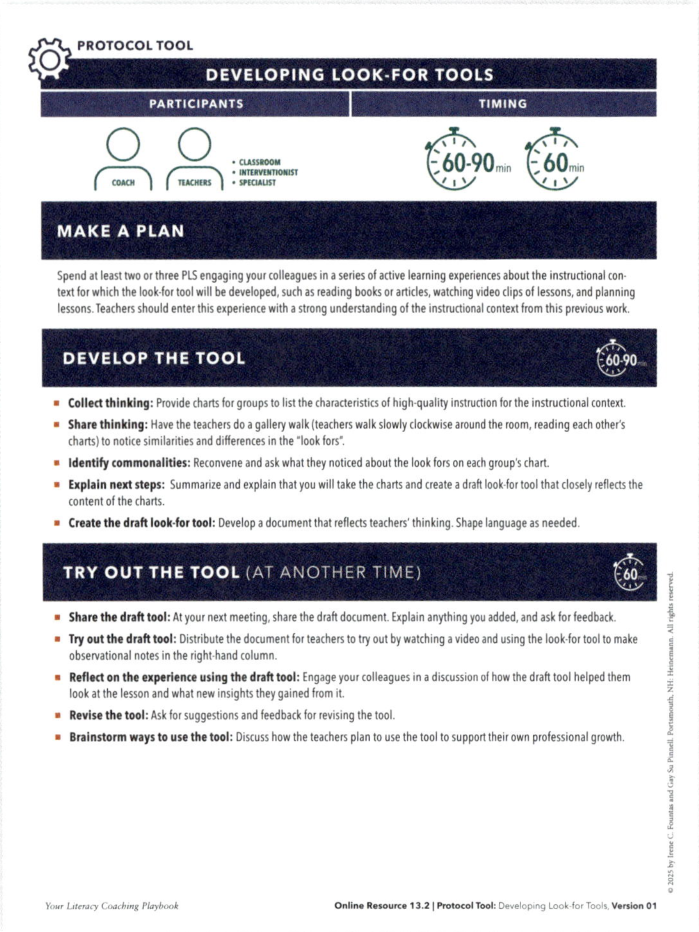
PROTOCOL TOOL

DEVELOPING LOOK-FOR TOOLS

PARTICIPANTS: COACH; TEACHERS
- CLASSROOM
- INTERVENTIONIST
- SPECIALIST

TIMING: 60-90 min; 60 min

MAKE A PLAN

Spend at least two or three PLS engaging your colleagues in a series of active learning experiences about the instructional context for which the look-for tool will be developed, such as reading books or articles, watching video clips of lessons, and planning lessons. Teachers should enter this experience with a strong understanding of the instructional context from this previous work.

DEVELOP THE TOOL (60-90 min)

- **Collect thinking:** Provide charts for groups to list the characteristics of high-quality instruction for the instructional context.
- **Share thinking:** Have the teachers do a gallery walk (teachers walk slowly clockwise around the room, reading each other's charts) to notice similarities and differences in the "look fors".
- **Identify commonalities:** Reconvene and ask what they noticed about the look fors on each group's chart.
- **Explain next steps:** Summarize and explain that you will take the charts and create a draft look-for tool that closely reflects the content of the charts.
- **Create the draft look-for tool:** Develop a document that reflects teachers' thinking. Shape language as needed.

TRY OUT THE TOOL (AT ANOTHER TIME) (60 min)

- **Share the draft tool:** At your next meeting, share the draft document. Explain anything you added, and ask for feedback.
- **Try out the draft tool:** Distribute the document for teachers to try out by watching a video and using the look-for tool to make observational notes in the right-hand column.
- **Reflect on the experience using the draft tool:** Engage your colleagues in a discussion of how the draft tool helped them look at the lesson and what new insights they gained from it.
- **Revise the tool:** Ask for suggestions and feedback for revising the tool.
- **Brainstorm ways to use the tool:** Discuss how the teachers plan to use the tool to support their own professional growth.

Your Literacy Coaching Playbook — **Online Resource 13.2 | Protocol Tool:** Developing Look-for Tools, **Version 01**

Figure 13-4

Use Look-for Tools in Learning Walks

You may find it helpful to integrate the look-for tools your colleagues have developed in learning walks (Chapter 14). As your colleagues observe for a short time in several classrooms, they can look for evidence of the teaching moves identified on the tool. The tools, however, are not designed to be used in an evaluative way. They aren't a checklist for teachers to critique their colleagues' instruction, but they are a way for everyone to use shared examples to reflect on their own instruction and identify further goals for professional learning.

A Word About Administrators Using Look-for Tools

Administrators, coaches, and teachers as partners can use the tool as a focus for continuous growth. The school principal will have the criteria for instruction stated explicitly, and the teacher will be able use it to identify specific goals. With common language, common goals, and common understandings, the main focus for the administrator can be the teacher's goals and concrete evidence of growth.

We're certain you will discover many more uses for look-for tools once you begin using them in your coaching. They are valuable because they have been collaboratively developed and are fundamentally focused on high-quality instruction. Teachers grow in expertise as they develop them, use them, and refine them. They are the gift that keeps on giving.

Up **Next**

In Chapter 14, we turn to the topic of learning walks, powerful tools for opening metaphorical windows and literal doors on what teachers' colleagues are doing in classrooms around the school. Learning walks are perhaps one of the most valuable forms of professional learning because they emphasize that excellent teaching is possible in every classroom.

Chapter 14

The Play: **Learning Walks**

Classrooms tell stories. Displays of students' writing on the walls, anchor charts that capture students' thinking, the arrangement of the furniture, the organization of the classroom library—every detail reveals a teacher's beliefs and values about teaching and learning. Now, think about what you would learn if the classroom were filled with kids and you had the chance to briefly watch the teacher and students working together. You'd be able to link the details in the classroom environment to what the teacher does with the students. And if you'd had a chance to spend a few minutes in multiple classrooms, you'd come away with a picture in your mind of what is happening in literacy classrooms throughout the school. Together, those classrooms would tell the story of where your school is in realizing its vision for literacy learning—and where there is room for growth. Several walks will begin to reveal patterns and trends that build a picture of the school you and your colleagues are creating.

BENEFITS OF LEARNING WALKS

- Inspire teachers to learn from the instructional practices they observe
- Allow collection of specific data about the literacy opportunities available to students across the school
- Give teachers ideas for how to organize their classrooms to reflect what they believe is best for student learning
- Strengthen a culture of trust, transparency, inquiry, and collaboration about instruction
- Reveal patterns and trends of how teachers reflect their values and beliefs about education
- Identify topics and interests for continued professional learning

What Are Learning Walks?

A learning walk is a short time spent in a classroom to observe teaching and learning. Learning walks typically involve a group of four to six participants (some combination of the coach, two to four teachers, one or two specialists, and often an administrator) who visit a predetermined number of classrooms (usually between three and five) for about five to ten minutes each. Typically, learning walks are focused on a particular goal that has been shared with participants in advance. Learning walks rely on and promote an open-door culture in which teachers feel comfortable sharing with and learning from their colleagues. Learning walks often result in plans for future professional learning, implementation of new teaching techniques and, in some cases, the generation of solution-based ideas for school-wide problems of practice. The purpose of a learning walk is to learn.

A Framework for Learning Walks

The suggested general framework for a learning walk in Figure 14–1 is designed for participants to have multiple opportunities to collect evidence across classrooms and have meaningful, nonevaluative conversations.

FRAMEWORK FOR A LEARNING WALK

PRE-WALK MEETING

Meet with the team and briefly discuss the focus of the observations and relevant data to collect. Talk briefly about how to share findings afterward. Review guidelines for observation.

5-10 min

THE WALK-THROUGHS

Observe and collect evidence related to the focus. Engage the team in quick hallway conversation after each classroom to summarize noticings or have them jot notes to discuss later.

5-10 min

per classroom for a total of approximately 30-40 min

POST-WALK MEETING

Share observations. Write action plans based on the data gathered. Confirm how and when the data will be shared. Ask for feedback and ideas for future learning walks.

10 min

Figure 14–1

Plan and Prepare for Learning Walks

Learning walks require some logistical planning, but once they are planned, the team has a lot to gain from a relatively short investment of time. In about an hour, your colleagues can visit and discuss what they see across several classrooms. Work with your administrator and/or literacy team to figure out timing, coverage, and the focus of the walk.

Choose Topics for Learning Walks

If it makes sense in your situation, decide on the focus for your team's first few learning walks while they are getting comfortable with the process. Here are some ideas to get you started:

- Different instructional contexts (e.g., interactive read-aloud, small-group reading instruction, phonics lessons)
- Aspects of the school improvement plan or specific school initiatives
- Use of new technology
- Literacy across content areas
- Use of visuals to support multilingual learners during literacy lessons
- Independence in reading and writing
- Student engagement in reading and writing

> ***Knock Out Problems***
>
> Instructional rounds, a type of learning walk, focus on problems of practice and involve teachers working together for solutions, much in the same way doctors collect information about patients to make diagnoses and form treatment plans. City, Elmore, Fiarman, and Teitel (2009) describe instructional rounds as a process that builds a coherent learning environment for adults and students. The power of all learning walks lies in the way they bring colleagues together to learn from one another and develop action plans that will get the school closer to its shared vision for successful literacy learning.

Sometimes, learning walks are focused on a problem of practice. For example, you and your colleagues might have expressed concern that multilingual learners are not as involved in talking about books as other students in class. In that case, you might coordinate a learning walk to gather data to learn more about the issue. Learning walks that focus on school goals and initiatives might be about looking at student engagement during independent reading. Some coaches set up periodic learning walks with a particular focus for the time of the year. Early in the year, learning walks might focus on how classrooms are set up to promote independence and easy transitions, while learning walks in the middle of the year might focus on student engagement and motivation. The most important thing is that learning walks address topics that are aligned with your school's goals and vision for literacy learning and are of immediate interest to your colleagues.

Invite Participants

Keep in mind that you are assembling a team of people who will participate in the learning walk and then work collaboratively to synthesize their findings. Try to select people you think might contribute varied points of view and who are likely to collaborate well with one another. There are many ways you might go about assembling a learning walk team, such as the following:

- Send targeted email invitations to colleagues who would be interested in or would benefit from being a part of the learning walk. If the participants are new to learning walks, explain their purpose and share the framework.
- Advertise the topic and ask for volunteers.
- Invite grade-level teams to participate.
- Invite an established team like the literacy leadership team or English language arts team.
- Invite your administrator to participate whenever possible.

Classroom Environment Walk

A classroom environment walk is one kind of learning walk. It is designed to gather information about the physical space of the classroom without the students present. Some of the ways you might focus this type of learning walk include looking at the following:

- Placement of furniture to promote independence
- Layout and organization of classroom libraries
- Quality and quantity of books in the classroom library
- Types and amount of student writing and artifacts on the walls
- Ways in which students' identities are valued in the classroom
- Displayed anchor charts–types, accessibility, visual quality

Classroom environment walks can be helpful to new teachers, especially if the classroom teacher is there to explain the decision-making behind the set-up. They can also be a more comfortable way for teachers to begin inviting colleagues into their classrooms. This type of walk is also easy to plan because it can be done before or after school or while students are elsewhere.

Schedule Time for Learning Walks

The timing of a learning walk matters because you will want to be in each classroom to see the instructional context or to access the data about a particular topic. It's a matter of coordinating the approximate times each host teacher will be involved in the specified teaching.

Once you have selected a topic for a learning walk, work with your administrator and colleagues to determine the observation classrooms you will visit and when you will be in each room. In some cases, you'll need to ask the host teachers to stagger their teaching of the lessons (especially shorter ones) so that you can walk in and out of classrooms and not miss the lesson entirely. If you enter a lesson midway through, that's fine, but you will certainly want to be in the classroom for at least part of the instructional context you are exploring.

Work with your administrator to determine the best times for the pre-walk and post-walk meetings. Ideally, the pre-walk meeting happens right before you visit the classrooms and the post-walk meeting shortly after. If you can only manage to schedule these meetings before or after school, try to plan them for the same day as the walk-throughs.

NEW TEACHER

New teachers can be a huge asset on a learning walk. They can help the team see things with fresh eyes. New teachers also benefit from seeing different ways their colleagues approach a topic or teach within an instructional context. All teachers gain from viewing even small snippets of teaching because they see different teaching styles and gather small tips and ideas that spark other ideas.

The Learning Walk: What to Say and Do

You are the facilitator of the learning walks. It's your job to help the team identify the evidence they will collect, discuss what they saw, and think about the action steps they will take as a result of their learning.

The Pre-walk Meeting: Sharpening the Focus

One effective way to narrow the focus within an instructional context is to use a section of an observational tool as a guide. If you have developed a look-for tool (Chapter 13) for a particular instructional context, provide teachers with a copy, ask them to skim the criteria listed for high-quality instruction, and identify one to focus on for the learning walk. With this focus in mind, the group then brainstorms ideas for the evidence they might collect during the walk. Figure 14-2 shows how one group selected interactive read-aloud as their focus and identified the evidence they would look for on the walk-through.

Remind the team to be detailed in their note-taking across classrooms. Being specific helps the team see patterns. For example, observers might note, "I counted ten pieces of student writing displayed on the walls, one piece of shared writing on chart paper, and a writer's notebook in each student's book box."

Start Learning Walks with an Open-Ended Approach

Renwick (2022) starts what he calls "instructional walks" by simply inviting people to record what resonates with them. This open-ended focus immediately emphasizes strengths and builds trust within the school community. As teachers become more comfortable with the idea of learning walks, you can begin to integrate a more focused approach.

Learning Walk Topic
Interactive Read-Aloud

Identified Focus
Quality of discussion during turn and talk

Evidence to Collect

- Teacher's prompts for the turn and talk
- Teacher's scaffolding of the discussion for reluctant contributors
- How and whether students initiate comments
- Students taking turns talking
- Students listening to their partner and building on the idea
- Students agreeing and disagreeing respectfully
- Students referencing the text during the turn and talk
- Students providing evidence for thinking
- Students seeking other perspectives

Figure 14-2

In addition to determining a specific focus for the learning walk, use the pre-walk meeting to remind teachers of the norms for entering someone's classroom (e.g., avoid student interactions, side conversations with colleagues, and touching or moving objects in the room). Lastly, discuss how and with whom you will share the team's findings. Knowing this ahead of time will make the post-walk meeting more efficient.

Learning Walks and Video

In each classroom you enter, capture (or ask an observer to capture) two minutes of video on the topic of the walk. You might use the video clip to review the experience during your final meeting with the learning walk team, show the clips to other teachers during a faculty meeting or professional learning session, add the clips to the video library, or quickly share one with a teacher when you are coaching on the run. Be sure to ask the teacher's permission before taking any classroom video.

The Walk-Throughs: Observe and Collect Data

During the walk-throughs, the team records noticings and interactions related to the identified focus. Consider providing a note-taking template to support them in noticing patterns across rooms. Figure 14-3 (p. 140) shows an example of how one teacher used a note-taking template. (You will find a blank, full-size Note-Taking Tool: Learning Walk Observations as **OR 14.1** in the Online Resources.) In this template, teachers record noticings and wonderings in the top section. Before they meet for the post-walk meeting, they fill in the bottom section with reflections on common practices they saw, strengths they noticed, and possible areas for future professional learning. In this example, notice the specificity of the observations of students engaged in independent reading.

ONLINE RESOURCE 14.1

After one or two walk-throughs, convene in the hallway to share noticings, calibrate how the group is taking notes, and focus everyone's attention on the next classroom. If you converse in the hallway, be sure the shared observations are neutral in case they are overheard.

Post-walk Meeting: Notice Patterns and Make Action Plans

Consider starting the meeting with a moment of reflection for the team to read over their notes and notice patterns across classrooms. Then open the discussion. Here is some sample language for how to start and facilitate the conversation:

Sample Language

- *What patterns did you notice across classrooms?*
- *What are strengths you saw that we can build upon as a school community?*
- *What are you thinking about what ____ noticed?*
- *You noticed ____. What do you think that means for future professional learning?*
- *What practices did you see that might benefit all teachers?*
- *What did you observe that you might try in your own teaching?*
- *Based on the learning walk, what are you thinking about trying in your own classrooms?*

After teachers have had the opportunity to discuss patterns and trends across classrooms, work together to form a feasible action plan. Briefly discuss how the team will share the findings of the plan in addition to the actions it will take based on these findings. Figure 14–4 (p. 141) shows an example of an action plan a group of teachers might make. (You will find a blank, full-size Note-Taking Tool: Learning Walk Action Plans as **OR 14.2** in the Online Resources.) Assigning a team member to accomplish the determined action goes a long way in making sure it gets done. It is also helpful to set a deadline.

Discussing a Classroom Environment Walk

If the team engaged in a classroom environment walk, pose some of the following questions during the post-walk meeting:

- What beliefs about student learning are reflected in the layout and design of the classrooms?
- What types of student artifacts are represented in the classrooms? What do they show you about the values and beliefs of the school?
- What physical changes to your classroom might you consider based on this learning walk?

ONLINE RESOURCE 14.2

Spend the last few minutes of the post-walk meeting soliciting feedback about the learning walk. Ask the team how they thought it went and ask for suggestions on ways it could be improved for the next time. Use their feedback to continue to refine your logistical planning and facilitation of the experience.

NOTE-TAKING TOOL

LEARNING WALK OBSERVATIONS		
DATE	**TOPIC/INSTRUCTIONAL CONTEXT**	**FOCUS**
3/18	independent reading	student engagement

NOTICINGS, SURPRISES, WONDERINGS

Classroom 1: About 70% of students are engaged in their books. About 5 students have been up changing their books. About 6 students are reading nonfiction. About 8 students are reading graphic novels. Most students are reading fiction. 4 students have books that appear too difficult—are pretending to read.

Classroom 2: About 80% of students engaged. All students have a short stack of books at their desks. Three students keep changing books or flipping through without reading. There is a balance of fiction and nonfiction being read. 4 students are engaged in writing in their reader's notebook.

Classroom 3: Approx. 70% are engaged in independent reading. Engaged students are reading longer novels. Over half are reading graphic novels. 5 students are reading nonfiction. 3 of them appear to be engaged and reading; 2 appear to be only reading the graphic pieces of the text. The teacher conferred with one student about a reader's notebook entry.

COMMON PRACTICES	STRENGTHS	POSSIBLE PROFESSIONAL LEARNING DIRECTIONS
In most classrooms, students chose books before independent reading and had them at their desks. Reader's notebooks are used. Graphic novels were a popular choice.	Students settle down with a book at the beginning of independent reading. Students are willing to write about their reading. Engagement in graphic novels	How to give a good book talk Using the reader's notebook to increase engagement Using interest in graphic novels to inspire reading in other genres

Your Literacy Coaching Playbook **Online Resource 14.1 | Note-Taking Tool:** Learning Walk Observations, **Version 01**

Figure 14-3

NOTE-TAKING TOOL

LEARNING WALK ACTION PLANS

DATE	TOPIC/INSTRUCTIONAL CONTEXT	FOCUS
2/28	shared reading	revisiting shared reading for explicit phonics teaching

ACTION PLAN	WHO WILL INITIATE THE PLAN?	HOW?	WHEN?	NOTES
Review using shared reading to reinforce phonics and word study understandings.	Literacy coach	Professional learning session followed by two weeks of coaching	Professional learning session: March 15 Coaching: March 22–April 13	After coaching, coach will initiate another learning walk and invite other teachers in the school. Perhaps follow up with a lesson study.
Literacy leadership team will look at resources for shared reading across grades K–4.	Grade 2 representative on the literacy leadership team	Send every grade-level team an inventory survey to fill out during common planning time to identify what resources are available and what more they need.	Send Survey: March 22	Determine needs and submit budget request if needed.

Your Literacy Coaching Playbook **Online Resource 14.2 | Note-Taking Tool:** Learning Walk Action Plans, **Version 01**

Figure 14-4

A Protocol Tool for Learning Walks

ONLINE RESOURCE 14.3

To help you facilitate learning walks, we offer a general protocol in Figure 14-5. (You will find a full-size Protocol Tool: Learning Walks as **OR 14.3** in the Online Resources.) The protocol tool is meant to provide a structure to frame the learning walks, but as always, vary the protocol to fit the teachers and the need. We recommend that you print out a copy to keep in your coaching notebook (Chapter 23).

A learning walk is aptly named. It truly gives you and your colleagues a way to learn about what is happening across classrooms and grades by walking through them. Learning walks promote the belief that your colleagues have so much to offer one another in experience and expertise. Building on the culture of trust and the belief that you are a learning school, learning walks give you one more play to add to your playbook and move your school closer to implementing its vision for literacy learning.

PROTOCOL TOOL

LEARNING WALKS

PARTICIPANTS: COACH; 2-4 TEACHERS; 1-2 SPECIALISTS; ADMINISTRATOR

TIMING: 45-60 min

PRE-WALK MEETING (5-10 min)

- Review the norms for entering a classroom as a team.
- Determine or review the specific focus for the learning walk.
- Work with the group to identify what evidence they plan to look for as a team.
- Agree on how information from the walks will be shared and with whom.
- If appropriate, distribute observation tools to record data.

THE WALK-THROUGHS (5-10 min per classroom for a total of approximately 30-40 min)

- Everyone observes silently and attentively.
- Everyone makes notes of observable evidence related to the focus.
- After visiting a few classrooms, engage in a brief, reflective conversation in the corridor or jot notes for later to summarize noticings.
- Note questions.
- Have each participant describe in concrete terms the evidence observed across the classrooms.

THE POST-WALK MEETING (10 min)

- Share highlights, observations, and patterns.
- Discuss any questions the team noted.
- Make sure the talk is rooted in evidence specific to the focus of the walk-through and is judgment free.
- Identify common practices, strengths, expertise, and possible areas for continued professional learning.
- Share evidence and wonderings from the learning walk as agreed upon formally and informally.
- Make an action plan.
- Decide as a team who will thank teachers whose classrooms were visited.

Your Literacy Coaching Playbook — **Online Resource 14.3 | Protocol Tool:** Learning Walks, **Version 01**

Figure 14-5

Up **Next**

What type of professional learning session results in practical, classroom-tested lessons teachers can try out right away and builds professional capacity for improved instruction at the same time? In Chapter 15, we welcome lesson study to your playbook.

Chapter 15

The Play: Lesson Study

Do the teachers in your school have go-to colleagues for bouncing off lesson ideas? Or a few people who can help them think about a tweak or an adjustment to a lesson that they couldn't quite see on their own? If so, good for them! When colleagues develop lessons together and use them with different students, they inevitably share what worked, what didn't, and what they might change for next time. These conversations can have a profound influence on teachers and the instructional decisions they make.

We're sure that some teachers in your school regularly collaborate on lesson planning because they are friends and they trust one another. But that leaves out others who are not benefiting from that kind of collaboration.

We hope this chapter will put lesson study on your radar because it is a very effective way to broaden existing circles of collaboration around lesson design so that everyone benefits from the support of colleagues and the stronger lessons that result.

BENEFITS OF LESSON STUDY

- Focuses on the art and science of teaching
- Results in practical, classroom-tested lessons teachers can try out right away
- Produces a generative process for thoughtfully designing, refining, and planning effective lessons
- Creates an exciting buzz in the school as teachers talk about how to improve their craft with each other
- Builds professional capacity for improved instruction
- Builds common language and understandings

A Tradition of Collaborative Learning

Stigler and Hiebert (2009) introduced North America to a modified version of the Japanese practice of lesson study, a collaborative model for shaping instruction. In Japan, the facilitator guiding the lesson study is called "the knowledgeable other." Think of yourself in this role. You facilitate and act as another participant, but you also have expertise you can share to lift your colleagues' thinking during the study.

What Is Lesson Study?

Lesson study, a type of professional learning with a long history in Japan, can give all your teachers the opportunity to co-plan and refine lessons with colleagues. Based in collaborative inquiry, it involves a small group of teachers, usually at the same grade level, shaping a lesson together. One teacher teaches the lesson while the others observe to notice the teaching decisions and their effects on student learning. Then they use their observations to refine the lesson plan collaboratively and teach it in their own classrooms. The group reconvenes later to share their varied experiences with the shape of the lesson and make further adjustments. Though teachers do walk away with practical, classroom-tested lessons, the goal is for them to learn a generative process for thoughtfully designing and planning effective instruction. Teachers get almost immediate feedback on how their lesson design worked as they observe students' reading and writing behaviors during the lesson. This teacher-driven, collaborative inquiry focuses on the craft of teaching and develops professional knowledge, which in turn leads to improved instruction. The important thing to remember is that the goal is not to create perfect lessons that will be effective for all students because there is no such thing as a perfect lesson and because all students are different from one another. But, refining the way we think about collaborative expertise can expand teachers' capacity for responsive teaching.

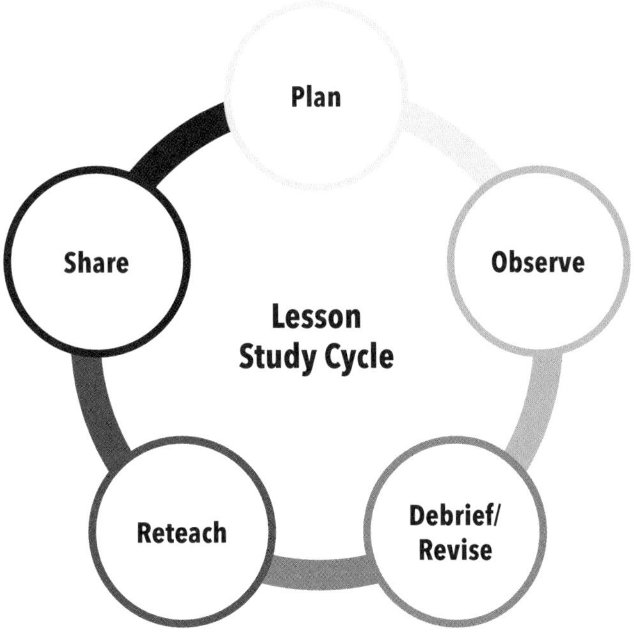

Figure 15-1

A Framework for a Lesson Study

There are five distinct parts to a lesson study cycle (Figure 15-1) which can take place over several days (Figure 15-2). Through careful observation, purposeful conversation, and bold revision, teachers move closer and closer to the results they want to see in their students' learning outcomes.

Plan and Prepare for Lesson Study

Organizing a lesson study requires careful planning because you'll need to coordinate the schedules of three to six teachers to co-plan and observe teaching together. You and your administrator must be quite creative in how you plan to accommodate the parts of the framework. Your first step, then, is to meet with your administrator to determine what is possible.

FRAMEWORK FOR A LESSON STUDY CYCLE

LESSON PLANNING

Help the group decide the focus. Guide the group in planning a lesson, determining who will teach the lesson and identifying the data or evidence observers will try to collect.

40-60 min

LESSON OBSERVATION

The host teacher teaches the lesson. Observers note evidence of the impact of the teaching on student learning. Encourage them to note spontaneous, unplanned teaching decisions.

20-60 min

LESSON DEBRIEFING AND REVISION

Invite the group to revisit the lesson goals, analyze teaching decisions, and discuss evidence of student learning. Guide discussion on how to modify or re-envision the lesson to make it more effective. Address spontaneous teaching decisions and how they reflect the group's shared beliefs about learning.

25-40 min

LESSON RETEACH

Each group member teaches the revised lesson to their own students without other teachers present.

20-60 min

SHARE AND EVALUATION

Invite teachers to share their experiences with the modified lesson. Help teachers reflect on what they learned from the process. Discuss how to share the final lesson and insights from the study with school leaders and other colleagues.

15-20 min

Figure 15-2

Schedule Time for a Lesson Study Cycle

The amount of time needed to complete an entire lesson study cycle depends on the instructional context on which the group is focused. Set realistic expectations about the amount of time needed for planning and teaching the lesson because different instructional contexts require more time to plan and teach than others. Regardless of the focus of the lesson, carve out a time for the group to plan the lesson together. We have seen lesson study groups meet before school, after school, or during common planning times. Utilizing common planning time works particularly well if you are working with a grade-level team. We find this configuration to be the most effective, though it can be modified.

The lesson study cycle might be completed in three or four days, but in rare cases it might stretch to a little over a week depending on how long the group decides they need to try out the lesson with their own students. We recommend keeping the planning, observation, and debriefing/lesson revision close together so you don't lose momentum or forget the details of the lesson. Work with your

NEW TEACHER

Lesson study is a wonderful way for new teachers to get to know their colleagues as well as learn how to efficiently and thoughtfully plan and revise lessons. New teachers benefit from listening to more experienced teachers share their rationales for shaping the lesson. However, do not underestimate the contributions new teachers can make to this process. Fresh thinking often yields innovative solutions and enthusiasm for thinking out of the box.

administrators to find coverage as necessary for the time teachers will be out of their classrooms, especially to observe the lesson. We recommend trying to engage teachers in one lesson study each semester or three times a year if time allows (e.g., beginning, middle, and end) to make the scheduling process manageable.

Establish the Goals of the Lesson Study

Work with teachers to identify the goals or focus of the lesson study. A lesson study might have a very specific goal, like teaching students how to write strong summaries, or a more general goal, like exploring how to engage children in talk during interactive read-aloud. The goals or focus might develop in the following ways:

- Talk with a grade-level team to determine what they would like to work on in a lesson study. Consider using student data or observations to help select a focus.
- Follow up on a professional learning session with a lesson study on the same topic.
- Suggest a lesson study after coaching several teachers in a particular instructional context.
- Choose a lesson study topic to address a school improvement goal, and ask your colleagues to sign up if they are interested.

Figure 15-3 shows some topics teachers have addressed through lesson study.

Examples of Lesson Study Topics

- Promoting deeper, more meaningful discussion during interactive read-aloud lessons
- Using facilitative language during book club meetings to deepen comprehension
- Using close reading with complex texts in book clubs or read-aloud
- Revisiting shared reading for phonics and word study
- Making connections between books in a text set
- Using precise language in reading, writing, or phonics lessons
- Supporting multilingual learners through interactive writing
- Helping students notice and name a text structure in nonfiction

Figure 15-3

The Lesson Study: What to Say and Do

We recommend that you serve as the facilitator for the lesson study. At some point, you might share this role with a colleague, but at the beginning, you can best guide the group to move through the lesson study efficiently and keep the focus on student learning.

At the first lesson study meeting, review the agreements that your school has established for working together and for observing in classrooms. For example, remind your colleagues to make sure all voices are heard during discussions, avoid interaction with students during the observation, and use nonevaluative language to comment on the lesson.

> ### *Reflection Journals*
> Ask teachers to bring their reflection journals to each lesson study. When they take notes, they can take a step back and reflect on the process and what they are learning about designing a lesson to meet their students' specific needs.

Lesson Planning: Learning a Process

Make sure teachers come to this part of the lesson study prepared to be active participants. Ask them to bring any necessary curriculum materials and their own students' data related to the topic of the lesson study. Provide any additional materials (including reading passages, articles, and blogs) that you think might facilitate the planning process. Ask someone to be the note-taker for the lesson planning and debriefing.

During the lesson planning process, your role is to set the stage for learning that takes teachers beyond this one lesson. Help them stay grounded in the lesson specifics while also reflecting on what they are doing so it is transferrable to their planning for future instruction. Following are five coaching moves you can make as the facilitator to accomplish these goals along with language you might use throughout the lesson study cycle to facilitate the discussion, deepen thinking, and keep the process generative.

1. **Keep teachers grounded in student data.** You cannot plan lessons without the specific students in mind. Because all lesson study group members will eventually teach this lesson with their own students, it is important that they share information about students across classrooms even though the initial

lesson will be taught in one classroom. Chapter 19 offers some specific ideas for how to help teachers collect and use data effectively. Here are some ways to ground a conversation in student data.

Sample Language

- *What do you need to know about the students' current knowledge and skills?*
- *What are some common goals you have for your students?*
- *What are the goals for this lesson, and how do they match the goals you have for the group of students?*
- *How will you provide support to multilingual learners?*
- *If many of your students are demonstrating ____, what does that mean for your planning?*
- *Many of your students are exhibiting strength in ____. How can you build on that strength in your lesson planning?*
- *____ is a next step you have identified for many of your students. How will you plan to address this goal?*
- *What unique learning needs should you be thinking about?*

2. **Summarize and reflect on the decision-making.** While teachers are engaged in lesson planning, occasionally summarize the decisions they have made and the reasons for them. This allows teachers to consider the forest and the trees as they make specific decisions for the lesson but also think about what those decisions mean for their future lesson planning.

   Sample Language

   - *So far, you've decided ____ because ____.*
   - *You considered your students' data in making that decision.*
   - *I noticed the group chose to ____ because ____.*
   - *Talk about what the group has decided about using ____ (resource). How are you thinking that will help the students learn ____?*
   - *What do you think about using ____ to help ____?*
   - *Is there another way to think about that?*
   - *Talk about why that is a priority for you.*
   - *What else could help?*

   Notice how these language stems focus on the rationales for the decision-making. By helping teachers articulate their rationales, you add another layer to the planning process that will impact how they make decisions on their own to respond to the strengths and needs of their students.

3. **Ground their teaching decisions in research.** As the facilitator or the knowledgeable other, direct teachers to helpful resources that will enhance the planning process without bogging them down. The idea is to keep the reading

brief and targeted. When you offer teachers a resource, they gain information, consider its use in planning the lesson, and have it for reference. Here are a few examples of how you might refer teachers to pieces of relevant text.

Sample Language

- *Read the abstract of this article. Highlight anything that you might consider when planning a lesson.*
- *Read the first two paragraphs of this section. What does that mean for the lesson planning?*
- *Read the summary at the end of this article. What points might you want to consider in planning?*

4. **Guide teachers in deciding who will host the lesson study.** Once the lesson is planned, have the group decide who will teach the lesson while colleagues observe. Be sure teachers understand that this process is nonevaluative. The focus is on the decisions they have made together and on the impact on student learning. Here are some ways to extend this invitation.

   Sample Language

   - *As you know, our goal is to think together about how to plan effective lessons. One colleague will teach the lesson so we can observe and think about what we planned together. Who would be willing to teach the lesson?*
   - *Let's think together about our group. Who has experience in this area and might be willing to teach the lesson?*
   - *This is new to everyone in our group. Who would be willing to teach the lesson so we can all learn?*

5. **Decide what evidence to collect.** Guide the group to think about evidence that will show whether students are learning and meeting the planned goals.

   Sample Language

   - *What are you hoping to see from students if the teaching is effective?*
   - *What particular behaviors will you be looking for as evidence of student learning?*
   - *What artifacts might you collect to help analyze the impact on student learning?*
   - *If the students are successful, what might that look like?*

The Lesson Observation: Seeing the Plan in Action

As the host teacher teaches the lesson, the rest of the group observes attentively, avoiding potential distractions like interactions with students or side conversations with colleagues. Ask teachers to note the impact of planned teaching decisions on student learning. They might do this in a two-column chart—one side to record the teacher's language and the other to note the students' responses. Ahead of the observation, mention that spontaneous teaching decisions will always surface throughout a lesson. Encourage the observers to note these decisions so the group can later discuss how they reflect the group's shared goals for literacy and student learning. The more teachers have the chance to discuss teaching decisions, the better they will be able to develop common rationales. The most exciting thing about lesson observation is the opportunity for almost immediate feedback on the effectiveness of their collective planning.

The Lesson Debriefing and Revision: A Chance to Rethink

The beauty of lesson study is the ability to revise and refine a lesson. Guide the group to rethink the lesson based on feedback from observing the effect of the teacher's decisions (both planned and unplanned) on student learning. Help the group analyze the evidence of student learning and discuss the teaching decisions they observed. Be sure to have the teachers offer their reflections on the lesson before you offer yours.

Sample Language

- *What do you think worked well in the lesson?*
- *What evidence did you collect that demonstrated student learning?*
- *What did you notice about the spontaneous decisions ____ made while teaching the lesson?*
- *What else might ____ have tried?*
- *How did students contribute to the lesson in unique ways?*
- *How did the decision to ____ impact student learning?*
- *What if ____ had responded with ____? How would that have changed the lesson?*
- *Are there changes you would make to the lesson based on your observations?*
- *What was in the way of (student's name) success?*

Help the group make any changes or adjustments to the lesson based on their observations. Ask the note-taker to record these changes and modify the lesson based on the group's feedback. Offer resources or readings that might be helpful in guiding this process. Once the group has finalized the lesson, it is ready for the observing teachers to teach the revised lesson to their own students before the next meeting.

The Lesson Reteach: Everyone Gives It a Try

Offer your colleagues support as they try out the lesson with their own students. Collect needed resources or meet with individuals who need clarification about the lesson. Encourage your colleagues to spend a few minutes right after teaching the revised lesson to note their reflections. By capturing their thinking right after the lesson, they will be able to share more details when you gather as a whole group. Before they reconvene, ask individuals to reflect on their own feelings in preparation for the debriefing. Here are possible reflection questions to help teachers think about their experience.

Sample Language

- *Which parts of the lesson did you find the most effective in shifting your students' reading (writing) behaviors?*
- *In what ways did the revisions to the lesson work? What further tweaks might you suggest?*
- *What student behaviors showed evidence of student learning?*
- *What in-the-moment decisions did you make in your teaching?*
- *What are you thinking you might do next?*
- *What was your most important learning?*
- *What were surprises for you?*

Go Deeper with Video

Consider having the teachers make a video recording of themselves teaching the revised lesson. Ask them to bring a one- or two-minute clip of the lesson to share a part they think was particularly effective or that demonstrates a particular area of focus for the group. If you choose to have teachers use video in this way, they can show the clips and discuss them during the final meeting.

Share and Evaluation: Closing the Lesson Study Cycle

Once each group member has taught the lesson and had a chance to reflect, gather the group for a brief meeting to discuss everyone's experiences. Use some of the questions above to start this conversation. Based on the discussion, the group might choose to further refine the lesson. While talking about the specifics of the lesson, keep zooming out to some of the bigger ideas or takeaways using some of the sample language provided below.

Sample Language

- *What have you learned about lesson planning from this work?*
- *What have you learned about your students from teaching this lesson?*
- *What have you learned about in-the-moment teaching decisions that you will bring to future teaching interactions?*

Besides providing time for this type of reflection, ask the group how they plan to share the final lesson and the new learning from the lesson study with school leaders and other colleagues so that all the educators in the school can benefit.

Lastly, solicit the group's feedback about the lesson study. Invite them to share what worked and what they would like to change for the next lesson study cycle.

A Protocol Tool for Lesson Study

We have summarized the process for conducting a lesson study in a protocol tool shown in Figure 15-4. (You will find a full-size version of Protocol Tool: Lesson Study as **OR 15.1** in the Online Resources.) We recommend printing it out for your own use and offering it to teachers who help facilitate a lesson study with you.

ONLINE RESOURCE 15.1

Lesson study is an excellent way to develop teacher agency because it relies on teachers' experience, contributions, and collaboration. Teachers learn about teaching from each other. It is also a reminder that you are not the only knowledgeable other in your school. You have a deep well of other leaders in the school ready to share their skills, information, and knowledge. Lesson study is one way to invite them to both share and grow their expertise. It is a way to develop your colleagues' belief in themselves as leaders who can make significant change in the school one lesson at a time.

PROTOCOL TOOL

LESSON STUDY

PARTICIPANTS	TIMING
COACH OR FACILITATOR; 3-6 MEMBERS • TEACHERS • SPECIALISTS	2-4 hours over 3-7 days

LESSON PLANNING (40-60 min)

- Review established norms for discussion and observing in the classroom.
- Guide the group in discussing the goals of the lesson (based on a previously chosen topic) and how they align with student data.
- Provide any relevant reading that supports the planning process.
- Guide the group in planning a lesson and considering teaching moves.
- Help the group decide how they will observe and collect evidence of student learning.

LESSON OBSERVATION (20-60 min)

- The host teacher teaches the lesson.
- Observers note evidence of student learning from planned teaching as well as spontaneous, unplanned teaching decisions.
- Invite observers to reflect on the planned decisions that had an impact and to note questions/wonderings about in-the-moment teaching decisions.

LESSON DEBRIEFING AND REVISION (25-40 min)

- Guide the group to revisit lesson goals, analyze teaching decisions, and discuss evidence of student learning.
- Facilitate a discussion about how to modify or revise the lesson to make it more effective for students.
- Help teachers reflect on the spontaneous teaching decisions the teacher made by sharing their questions and wonderings.
- Discuss whether the spontaneous teaching decisions are grounded in the group's shared literacy beliefs and whether they should be incorporated into the lesson plan.

LESSON RETEACH (20-60 min)

- Have each teacher teach the revised lesson in their own classroom with no observers.
- Assist teachers as needed.

SHARE AND EVALUATION (15-20 min)

- Invite teachers to share their experiences of reteaching the modified lesson.
- Make modifications to the lesson as needed.
- Discuss how to share the final lesson and insights with school leaders and other colleagues.
- Help teachers reflect on what they have learned from the process for future lesson planning.
- Ask for feedback on the lesson study process.
- Invite teachers to share what they would like to focus on for a future lesson study.

Your Literacy Coaching Playbook

Online Resource 15.1 | Protocol Tool: Lesson Study, **Version 01**

Figure 15-4

Up **Next**

If you really want teachers to dive into professional learning, have them select the topics themselves. In the next chapter you'll learn about study groups, another form of collaborative inquiry in which a handful of teachers work together to learn about a topic in depth, solve a problem, or accomplish a goal.

Chapter 16

The Play: **Study Groups**

Quick: What topics are teachers in your school burning to learn more about? If you can't easily answer that question, this chapter is for you—and, we hope, study groups are in your future. With study groups as a structure for professional learning, you and your colleagues can enjoy self-selected, self-directed study of relevant topics, issues, or resources that will result in purposeful actions in the classroom. That's because in a study group the participants pick the topic, so it is always relevant and meaningful to them.

In study groups, your colleagues have more control over learning about topics that interest them. There is no better way to build collegial relationships, professional knowledge, and effective instructional practices than to set up structures for teachers to engage in learning together. Study groups are examples of

BENEFITS OF STUDY GROUPS

- Provide an opportunity to investigate a topic, an issue, or a problem of practice, or to accomplish a project
- Engage participants in cooperative work tasks
- Build teachers' agency
- Expand teacher knowledge of content and pedagogy
- Build deep knowledge of curriculum, assessment, and instruction
- Provide time to explore new resources
- Create a program of differentiated professional learning for teachers
- Provide a time for exploring current research

teachers assuming responsibility for and committing to their own growth as professionals. They contribute to improvement for all the students in the school. Finally, study groups allow you to be a learner alongside your colleagues.

What Is a Study Group?

A study group (sometimes called a "collaborative inquiry group," "task force," or "project group") is a small group of teachers with the same interest (generally about four but no more than eight) who have volunteered to meet for a limited period of time (usually a few weeks or a few months) with their colleagues to investigate a particular topic, issue, or problem of practice, or to accomplish an important project (Figure 16-1). Use your imagination to consider the wide variety of study groups that can be productive within your school or district. Groups can consist of teachers from a single grade level or from multiple grade levels but who have a common interest. Professional book clubs (Chapter 17) are a specific type of study group formed when the group has a common interest in reading and discussing a professional book to explore a topic.

The length of a study group meeting is ideally about an hour because it is enough time for an in-depth exploration of a topic or problem or for working on

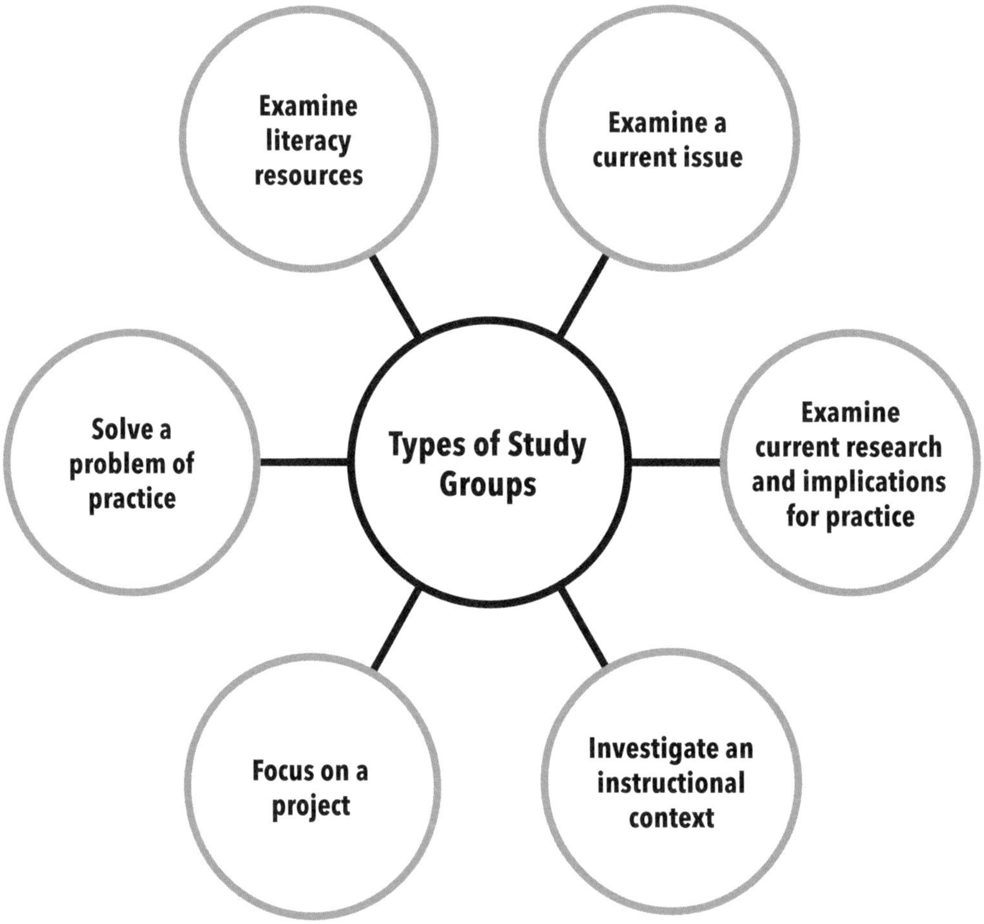

Figure 16-1

components of a project without requiring too much of a time commitment. A monthly or bimonthly meeting (on the same day of the week) is often manageable. A project or study can be carried out across several of these meetings. Work with the group to figure out what can be accomplished during a meeting and develop a strategy for completing a study or project over time.

As a goal-directed group, study group participants gather information, engage in cooperative work tasks, and discuss and share their learning. They share their insights and recommend specific actions to the school team so that the changes can be discussed and possibly implemented for school improvement.

A Framework for Study Group Meetings

We have provided a broad framework for a study group meeting (Figure 16–2). Adjust it as needed to suit different types of study groups.

FRAMEWORK FOR A STUDY GROUP MEETING

INTRODUCTION

If you have met on the current topic before, start by asking participants to summarize what was discussed at the last meeting. The group leader then shares the goals and agenda for the meeting as determined ahead of time.

10 min

ENGAGEMENT IN STUDY

The leader engages the group in the study, whether that involves working toward a solution to a problem of practice, exploring a new resource, reading about research, or tackling a task in a multi-step project.

40 min

SUMMARY AND NEXT STEPS

The group identifies what they learned or notes their progress on a project. They decide any actions needed in the interim and sets goals for next time. At the final meeting, the group generates a plan for reporting their findings to the school team.

10 min

Figure 16–2

Plan and Prepare for a Study Group Meeting

There are always logistics to settle ahead of any meeting, and study groups are no exception. Start by meeting with your principal to identify possible times for study groups to meet and to be sure that you are honoring teachers' contractual agreements. Find out if time is available during school hours or whether study groups will need to meet after school or even occasionally by distance technology, outside of school hours. If the latter is the case, you'll want to investigate whether it's possible to offer a small stipend. Consider budget implications if resources are needed.

Identify Topics of Interest

Keep a list of study group topics that interest multiple teachers or for which there is a strong need as evidenced by data analysis or by teachers' request. Topics of interest and need will surface throughout your interactions with colleagues, from your observations in classrooms, conversations in professional learning, and from your monitoring of school data. Teachers might also request a study group to solve a problem of practice they are experiencing in their classrooms. Figure 16-3 shows a sample of study group topics that emerged in some of the schools in which we worked. Some of the study group topics emerged as problems of practice in these schools, some involved an examination of research, and others became study group projects.

Study Group Topics

- Increasing student engagement
- Learning effective practices for teaching phonics skills
- Creating classroom libraries (grade by grade) that represent all students
- Teaching emergent readers strong skills for looking at print
- Investigating the effects of book club discussions on student identities
- Examining research on early literacy with a critical lens
- Researching the effects of reading complex picture books on student writing
- Identifying exemplars for student writing assessment by grade level
- Using interactive writing to develop phonics skills
- Examining the quality of nonfiction resources
- Minimizing achievement gaps in different sectors of the school population

Figure 16-3

Announce the options for study groups, with an explanation of how the topics were chosen, and invite interested teachers to join. Encourage them to sign up for a short, preliminary planning meeting to discuss a regular meeting time. We suggest that the dates, location, and times be established by group members at that first meeting and put on the calendar.

If several study groups are planned for the year, announce them all at once so teachers know their options. We have found that setting an expectation in a school that every teacher will join at least one study group each year worked well, but that needs to be a principal, coach, and team decision. If you don't get enough volunteers, talk with teachers that you feel might enjoy a particular study group and encourage them to join.

A comfortable meeting space and enjoyable refreshments are a must. A small budget for refreshments after school will be appreciated, though teachers could volunteer to provide refreshments on a rotating basis.

Schedule a Time for Study Group Meetings

Depending on the type of group, decide how many meetings will be needed to accomplish the group's goals. We suggest you schedule an hour for each meeting so there is enough time to get to all the agenda items without keeping people too long.

The voluntary nature of the group is essential whether it meets during school time or after school. Mandated attendance will most likely defeat the purpose of teachers taking charge of their own learning.

Assign Roles

Before a study group meeting, identify the group leader (a volunteer for the duration of a series of meetings) and a note-taker (a volunteer for the entire series or a rotation of members). The group leader will create the agenda and facilitate the meeting. The note-taker takes notes and posts them in a document after the meeting. Before each meeting, the group leader sends out the agenda, a reminder of the agreed-upon actions, and any resources necessary to have at the meeting.

Study Groups: What to Say and Do

As much as possible, plan to join the study groups as a participant so you can provide resources, contribute to the discussion, and learn alongside your colleagues. Sometimes, you might feel that you don't need to attend because of the focus, but it is highly beneficial to participate when the topic is related to literacy. Participating in a study group is a wonderful opportunity to position yourself as a learner and a colleague and to build a trusting relationship with members of the team.

Avoid being the facilitator of a study group yourself so you can be a co-learner and a participant. If you are inclined to lead a group, engage a colleague as a co-facilitator. However, if study groups are new to the group or the leader is new to the experience, you may need to provide more support. With a little support from you, teachers will develop their ability to lead the group discussions effectively, and many will already have such skills developed in other contexts. Their talents can be tapped. Figure 16-4 contains a few tips and sample language that a group leader might find useful for any type of study group.

Introduction

The group leader starts every study group by linking the meeting to previous learning and sharing the meeting goals. If the study group is focusing on a project, the group leader might ask for an update on action items from the last meeting. At first, you might find it necessary to meet with the group leader ahead of the meeting to make sure the goals are clear and feasible in the time you have. The group leader asks the group for any questions or feedback on the goals and can create a parking lot for issues that can't be addressed immediately.

TIPS FOR STUDY GROUP LEADERS

Allow wait time. Remember, silence is space for thinking.

Listen and learn. Show active listening by attending to each person to understand their perspective whether or not you agree.

Paraphrase by restating the most important points in what participants have said to check understanding.

- *So you are saying . . .*
- *Let me check my understanding.*
- *(Restate) Did I get that right?*

Clarify by asking genuine questions and encouraging others to ask questions to understand more.

- *Talk more about what you mean.*
- *What else could you have done?*
- *Why do you think that happened?*

Invite thinking to gain a variety of perspectives.

- *What do you think?*
- *What do the rest of you think about this issue?*
- *Is there another way to think about that?*
- *Talk us through your thinking about that.*
- *Let's hear more voices on this.*

Figure 16-4

Engagement in Study

The heart of the process is the engagement in the study–the investigation and discussion of content (e.g., research on a current issue), the collaborative inquiry around a problem of practice, the planning and implementation of a project, or the exploration of valuable resources. The activities and content of the study group depend on the type of study group. Let's look at examples of a few different types of study groups to better understand what might be possible.

A PROBLEM OF PRACTICE STUDY GROUP

During a problem of practice study group, the group leader invites a teacher to share the details of a dilemma. As the coach, you play a role in helping teachers determine whether a problem is worth pursuing through a study group.

After the teacher presents the problem, the group leader invites questions, which often help the teacher further analyze the problem. The next step is for the group to analyze the problem while the teacher listens and takes notes. We recommend that the teacher listens instead of participating during this time to remain fully open to the ideas generated by the group. Following is a brief snapshot of a problem of practice study group meeting. It begins after the group leader has made a link to the previous meeting:

Selecting a Problem of Practice

You can help teachers assess dilemmas and decide if they are appropriate for a study group. To select a problem of practice, it should be something that persists in bothering you, is within your control to change, and is something that you truly care about and are willing to work at (Dunne, Evans, Thompson-Grove, 2024).

Group Leader: *Thank you for sharing some of the work you have done since our last meeting. Today we will work through another problem of practice that Ms. S. will be presenting. I know many of you have expressed a similar challenge, so hopefully we can put our heads together today and come up with some ideas for addressing the issue. Ms. S., please share the problem with the group.*

Ms. S.: *I have noticed that many students in my class are routinely picking fiction for independent reading and never seem to select nonfiction texts.*

Teacher 1: *How do they select their books for independent reading?*

Ms. S.: *They usually go over to the classroom library and flip through bins.*

Teacher 2: *How do you have your classroom library organized?*

Ms. S.: *I have bins marked fiction and nonfiction. I wonder if I should rethink that.*

Teacher 3: *What types of fiction books do you notice they often choose?*

Ms. S.: *They love graphic novels. They are definitely the most popular.*

After teachers ask a few more clarifying questions, the group leader summarizes the problem and invites the group to brainstorm some ideas.

Group Leader: *Ms. S. would like us to think about how she might get her students to select more nonfiction texts for independent reading. Let's take a few minutes to talk about some ideas while Ms. S. records some notes.*

Study group members share ideas including organizing the classroom library nonfiction collection in bins labeled with engaging themes, giving a survey to students to identify content that interests them, giving book talks on different nonfiction texts, borrowing some nonfiction graphic novels from the library, and increasing the number of nonfiction read-alouds she selects. The study group leader summarizes the suggestions, asks for Ms. S. to reflect on the new learning, and guides the group to form an action plan. Notice how even the teachers' clarifying questions at the beginning get the teacher and the group thinking about possible solutions. As an active participant in the group, the coach might recommend helpful readings in the follow-up, offer to send video clips of book talks, and ask if any of the teachers would like to be coached as they try out some of the action plans. The problems of practice study group is focused on getting results for that teacher, but other teachers will walk away with new insights.

A PROJECT-BASED STUDY GROUP

The challenge of the project-based study group is determining the scope of the project and the method or steps to approach it over the course of several meetings (if necessary) without losing momentum. Careful planning with the group should create a workable plan. Examples of projects might be to improve and update classroom libraries, create closer ties with the community, make the school more welcoming to parents, or any other goal important to the staff. Following is an example of how a first meeting might go for a group planning a project to evaluate and update classroom libraries across the school to make sure they are more representative of diverse identities:

Group Leader: *We have decided as part of our school improvement plan that one of our goals is to make sure our students see diverse peoples in the books they read. That means we need to make sure our classroom libraries have diverse representation. Alyssa and I thought this would be something we could do as part of a study group. Let's start by brainstorming how we might organize this project. Turn to the person next to you and talk for a few minutes about how you think we might want to tackle this project over a series of study group meetings. Jot down your thinking to share with the group.*

After teachers share ideas in pairs, they share out with the group:

Teacher 1: *We were thinking we can tackle one grade level per meeting. For example, we could work in pairs in each first-grade classroom to survey the classroom library collection.*

Teacher 2: *We thought the same thing, but we were wondering what criteria we'll use to evaluate the collections. I don't think I have a good understanding of the qualities we are looking for.*

Coach: *I can offer the group a few different tools I have in my files for evaluating representation in text collections. Maybe at our next meeting, we can look at those and decide if we want to use one to guide our survey of the libraries.*

Group Leader: *That would be helpful. What does everyone think about the idea of working in a single grade level at a time?*

The group decides to go forward with the suggested plan and spends the next meeting evaluating tools for the project. They decide it will take approximately eight meetings to survey the libraries across the grades, analyze their findings, and take action to diversify their collections.

In this example, you see evidence of the collective planning that happens during project-based study groups. You also see how the coach, acting as a fellow participant, offers resources to scaffold the project. Notice also how the group breaks a project down into manageable pieces. Project-based study groups are a practical way to get things done without a huge time commitment.

A STUDY GROUP TO EXPLORE RESOURCES

As the coach, you may take a more active role in a study group dedicated to exploring resources because you are likely to be the person who is the most familiar with them. We recommend that you select a co-leader so others feel ownership and investment in exploring and using the resource. Resources can include materials like curriculum guides and texts or physical spaces like the school's media center or book room. You can certainly meet with teachers individually to explore these resources, but a study group (or a bite-size study group!) allows teachers to generate excitement as well as a variety of ideas for using the resources. Here are some ideas for exploring a physical space, like a book room:

- Design a scavenger hunt that will help teachers explore the space.
- Have teachers role-play several scenarios to show how to use the space.
- For larger spaces, form two or more groups. Assign each group a different part of the room to explore. After a set amount of time, have each group give a tour of their space to the other groups.

Here are some ideas for exploring materials and supplies:

- Form two or more groups. Assign each group a set of materials or supplies to explore. After a few minutes, have representatives from each group explain what they learned to the other groups.
- Alternatively, after the groups spend time with their assigned resources, have them make an anchor chart to explain what they learned. An anchor chart is a visual display of the most important content.

NEW TEACHER

You might sometimes suggest exploring underused resources as well as new ones. This type of study group can be particularly helpful for new teachers who are still learning what resources are available to support their teaching. Taking the time for all teachers to discover the value of resources already in their possession or that are available through the district is time well spent in a study group.

- Form groups to look at the resources through the lens of focus questions such as the following.
    - *How is this resource organized?*
    - *What do you see as the value of this resource?*
    - *How might you use this resource with your students?*
    - *In what ways would this resource enhance what you are already teaching?*

No matter how you choose to guide the inquiry, give teachers plenty of time to become acquainted with the resource through study and discussion. The more they talk about it, the higher the chance that they'll use it.

Summary and Next Steps

At the end of any type of study group, it is important that the group leader leaves time during the final meeting for a summary of what participants have learned. Scaffold this process by offering group leaders some language prompts.

Sample Language

- *What are your three biggest takeaways from our work today?*
- *What has this study made you think about that will impact your teaching?*
- *What progress did we make today toward our project goals?*
- *What might we want to share with the rest of the school about our work?*
- *What are implications from our work that may need to be considered by the school team?*

ONLINE RESOURCE 16.1

Finally, the group leader guides the group in determining their next steps or action plans. The note-taker can record notes in the Study Group Notes template as shown in Figure 16-5. (You will find a blank, full-size Note-Taking Tool: Study Group Notes as **OR 16.1** in the Online Resources.) Assist the group leader in getting feedback on the study group session by encouraging teachers to informally share what they felt worked and what could be improved. You can also offer to follow up with a survey for the group.

NOTE-TAKING TOOL

STUDY GROUP NOTES

DATE	NEW LEARNING	ACTION ITEMS
11/2	Classroom libraries need to be inventoried and evaluated for diversity and representation.	1. Choose a tool to review classroom libraries in GK–1 (Mrs. R.) 2. Find out budget for classroom libraries in GK–1 (Kristin) 3. Order books according to need (Mrs. R.)

Figure 16-5

A Protocol Tool for Study Groups

Throughout this part of the book, we've provided protocol tools. In Figure 16-6, we show one for study groups. (You will find a full-size version of Protocol Tool: Study Groups as **OR 16.2** in the Online Resources.) Vary the tool as needed to suit particular topics of study.

ONLINE RESOURCE 16.2

Study Groups Across the Year

As part of your design for school-wide professional learning, consider including a few study groups across the year to provide your colleagues the many benefits of steering their own professional learning and to address the variety of professional learning needs in your school.

PROTOCOL TOOL

STUDY GROUPS

PARTICIPANTS	TIMING
GROUP LEADER; TEACHERS (4-6); COACH; NOTE-TAKER	60 min

INTRODUCTION

Link to Previous Learning (5 min)	▪ Link to last meeting and goals–participants talk about what people tried or learned since the last meeting.
Goals (5 min)	▪ Identify the goals for today's meeting as decided in prior meeting.

ENGAGEMENT IN STUDY

Type of Study Group	Solving Problems of Practice	Working on a Project	Exploring Resources	Examining Research/ Current Issues/ Literacy Practices
Study Group Engagement (40 min)	Group leader invites the teacher to share a problem of practice. Group members ask the teacher questions. The group brainstorms ideas while the teacher takes notes.	Group leader engages members in deciding how to organize the project, what resources/tools they will need, and how to divide the tasks. Each meeting, the group accomplishes one task toward the completion of the project.	Coach and a co-leader invite the group members to explore a physical space or a resource, using activities such as scavenger hunts, dividing up parts of the resource and teaching one another, charting, etc.	Group leader and coach engage group in readings, observing video clips, or reviewing other resources to examine the issue. The note-taker records significant points from the discussion of the issue.

SUMMARY AND NEXT STEPS

Summary (5 min)	▪ Group leader guides the group to identify what was learned and the implications.
Action Steps (5 min)	▪ Group decides on any actions needed in the interim and sets goals for next time. (See Study Group Notes template to assist with notes.)

Your Literacy Coaching Playbook **Online Resource 16.2 | Protocol Tool:** Study Groups, **Version 01**

Figure 16-6

Up **Next**

You're probably familiar with the idea of book clubs for students, but how about professional book clubs for teachers? In the next chapter, we'll show you how to organize and involve your colleagues in book clubs centered on relevant topics that can further expand their expertise in the classroom.

Chapter 17

The Play: **Professional Book Clubs**

Think about the last time you sat in on a book club discussion among a small, heterogeneous group of children. As they shared their thinking with one another, you may have been struck by how the club environment helped everyone in the group build richer understandings of the book than any one child might have gained from independent reading alone. You also may have observed that as an instructional context, the book club seemed to extend students' thinking as they processed and interpreted the perspectives and opinions of their peers, expanded their ability to express their ideas orally, and provided an authentic context for applying norms for listening and speaking. If book clubs can do all this for students, why shouldn't teachers benefit from them as well?

What Are Professional Book Clubs?

Professional book clubs, a specific type of study group (Chapter 16), are a comfortable, enjoyable, and supportive way to develop a strong sense of community and collegiality as well as expand teachers' collective professional knowledge. The rich experience of discussing a book leads to multiple interpretations and takeaways as people filter the information they read through their unique personal experiences and varied knowledge. The entire group benefits from hearing the perspectives of each participant and develops a deeper understanding of the text than any one reader could gain alone.

In this chapter, we explore how to get professional book clubs up and running in your school, provide suggestions for how to facilitate the book club discussion, and offer recommendations for how to empower teachers to co-facilitate professional book clubs with your support.

BENEFITS OF PROFESSIONAL BOOK CLUBS

- Foster collegiality as participants share their own experiences related to the text
- Build a common vocabulary for discussing literacy teaching
- Keep up with current educational research and cutting-edge teaching techniques
- Reflect on how new understandings gained from the text might translate into shifts in practice
- Develop common understandings and beliefs about teaching and learning
- Add to the collective expertise of the educators in the school

A Framework for Professional Book Clubs

The more relaxed and enjoyable the book club experience is, the more colleagues will want to join, so we encourage you to look at the framework with a flexible lens (Figure 17–1). We provide it merely as one way to structure the time with colleagues. Even the relaxing, enjoyable environment of a book club takes up valuable time in your colleagues' schedules, so make sure it is time well spent. Planning and organizing in advance minimize stress and deepen the experience for everyone, including the facilitators.

FRAMEWORK FOR A PROFESSIONAL BOOK CLUB

PLANNING AND PREPARATION (15-20 min)

- Select a great book that will support the school's literacy goals.
- Meet with administrators (as necessary) to request funding for books and refreshments.
- Schedule book club times and choose a meeting space.
- Advertise the book and meeting times, and invite colleagues to join.
- Assign what to read for the meeting.

BOOK CLUB DISCUSSION (40-50 min)

- The group meets and the facilitator of the book club guides the discussion, asking questions and prompting discussion.
- The facilitator keeps members grounded in the text, helps the members build on one another's ideas, and helps them link their thinking to current classroom practice.

WRAP-UP AND EVALUATION (5-10 min)

- The facilitator provides time for the group to reflect on how the discussion might impact their teaching.
- The group briefly discusses what went well and what they might do differently next time.

Figure 17-1

Plan and Prepare for a Professional Book Club

Any member of the school team is encouraged to suggest a great book for a professional book club, though you, as the professional learning leader, will want to take the primary role in organizing it. It will be exciting for you when your colleagues begin to suggest books and express interest in co-facilitating a book club because both behaviors demonstrate their growing investment and interest in professional learning.

The more relaxed and enjoyable the book club experience is, **the more colleagues will want to join.**

How can you boost teachers' interest in participating in a book club? You might start by inviting a colleague to partner with you in facilitating a book club as early in the year as possible. Doing this will provide a colleague with an enjoyable opportunity to build a relationship with colleagues and foster leadership skills.

Be Creative with Book Clubs: An All-School Read

Think about different ways you can energize your staff using professional book clubs. One way might be to choose an annual all-school read, in which every staff member and administrator read the same book. Organize groups of four to eight people to discuss the book and assign a meeting facilitator for each group. Attend the meetings when possible to support the group leaders. An all-school read can create a lot of energy around a literacy topic and get everyone thinking about and brainstorming ideas. The momentum for change that this kind of initiative can create has exciting potential for improvement in teaching and learning across classrooms and grade levels in addition to building community.

Select a Book for a Professional Book Club

You are equipped to make a great book selection for a book club. As a professional learning leader, you are in tune with the needs of the school—from your observations, from the school's data, and from the teachers' identification of their professional learning needs. We encourage you to read as many professional books as your time allows so that you stay current with the content and with high-quality professional resources in the field of literacy. The selection will need to be an engaging and well-written book on a topic that teachers feel is relevant and of high priority in their professional learning. Strive to get recommendations from your colleagues inside and outside of your school.

Anyone suggesting a book must have read the book. We recommend that you read any books that are on the short list of possibilities. Engage in a discussion with any teacher who has recommended a particular title.

As you consider the possibilities, ask yourself the following questions:

- *How will this book enhance other professional learning opportunities?*
- *How might it become a resource to support coaching goals?*
- *How does the book support and/or contradict other literacy initiatives?*
- *How does it match with your school's literacy improvement goals?*

Though current journal articles and blog posts are important for you and your teachers to read, we recommend you reserve professional book clubs for reading books. Use professional learning sessions, study groups, and other opportunities to explore short texts.

Choose the Right Books for the Right Reasons

- Think about your instructional practices and your goals for professional learning, and align your choices with them.
- Be sure the book is relevant to teachers' interest and their instructional practices.
- Choose books that are well written, rich in content, engaging, and enjoyable to read.
- Read reviews to make your initial selections, but make sure to read the book before choosing it for a book club.
- Choose books that include current research and address timely, relevant topics.
- Occasionally, instead of a professional book, you may want to select a young adult novel or a text set of thematically linked picture books. Discussions can focus on how to use these texts as mentor texts for children in reading and writing or on how the books can be used for critical examination related to social justice goals.

Order Books and Schedule Book Clubs

Once you make an excellent choice with strong rationales, secure funding to order one book for each teacher who joins the book club. If you don't have control over your own budget, share your recommendation with the school principal or your district administrators and request that the book be ordered. And, invite them to join!

You will also need to discuss scheduling with your administrator. We recommend scheduling a series of meetings before or after school, each lasting forty-five to sixty minutes. If the group meets outside of the school day, discuss the possibility of an honorarium with your administrator. Though it is possible to meet during the school day, teachers tend to be less distracted and more relaxed when students are not in the building. Some groups decide to meet once a week or once every other week for a period of four to eight weeks depending on the length of the book. If you can afford the time, we find that teachers get the most out of reading smaller chunks of books and diving deeply into the content. However, there are situations when you might read a shorter book and spend one session discussing the whole text.

Talk with your administrator about possible locations for the meetings. Think about places in the school that offer comfortable, flexible seating arrangements to promote discussion. Also, ask if there are any funds for refreshments. Sometimes the family association can be a source of funding or teachers might be willing to rotate the responsibility of bringing snacks. We know members of a professional book club who gave their meeting space a clever name, resembling a coffee shop. They carried the theme through the space, setting it up with a coffee machine, mugs, and ambient lighting. Of course, book club setup can be much simpler than that. The point is that book club is a time for professional learning, but it is also a time for a relaxing respite from the pressures of the day.

QUICK TIP

As you choose where to meet, think about where you might be able to arrange chairs in a circle to promote discussion and community.

NEW TEACHER

Book clubs are a great way for new teachers to get to know their colleagues. The relaxed setting can make it feel less intimidating than other professional learning scenarios. If you have several new teachers in your school or district, consider facilitating a book club uniquely suited to them with topics that are tailored for them. The more opportunities new teachers have to connect with colleagues, the more supported they will feel.

Invite Participants

Now that you have figured out some of the logistics, it is time to share your wonderful recommendation with your colleagues. Send an email, post a flyer, and recruit by word of mouth. Share why the title was selected and provide a few highlights of the book. Promise each teacher a copy of the book and announce the meeting schedule. Explain that if they join, they need to commit to all the meetings. You might have some schedule flexibility which could be addressed at your first meeting if needed. But it is important that teachers know the schedule so they can get it onto their calendars and complete the agreed-upon readings.

The Book Club Discussion: What to Say and Do

As a facilitator or co-facilitator of a book club, your role is to guide the discussion so teachers stay grounded in the text, think about implications for their teaching, and build on one another's ideas.

Start the book club with a welcome and a quick reminder that book club is a time for thinking together and developing new insights through a group inquiry: every member's voice is valued, and everyone should have a chance to share. Encourage the group to stay with an idea until it is thoroughly discussed. Remind members to refer to page numbers as they share so all can turn to the relevant page and stay deeply embedded in the text. Come prepared with a few probing questions about the important ideas in the book but also be open to following the direction the group takes. Here we suggest some tips for a productive conversation:

Start with an open-ended invitation into the conversation. Use open-ended questions to move the conversation forward right from the beginning.

Sample Language

- *What stood out to you in the reading?*
- *What resonated with you and your teaching?*
- *What were points of disagreement? What were the points of agreement?*
- *What are you thinking about after reading this text?*
- *What assumptions did the author make?*

Guide the group to connect what they have learned from the text to actions in their classrooms. The following questions may be helpful in keeping participants thinking about how to link the new learning to their daily instruction.

Sample Language

- *Look at page ____. What would that look like or sound like in your classroom?*
- *What are you already doing that these ideas might enhance?*
- *In what ways might these ideas address our students' needs?*
- *How are these ideas consistent with our school-wide improvement plans or our vision for literacy learning?*

Use facilitative language to help the group build on one another's ideas. Once teachers are facilitating book clubs on their own, provide them with a list of helpful prompts, such as the following, to move the conversation forward, ground the talk in the text, and come to deeper understandings.

Sample Language

- *What do you think about what ____ said?*
- *What are you thinking about that idea?*
- *So, you are saying ____. Is that right?*
- *Does anyone have an example that fits with the idea we are reading about?*
- *How does this idea fit with your experience in teaching?*

Wrap-Up and Evaluation

Wrap up the session with a reflection and a reminder about how to prepare for the next meeting.

Ask questions to generate meaningful discussion to carry the learning from the book club into the classroom.

Sample Language

- *How did the book make you think differently about teaching and learning?*
- *What did you learn that has you thinking about your own experiences in the classroom?*
- *How can our book club members support one another in implementing new ideas?*

Invite your colleagues to jot down their goals and ask how you can support them as they try out some of the new ideas. Lastly, use questions such as the following to invite the book club members to evaluate the discussion—what went well and what could be done differently the next time.

Sample Language

- *What are your thoughts about our discussion? How well were we prepared for the discussion?*
- *What did we do to make sure everyone had a chance to talk?*
- *How well did we listen and respond to the ideas of others?*
- *How did we help each other clarify understandings?*
- *How did we encourage different points of view?*

If your goal is for your colleagues to begin leading book clubs themselves, ask them to reflect on what they noticed about the role of the facilitator.

Sample Language

- *What did you notice about how the facilitator guided the conversation?*
- *How did the facilitator keep the group grounded in the text?*

- *What was the most helpful thing the facilitator did to keep the discussion flowing?*
- *How did the facilitator bring in different voices?*
- *What is something you learned for a time you might serve as a facilitator?*

A Protocol Tool for Facilitating Professional Book Clubs

We have summarized the process for facilitating a book club in a protocol tool as shown in Figure 17-2. (You will find a full-size version of Protocol Tool: Professional Book Clubs as **OR 17.1** in the Online Resources.) We recommend printing it out for your own use and offering it to teachers who help facilitate book clubs.

Remember, the framework highlighted in the protocol is just a suggestion for how you might structure and facilitate book clubs. It is not rigid and should not feel forced in any way. Professional book clubs should be a nurturing time for teachers to get and give ideas without feeling the pressure to add one more thing to their teaching schedule. The overarching goal of this time together is to enjoy learning and growing together.

ONLINE RESOURCE 17.1

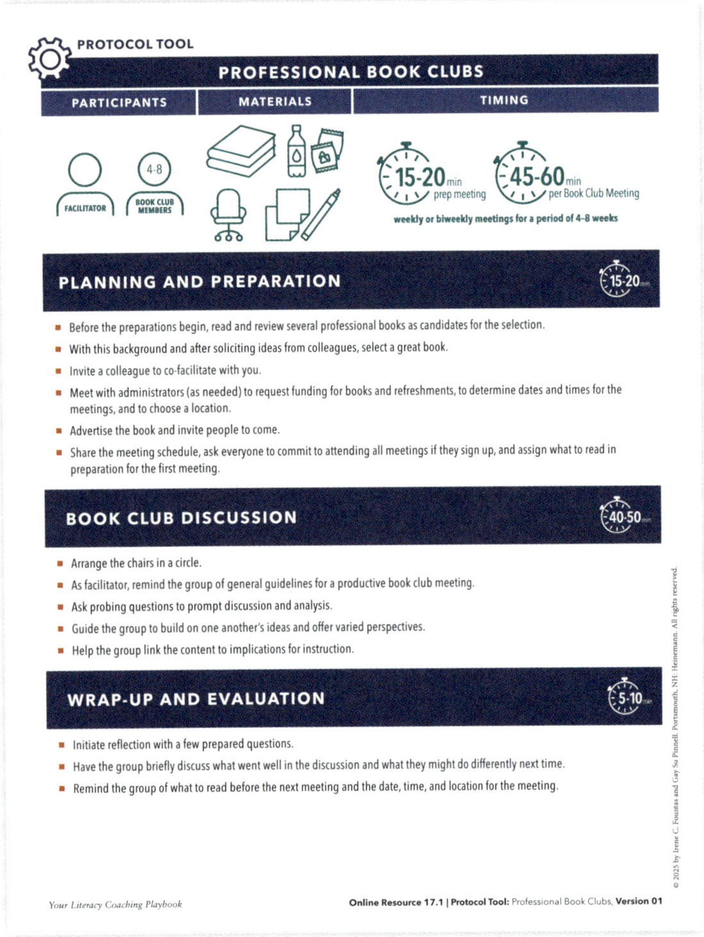
PROTOCOL TOOL

PROFESSIONAL BOOK CLUBS

PARTICIPANTS	MATERIALS	TIMING
FACILITATOR; 4-8 BOOK CLUB MEMBERS		15-20 min prep meeting; 45-60 min per Book Club Meeting; weekly or biweekly meetings for a period of 4-8 weeks

PLANNING AND PREPARATION 15-20 min

- Before the preparations begin, read and review several professional books as candidates for the selection.
- With this background and after soliciting ideas from colleagues, select a great book.
- Invite a colleague to co-facilitate with you.
- Meet with administrators (as needed) to request funding for books and refreshments, to determine dates and times for the meetings, and to choose a location.
- Advertise the book and invite people to come.
- Share the meeting schedule, ask everyone to commit to attending all meetings if they sign up, and assign what to read in preparation for the first meeting.

BOOK CLUB DISCUSSION 40-50 min

- Arrange the chairs in a circle.
- As facilitator, remind the group of general guidelines for a productive book club meeting.
- Ask probing questions to prompt discussion and analysis.
- Guide the group to build on one another's ideas and offer varied perspectives.
- Help the group link the content to implications for instruction.

WRAP-UP AND EVALUATION 5-10 min

- Initiate reflection with a few prepared questions.
- Have the group briefly discuss what went well in the discussion and what they might do differently next time.
- Remind the group of what to read before the next meeting and the date, time, and location for the meeting.

Your Literacy Coaching Playbook **Online Resource 17.1 | Protocol Tool:** Professional Book Clubs, **Version 01**

Figure 17-2

Up **Next**

In Chapter 18, we turn to a discussion of lab classrooms, designated classrooms in the school where you and a small group of colleagues can gather to observe a colleague in action. Given today's renewed emphasis on the science of teaching and learning, the notion of "classroom as laboratory" is a not-so-new idea that has taken on new significance. Read on to learn how your school can benefit from this emerging trend.

Chapter 18

The Play: **Lab Classrooms**

For teachers, there is no substitute for watching a talented colleague in action. When teachers have the chance to observe all aspects of literacy teaching in a real classroom with real kids in their own school community, they quickly get the message that effective teaching can happen anywhere in the school. Not only that, but seeing it unfold right in front of them can't help but boost confidence in their ability to excel as teachers in their own classrooms.

In this chapter, we help you think about how to increase access to live teaching within your school through the development of a "lab classroom" that engages teachers in learning from each other. We hope you will consider developing such a classroom, as it will provide a rich asset for continuous professional learning.

BENEFITS OF LAB CLASSROOMS

- Provide a model of teaching to make ideas concrete
- Support new teachers in seeing what a type of practice looks like and sounds like in real life
- Provide the opportunity for teachers to view student work
- Offer examples of the language teachers might use in teaching
- Offer teachers the opportunity to see the social and physical environment, including time transitions and movement from one activity or space to another
- Create a welcoming classroom for scheduled observations and discussion

What Is a Lab Classroom?

A lab classroom, sometimes referred to as an "observation" or "demonstration classroom," is a regular-size classroom or any place in the school where a teacher is providing instruction that aligns with the school's values and beliefs about literacy instruction. The teacher in the lab classroom volunteers to host colleagues to observe teaching and learning. Thus, the term *host teacher*. The host teacher has had the opportunity to develop accelerated expertise in implementing the school's high-quality literacy program with the support of the coach. Host teachers continue to problem-solve and find ways to improve their instructional practices as they position themselves as professionals who always have more to learn. A lab classroom is also a great vehicle for supporting the understandings and observational skills of principals. However, remind everyone in the school that a lab classroom is a place for collegial learning, not a perfect example to imitate.

The Role of Host Teacher

The host teacher is a member of the staff who is willing to invite colleagues to observe instruction in their classroom for the purpose of learning more from each other.

Schools sometimes have more than one lab classroom. Several teachers in the school who are experienced with particular techniques and practices may be willing to invite colleagues to observe their teaching. Or, you might choose a host teacher at a primary grade level and one at an intermediate grade level. The lab classroom is a place where everyone can extend their learning around a shared example that fosters thinking together about teacher decision-making.

Lab Classrooms: Modeling Real-Life Teaching

Your colleagues often want to see what teaching looks like and sounds like, particularly if they are entirely new to specific content or instructional practices. The host teacher brings learning to life for those teachers and others, makes concepts concrete, and offers examples of specific language they might use. The visiting teachers can observe the social and physical environment as well as the transitions and instructional practices. Plus, they get a close look at student work—all within their own school.

Think of lab classrooms as practical learning labs in which teachers can observe the organization and management of a vibrant literacy classroom and view expert teaching of reading, writing, and phonics with all its successes and challenges. They can see the real application of newly acquired knowledge in practice in their own school with their own students. While there is no such thing as perfect teaching, "on-the-job learning" in lab classrooms helps teachers develop a concrete picture of what they are working to achieve.

Our experience has been that lab classrooms almost always become prime examples of learning in action that results in long-term systemic improvement. Many of our coaches have developed a classroom within their schools that can be a place of observation and collaborative inquiry by individuals or small groups of teachers. Sometimes, it's the coach's own classroom (when the coach teaches part of the day), and other times the coach partners with an experienced colleague or a new teacher.

Plan and Prepare for Lab Classrooms

Many school leaders have found that lab classrooms can be the scene of powerful learning, and they have partnered with the school coach to make them happen. As a coach, you can begin by engaging a host teacher who is both interested in this powerful learning opportunity and willing to show remarkable generosity by opening the classroom door to create a dynamic learning space for colleagues.

Your first goal is to work with your principal to identify a teacher who may be willing to become a host teacher. Alternatively, you might be able to co-teach with a prospective host teacher so your colleague has daily opportunities to observe and discuss teaching with you.

Whether or not you co-teach with the host teacher, make sure the lab classroom is well resourced and that the host teacher's learning is supported through your frequent coaching and offering of other professional learning opportunities. The idea is to accelerate the learning of host teachers in advance of the full implementation of the school's plans for curriculum, assessment, and instruction. The host teachers provide a model of what teachers need to see in action.

You might co-plan with the host teacher, helping to ensure the lab classroom provides a good example for colleagues. Here, "good" simply means a clear example of the lesson without distracting departures from what is intended for teachers to see. This leaves observers to notice the teacher's decisions and the language that supports student learning.

NEW TEACHER

The lab classroom provides a concrete example for teachers new to teaching and new to the school. The observation experience supports their development of collegial relationships and helps them become a part of the community.

Lab Classroom Demonstrations: What to Say and Do

Once your lab classrooms are established and you feel confident that your other colleagues will benefit from observing the teaching and learning happening in them, you can begin scheduling classroom visits. Once again, it is important to note that the demonstration will not be a perfect model because there is no such thing as perfect teaching. Your colleagues should be aware that the host teacher is on a learning journey along with everyone else. The demonstration simply gives people a vision for what teaching and learning might look like.

Unlike peer and cluster coaching, which also involve colleagues observing a host teacher, the primary focus of demonstration lessons is not to lift the expertise of the host teacher. Of course, learning happens whenever colleagues have opportunities to talk about a lesson, but the focus is different in this context. The host teacher is simply providing an example for group discussion. If possible, the host teacher is a part of the preparation discussion and the discussion after the lesson in order to offer perspectives on and rationales for instructional decisions.

A Framework for Demonstration Teaching

As with any type of professional learning, it is helpful to have a reliable structure to frame the experience for your colleagues. However, you'll need to vary the framework somewhat in order to best serve the needs of your colleagues and the host teacher. For example, you may not always find it necessary to co-plan with the host teacher, though it is certainly beneficial to know what your colleagues will be observing so you can guide their observation with a few focused prompts. Having access to a lab classroom within your school allows for more informal visits as well. Ideally, you always have time to discuss what your colleagues observed, but they will gain from the experience even if this is not always possible. Lab classrooms allow for this kind of flexibility. Now take a look at Figure 18–1.

**FRAMEWORK FOR
LAB CLASSROOM DEMONSTRATION AND OBSERVATION**

CO-PLANNING

Determine a focus for the demonstration based on the needs of the observing teachers. Before meeting with the group, co-plan the lesson with the host teacher (when possible). Become familiar with student data to share with observing teachers in case the host teacher cannot attend the preparation meeting.

20-30 min

PREPARATION FOR OBSERVATION

Meet with the observing teachers to discuss what they will see. When possible, the host teacher shares the lesson and information about the students. Offer focus questions to guide the observation.

10 min

DEMONSTRATION/OBSERVATION

The host teacher teaches the lesson. Observers note evidence of the impact of the teaching on student learning. Encourage them to note spontaneous, unplanned teaching decisions.

15-30 min

DISCUSSION AND ANALYSIS

Invite the group to revisit the lesson goals, analyze teaching decisions, and discuss evidence of student learning. Participants discuss how the observation extended their thinking and share their wonderings. When available, the host teacher joins and shares personal reflections.

15-20 min

Figure 18–1

Co-plan with the Host Teacher

Co-planning with the host teacher is a helpful way to ensure that the demonstration lesson is in line with what your colleagues are learning in other professional learning contexts and so there isn't any confusion about what they will observe. Become familiar with the available student data so you can plan effectively and share what you know about the students with the observing teachers when the host teacher cannot be a part of the opening discussion.

Prepare for Observation

Before your colleagues observe the lesson, meet briefly to discuss what they will see. If schedules allow, have the host share the lesson plan and provide information about the students. You can serve this role if the host teacher is not able to join the group. Discuss a few things participants need to look for during the lesson. If you have worked with colleagues to develop a look-for tool (Chapter 13), review the criteria and identify one or two areas you want to focus on. Share one or two questions, such as the following.

Sample Language

- *How does the teacher engage the children during the interactive read-aloud?*
- *How does the teacher differentiate instruction during the interactive writing lesson to meet the needs of different writers?*
- *Notice the discussion after the students read the text. How does the text introduction set them up for the discussion?*
- *How does the teacher use the shared reading text to reinforce the phonics principles the students are learning?*
- *How does the teacher make the application of the phonics lesson engaging for different learners?*
- *What are some ways the teacher sets the students up for success during independent reading?*
- *How does the teacher use mentor texts during the writing lesson to teach the writing principle?*

Observe the Lesson

The observation might take only fifteen to thirty minutes, or it might be longer depending on the purpose of the observation. Encourage the visiting teachers to make notes on what they see based on the focus questions you and the host teacher offer. Advise them to refrain from judging what they see, and encourage them to capture the interactions in their notes. The more precisely they can capture what the host teacher and students say, the better the post-observation discussion will be.

Unless you have a one-way glass wall for observing (frequently used in schools set up for the purpose), the group of observers is probably limited to the number that can fit into corners or at the back of the room without interfering with the lesson. The group of visiting teachers may be made up of one or two teachers (possibly new to the process or to the school), a small group of grade-level colleagues, an invited group, or a group that initiated a request. The teachers may be a cross-grade-level group who are interested in observing a particular instructional context. If available, closed-circuit video may also be used effectively, and definitely has its place, although we have found that it is always best for teachers to be there in person. The teachers are seeing the instruction for just one moment in time, so they must be alert to capture the significant interactions. The process enables participants, freed from teaching, to notice the important teaching decisions and their effect on student learning.

Capture Teaching on Video

Consider recording a lab classroom lesson on video to share and discuss in your professional learning sessions. This way, the lab classroom can be "active" all year long.

Discuss and Analyze

The most powerful learning comes from the discussion after observation. Have participants share what they have noticed to produce a fuller picture of events and language. Together, they can discuss how the observation extended their thinking and share their genuine wonderings. When available, the host teacher joins in by adding personal reflections and thinking. All this discussion begins to build a bridge to classroom practice from participants' previous learning experiences, including the reading and study of professional resources, previous work with the coach, and their own work in the classroom.

Challenge participants to apply their insights to their own future work. The teachers might decide on some common instructional moves to try in their own classrooms and perhaps talk about a plan to share their results with each other in the future. Here is some language to invite reflection.

Sample Language

- *What will you take back to your own teaching from this experience?*
- *What instructional moves will you try with your own students?*
- *What is something you learned that surprised you?*
- *What is something you noticed that will affect your teaching?*

A Protocol Tool for Demonstration Teaching in Lab Classrooms

ONLINE RESOURCE 18.1

We have summarized a process for observing teaching in lab classrooms in Figure 18–2. (You will find a full-size version of Protocol Tool: Demonstration Teaching in Lab Classrooms as **OR 18.1** in the Online Resources.) Use the framework as a guide for making the most out of the learning in your lab classrooms. Print out the protocol and keep it handy in your coaching notebook (Chapter 23).

Grounding Teachers' Practice in a Strong Theory

Lab classrooms may be used to explore almost every aspect of classroom life. As teachers deepen their understanding, they profit from such visits and continue to expand their knowledge. For an experienced staff in a well-developed learning school, lab classrooms may become a major source of analysis and learning, and you may be able to develop more lab classrooms. Eventually, teachers may begin to visit the lab classroom without a coach. In fact, every new practice (or nuance of teaching) may be explored in this way. Lab classrooms can become a major vehicle for continual learning and an inspiration for the team.

The creation of a lab classroom in your school is a practical investment in the expertise of your team. It brings the learning of theory right into the classroom. Teachers often take university or

Demonstration Teaching Cannot Replace Coaching

Teachers are often more comfortable observing their colleagues teach than being observed themselves. But, it is important not to rely so heavily on lab classrooms that teachers think that they become a replacement for the experience of being coached. Demonstrations provide a vision, but coaching is really where change happens because teachers are engaged themselves in the analysis of decision-making that makes an impact on student learning.

online courses or attend in-service workshops but find it difficult to talk about theoretical ideas in the abstract. Yet, teachers do need to build a practical theory about what learning is, how it takes place, and how it changes over time. They need to think deeply about the interaction between their own teaching moves and student learning.

In the past, some teaching has been viewed as the implementation of a scripted series of actions. Teachers either weren't taught *why* they should engage in these actions or *how* students would benefit. Or, they were given a flat answer such as "research shows . . . ."

> **Link Research and Practice**
>
> The lab classroom is not a place where teachers experiment with instruction; rather, it is a place where they can see and participate in teaching based on sound research. They learn how to translate research into classroom practice. What an ideal opportunity to link research and practice!

In our experience, teachers need not only a repertoire of practical actions to take but a growing understanding of the *whys* and *hows* of their work. The coach can be key to filling the gap between theory and practice. A strong theory forms a core foundation on which teachers can make decisions; it's always tentative because teachers are learning about the complex work of the brain of each learner.

PROTOCOL TOOL

DEMONSTRATION TEACHING IN LAB CLASSROOMS

PARTICIPANTS	TIMING
TEACHER, COACH, 2-4 TEACHERS	60-90 min

CO-PLANNING 20-30 min

- Meet with the host teacher to schedule a time for the demonstration.
- Select a focus based on the needs of the visiting teachers.
- Review student data.
- Plan a lesson together with the needs of the students as well as visiting teachers in mind.
- Develop two or three focus prompts for the visiting teachers, or plan to use a look-for tool to focus the observation.

PREPARATION FOR OBSERVATION 10 min

- Host teacher (when available) shares information about the students, goals, materials, and plans for the lesson.
- Discuss what teachers need to look for during the lesson using either a look-for observational tool or the focus prompts.
- Invite genuine questions and wonderings.

DEMONSTRATION/OBSERVATION 15-30 min

- Have the observing teachers create two columns for note-taking, one for what teacher says and the other for what students say.
- Remind teachers to avoid evaluative language and to make specific notes to capture the interactions.
- Ask the group to note significant language from the lesson (teacher and students).
- Ask them to keep in mind the focus questions you have discussed.

DISCUSSION AND ANALYSIS 15-20 min

- Invite visiting teachers to share their observations and discuss the lessons.
- Encourage observers to share specific teacher and student interactions.
- Keep the discussion focused on the teaching decisions and impact on the students' learning.
- Ask the host teacher, if available, to share reflections and thinking about the lesson.
- Guide observing teachers to reflect on how the experience will influence their own teaching.

Your Literacy Coaching Playbook **Online Resource 18.1 | Protocol Tool:** Demonstration Teaching in Lab Classrooms, **Version 01**

Figure 18-2

At the same time, the theory must be linked to actual action in the classroom. It's the classic and oft-asked question, "But what do I do on Monday?" Teachers always want and need to know the answer. A strong understanding of learning will make them less vulnerable to practices that either won't work or may actually confuse learners. This critical way of thinking is a hallmark of the learning school. Practices and materials are not adopted without critical review and analysis of possible outcomes. They must fit with the collective vision. With the concrete vision of a lab classroom, teachers have a firsthand view of the school vision turning into reality.

Up **Next**

We've said it before and we'll say it again: Coaches must have a strong grasp of data about the rate of student progress over time. Discussing and analyzing data from formative and summative assessments with teachers helps them develop a process for and a habit of making data-informed instructional decisions. Chapter 19 will help you and your colleagues become data literate.

Chapter 19

The Play: **Data Conversations**

For many teachers, the word *data* still arouses feelings of anxiety and inadequacy. It's no wonder, really, because in many circumstances, test scores have been misused to place pressure and blame on schools and teachers when their students haven't met certain expectations for achievement. Sometimes only the numbers seem to count.

In this chapter and in all the work you do, we hope to shift your thinking so that you begin to think of different kinds of data as tools for illuminating constructive, actionable information about student progress and driving effective actions in the classroom.

Since the passage of the No Child Left Behind Act and the high-stakes assessments associated with that bill, American public schools have been required to report assessment scores that show "adequate yearly progress" in student achievement.

BENEFITS OF DATA CONVERSATIONS

- Support all teachers in understanding how to collect, analyze, discuss, and use data on student progress
- Ensure that data-informed decisions have the intended effects
- Promote reflection, accountability, and continuous learning on the part of all teachers
- Help teachers notice patterns in the data that might suggest inequities in learning opportunities
- Lead to more informed differentiation of instruction
- Allow for tracking of student achievement over time
- Foster increased teacher efficacy
- Promote collective ownership of student outcomes

Conditions for Effective Data Conversations

- Collective ownership of achievement data
- Predictable structures and defined times to review data
- Thoughtful analysis of data with an equity lens
- Application of an asset-based lens in looking at data and making instructional decisions
- A belief in the value of both hard and soft data

As a result, recent years have seen a growing focus on data literacy for all teachers, as test scores and other assessment data increasingly have come into the public forum. This chapter will help you think about your role in furthering the data literacy of your colleagues through the conversations you have across all the professional learning opportunities you provide.

Establish the Conditions for Effective Data Conversations

To have effective data conversations and change the way data is currently used (or not used) in your school, you'll want to start by engaging your principal. The two of you (or more if a team is involved) can work together to put conditions into place that will help your colleagues learn how to continuously gather, interpret, act on, and monitor evidence of teaching and learning. Just as important, data literacy helps you support everyone's understanding of the story it does or does not tell. And ultimately, data literacy means mining numbers and observations for actionable insights and helping teachers learn how to monitor the effects of those actions over time.

As a coach, you are in the best position to help the school leadership team develop the conditions that allow for these meaningful conversations about data and its effective use in driving instructional decisions. Here are five ways you can help establish and promote the conditions that support effective data conversations:

1. Build collective ownership of achievement data.

Help teachers, administrators, and specialists understand that everyone in the school needs to take responsibility for critically examining the data on the success of every child by name. The goal is for your colleagues to shift from saying "my" students to "our" students. This means that, as a school, you need to have systems in place for looking at the data of individuals, groups, classes, and the whole school.

MAKING DATA VISIBLE

One way you can build this collective ownership is to provide visual representations of data in spaces accessible only to teachers. A data wall is one method for putting "faces on the data" (Sharratt and Fullan 2012) that can help you and your colleagues throughout the school keep a close eye on shifts in learning. Data walls usually are displayed in secure places like the faculty room or on fold-out boards that can be opened for a group data meeting and then put away. Digital data walls can be made in online bulletin boards or virtual whiteboards. Spreadsheets can also be used to show data visually. We do not recommend the practice of using data walls with students to monitor their own progress or with parents. We suggest using data walls only as a teacher tool for monitoring large amounts of data.

Many types of data can be displayed on a data wall, whether it is a physical or digital display. You can display patterns in standardized test data (Figure 19–1) or in data from benchmark assessments (Figure 19–2) that look at individuals and also aggregate the data by subgroup. Every student in a grade level can be represented by an icon, which can be as simple as a sticky note with a child's first

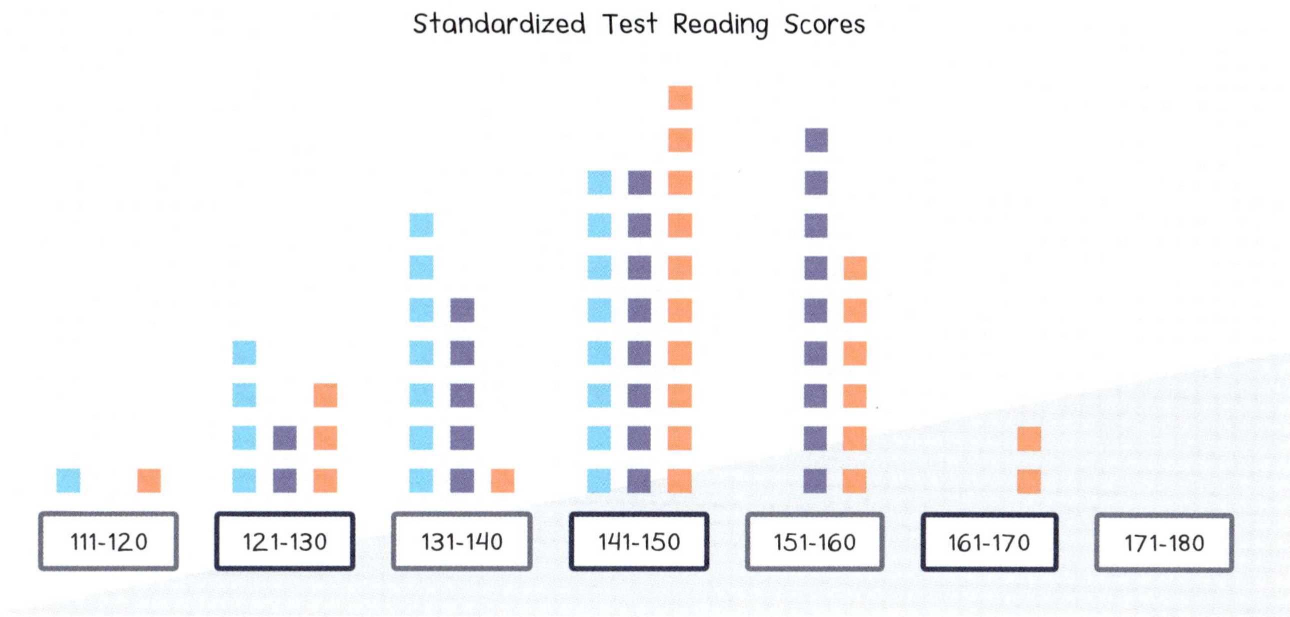

Figure 19-1

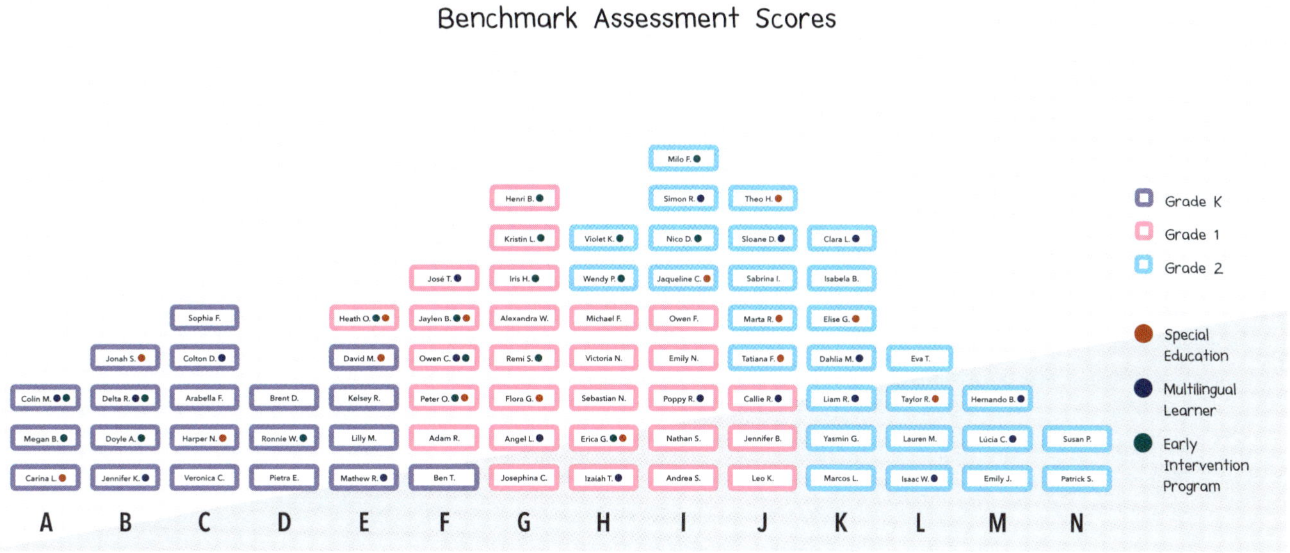

Figure 19-2

name on it. First names, student initials, or a numbering system can be used. The important thing is that the icon must be moveable, so it can be repositioned at intervals to show shifts in progress. At a glance, data walls can reveal students who need extra attention. They also allow teachers to view and discuss the progress of the group as a whole, as well as engage in collaborative problem-solving to address challenges.

We suggest that you photograph the data wall for a particular group of students before moving any of the icons or save previous versions of digital data displays. This way, you will have an easy way to compare the last iteration with any changes you make afterward.

Most important, visual displays of data provide a platform for collegial, collaborative conversations about student learning. The visual display of school-wide data reflects the belief that the entire school community cares for each student because they know they all hold responsibility for educating every child in the school.

2. Create predictable structures and defined times to review data.

Teachers need time to consistently review and interpret data to improve instruction and professional learning across the school. Rich opportunities for data conversations exist in most of the professional learning plays that we've described in this book (Figure 19-3). In coaching, you help teachers look at data to make instructional decisions as well as analyze the impact of those decisions on student learning. In lesson study, you help teachers use data to plan and refine lessons. Learning walks involve both collecting and interpreting data, and study groups that focus on problems of practice or projects use data to create solutions.

The teachers' examination of data and the actions in the classroom that follow their analysis can mean the difference between students who are consistently achieving at expected levels and students who are not. Besides embedding data review in the professional learning protocols, many schools also have regularly scheduled data meetings to look at trends and patterns to make school-wide decisions.

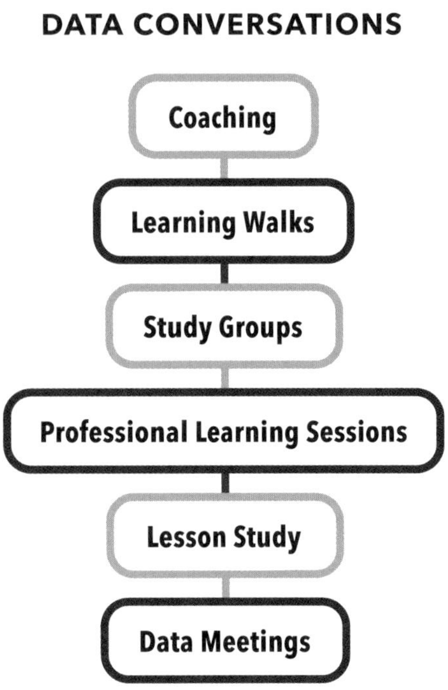

Figure 19-3

3. Apply an assets-based lens to data.

Promote a culture in which teachers look at strengths in data. Guide your colleagues in analyzing the factors that may have led to the success of high-achieving students to help other students achieve at higher levels. For example, ask what disparities among groups are revealed; then follow up by considering how to mitigate and resolve the issues holding students back.

Helping your colleagues hone the ability to identify strengths allows them to teach at the cutting edge of their students' learning. In each of the data conversations you have with your colleagues, think together about instruction that builds upon demonstrated strengths versus covering material to address deficits. Notice how a teacher and coach used this asset-based mindset to establish priorities for instruction in Figure 19-4. In this case, the student's writing was the source of the data, and the coach and teacher worked together to identify strengths in order to inform next steps. For example, Eva shows strength in using dialogue, so the coach and teacher determined that one next step for Eva would be to learn how to weave action into dialogue. Notice how each goal is tied to a strength the student has demonstrated.

4. Examine data with an equity lens.

Guide data conversations to detect how teacher beliefs, such as those about social class, language, gender, or race, may be getting in the way of effective instruction. No matter how you look at the data on student achievement in your school, always maintain a strong lens on issues of equity. To identify and understand systemic inequities that may be contributing to poorer outcomes in certain groups, discuss questions such as these with your colleagues: Does one group of students

NEW TEACHER

Some new teachers might fall into the trap of deficit thinking. They worry about their students' progress and then wonder if they are doing enough. Meet individually with new teachers for brief data conversations. Review student artifacts together and make instructional decisions based on demonstrated strengths. This assets-based mindset will impact the way they assess and plan across subject areas.

Name: Eva	Grade: 3	Genre: Memory Story	Date: 10/17
	Strengths	Next Steps	Plan
Genre	• Selects a meaningful topic. • Shares feelings about the memory. • Uses dialogue to add meaning to the story.	• Understand that memory stories include reflections from the writer about the memory. • Build on her understanding of dialogue by showing how to weave action with dialogue.	• Work with Eva, Katey, Yasmine, and Chansey on adding reflections.
Craft	• Writes a strong lead. • Uses dialogue. • Uses descriptive verbs (dangling, angled) • Uses some transition words.	• Learn how to reveal characters by what they say and do. • Expand her understanding of writing transitions	• Meet in an individual conference. Use mentor texts to model how to reveal characters through dialogue.
Conventions	• Punctuates dialogue correctly. • Writes many high-frequency words correctly.	• Learn about paragraphing to show speaker change. • Use words with the same letter pattern to write other words.	• Develop a whole-class lesson to address paragraphing.

Figure 19-4

consistently score lower on one measure? Is intervention or stronger (different) instruction needed? Is one group less engaged in the texts you read aloud or provide for reading, or are more culturally relevant texts needed? For students scoring lower in writing, what barriers (language or other) are interfering? Taking the following actions should ensure equitable outcomes for all.

- **Identify disparities.** First, look for patterns of disparity among subgroups of students (based on race, socioeconomic status, language background, disabilities, gender, etc.). Identify which of those groups may be facing needless barriers to success. Work with colleagues to identify the challenges evident in the data and investigate root causes for what is keeping some students from reaching their full potential.
- **Tailor support.** Provide interventions that respond to the unique needs of individual students and groups of students.
- **Identify systemic inequities.** Investigate whether there are systemic or institutional inequities contributing to the disparities in the data for particular subgroups. Work to actively disrupt policies and school-wide practices that may be negatively affecting learning for certain subgroups.
- **Promote fairness.** Ensure that resources, opportunities, and attention to individuals compensate for the disadvantages some children face.
- **Guard against unintended consequences.** Take care that data-driven instructional decisions do not inadvertently contribute to existing inequities.
- **Hold everyone accountable.** Convey the idea that every person in the school must view and respond to data through an equity lens.

Getting a More Complete Picture with Different Types of Data

Looking at a variety of data categories and cross-referencing them gives a full picture of a student's progress and growth as well as the effective instructional practices that yielded the results (Van Barneveld 2008).

Assessment Data: Data from formative, summative, and benchmark assessments, including standardized test data

Demographic Data: Data on students' race, ethnicity, socioeconomic status, language proficiency, special education needs, etc.

Contextual Data: Attendance records, behavioral data, data on individual students' growth over time, intervention data, if applicable, and data on student engagement and participation in class

Progress Monitoring Data: Data resulting from continuous progress monitoring of individual students over time

5. Value and use both hard and soft data.

As a coach, be sure to stay up to date on the learning progress of all the students in your school. State tests and other standardized assessments provide high-level summary reports that make it easier to keep the hard data they yield at your fingertips. It can be more difficult to stay on top of soft data (observational notes on reading and writing progress, student work samples like students' writing about reading, reading lists, writing across genres, etc.) and data that fall somewhere between the two, such as reading records, rubrics, writing students do in response to prompts, or benchmark assessments. Many systematic assessment procedures yield both hard and soft data that is valuable.

It's important for teachers to understand the difference between hard and soft data and to use each type for the important information it provides. It may be helpful to prepare a handout with a chart like the one in Figure 19–5 to share with your colleagues as you embark on reviewing data across professional learning situations.

Hard and soft data can be collected through both formative and summative assessment. The point of formative assessment is to inform instruction while the student is in the process of learning the material, while summative assessment gives teachers feedback on how much a student understands a concept or idea after the teaching is completed. In your role, you will often work with teachers on analyzing data collected through formative assessment so the information can directly impact teaching. Formative assessment might include a presentation, a draft of writing, or an audio recording of a student reading. However, you might find it useful to look at the results of summative assessment to identify trends and patterns across classrooms, grades, and the school. Summative assessment might

Types Of Data	
Hard Data (Quantitative) Expressed numerically, measurably, verifiably, factually	**Soft Data (Qualitative)** Focused on description
Sources of hard data include ▪ Standardized assessments ▪ State tests ▪ Benchmark assessments ▪ End-of-unit assessments ▪ Grammar assessments ▪ Phonics assessments ▪ Attendance records	Sources of soft data include ▪ Student work samples (e.g., reader's notebook entries, writer's notebook entries, writing samples) ▪ Anecdotal notes ▪ Progress notes ▪ Reading records ▪ Audio and/or video recordings ▪ Photographs ▪ Survey results ▪ Interviews ▪ Rubrics ▪ Teacher observations

Benefits	
Hard Data	**Soft Data**
▪ Provides quantifiable results ▪ Can be scored objectively by a computer ▪ Allows for comparison of scores over time ▪ Holds school accountable for results ▪ Can be analyzed statistically	▪ Can be accessed quickly ▪ Available at frequent intervals ▪ Can be linked to other data ▪ Shows information not evident in hard data ▪ Is immediately relevant to instruction ▪ Can provide context from behavioral data, data on student engagement and participation in class, and other types of contextual data

Figure 19-5

> *"Data-driven decision-making does not simply require good data; it also requires good decisions."*
>
> **–FREDERICK HESS** (2008, 12)

include a rubric that evaluates a writing assessment or a test at the end of a unit. Both types of assessment yield hard and soft data but are used for different purposes.

Your role in data conversations is to help teachers use hard and soft data to gain precise, objective, and qualitative insights to uncover root causes behind the data. The real power of data lies in how the facts are interpreted and how the insights are translated into more effective actions in the classroom. Together, both hard and soft data provide the full picture of a student's learning progress.

Each data conversation you have with colleagues further promotes the conditions that make for more effective data analysis. As you engage in conversations across professional learning experiences and in regular data meetings, build the idea that everyone is responsible for student achievement, look at the data with an equity lens, bring an assets-based mindset, and help your colleagues value different kinds of data so that everyone is working toward helping students reach their fullest potential.

A Framework for Data Conversations

We have made it a point to integrate the use of data in many chapters in this book. Here we offer a general framework specifically for looking at data with your colleagues (Figure 19–6), which you can apply in any of those situations. For example, use the framework with an individual teacher during coaching to look at the data of a small group of children to plan a reading lesson. Or, use it in a data meeting to frame a conversation with a big group as you review school-wide data on a data wall. Whatever the case, you can easily adapt this framework to suit the type of data you are analyzing and the context in which you are discussing it.

FRAMEWORK FOR A DATA CONVERSATION

LOOK AT THE DATA

Look at the raw data with your colleague(s). Ask for noticings and wonderings. Encourage your colleague(s) to identify patterns, trends, holes, and questions. Notice and name what the data says.

INTERPRET THE DATA

Now is the time to think about "why." Invite your colleague(s) to share possible explanations for the data to determine possible root causes of results. Work together to answer questions or determine what other information is needed to better understand the data.

DETERMINE NEXT STEPS

Summarize the main points from the discussion, identify next steps, and determine ways to monitor or evaluate the effectiveness of those actions.

Figure 19-6

Plan and Prepare for Data Conversations

To ensure that data conversations are productive and that the data is used effectively to improve student outcomes, you'll need to plan ahead.

Collaborate to Identify What You and Your Colleagues Want to Achieve

The goals for a data conversation will likely be based on the context of the meeting. For example, the goals you have for looking at data during a coaching session or a lesson study will be different from goals you have for a data meeting. Being clear about what you want to accomplish by looking at data will ensure that you are looking at the right data. Here are examples of some goals you and your colleagues might have for a data conversation:

- Plan changes to instruction based on summative data
- Analyze student work or formative assessments to inform lesson planning
- Identify trends in behavioral or attendance data
- Determine needs for intervention across a grade level
- Measure progress toward school-wide or grade-level goals
- Identify disparities in achievement across subgroups in a particular area
- Determine the factors contributing to high achievement

Gather, Organize, and Distribute the Data

Before a data conversation, determine the appropriate type of data as well as a way to present it. Sometimes you will collect and present the data. Other times, you will ask teachers to bring data from their classrooms. For example, you might ask teachers to bring a class set of writing to a professional learning session to analyze it to inform instruction. If you are coaching a colleague in small-group instruction in reading, you might ask your colleague to bring the most recent reading records from the group so you can think together about the best way to support the students' reading. You can also offer to look at student work ahead of a coaching session. Most important, be clear about what data will be helpful based on the goal of the conversation.

If you are responsible for gathering and preparing data for a data conversation, think about how you will present the data to others. Depending on your goals, you might do any of the following:

- **Disaggregate data.** Break the data into subgroups (e.g., grade level, demographics, specific classes) to help teachers focus on meaningful patterns and trends.
- **Prepare visuals.** Create graphs, charts, tables, and data walls to make the data easier to interpret and to help teachers more easily identify trends, learning gaps, or improvement. Choose the type of visual carefully. Different ways of representing data in a graph or chart will emphasize different aspects of the data.
- **Ensure accessibility.** Provide access to data ahead of time by sharing digital copies or printed pages so teachers can arrive prepared with questions, observations, or wonderings about the data.

With careful planning and preparation, the data conversations you lead will be focused, collaborative, and geared toward actionable outcomes.

The Data Conversation: What to Say and Do

Data conversations can be anxiety provoking for some teachers and simply overwhelming for others. For these reasons and others, we suggest you keep data conversations (no matter the context) simple and focused on four questions, which can apply to any type of data. These four questions are addressed through the three parts of the data conversation. In each data conversation, maximize your use of facilitative language as you lead the collaborative inquiry, summarize answers, clarify understandings, and discuss possible next steps.

> **Four Questions for the Data Conversation**
>
> - What does the data show?
> - What does the data mean?
> - What data is missing?
> - What should we do with what we've learned?

Part 1: Look at the Data

The first part of the data conversation is to look at the data and notice and name what the data shows. Before jumping into interpreting or analyzing the data, encourage your colleagues to spend time thinking about what they notice, wonder, or question about the data. Here is some language you can use to help them think about the first question:

Sample Language: What does the data show?

- *What patterns did you notice?*
- *What trends stood out to you?*
- *I noticed ____.*
- *Did you notice that ____?*
- *There is a pattern of ____.*
- *How would you summarize the information?*
- *I am wondering ____.*
- *Is there something missing from this data that you were wondering about?*

Part 2: Interpret the Data

The next part of the process is to spend time interpreting the data. If you are looking at student work, this might mean looking at a student's writing and noticing strengths you can build on for your teaching. If you are looking at a class set of writing, this might mean analyzing why some students took on a new behavior while others didn't, which informs how writing instruction might change. In a data meeting, interpreting the data could mean taking a close look at institutional inequities for different subgroups. Or, it could mean working together to determine what led to an increase in reading scores. Whatever the context or data set you and your colleagues discuss, the following language can help you think about the next two guiding questions:

Sample Language: What does the data mean?

- *What did you find interesting?*
- *What might the data imply?*
- *What might the pattern we see suggest?*
- *What might explain ____?*
- *What does the data make you think about?*
- *What questions do you have?*
- *The data suggests ____.*
- *I was thinking ____.*
- *So you're saying the data shows ____.*
- *What do you think could be the root cause of these outcomes?*
- *What did you find surprising? Why?*
- *What do you think that might mean for your teaching?*
- *I'm wondering ____.*

Sample Language: What data is missing?

- *What else do we need to know?*
- *What do you think is lacking here?*
- *Would it help to look at demographic data? Because?*
- *What might we learn from looking at student work?*
- *How does that correlate with what you see in the classroom?*

Part 3: Determine Next Steps

The last part of a data conversation is to take what you and your colleagues have learned from the data and make a plan. In a lesson study, this might involve looking at student artifacts after a lesson and using the data to adjust the lesson. In a data meeting, it might mean creating new goals for school improvement.

Besides determining action steps, discuss how you will continue to collect data to monitor progress toward goals. This can happen on a short timeline. For example, during a pre-observation conversation, you might ask what outcomes the teacher will be looking for to reach the goals that were determined based on data. After the observation, look at data (observational notes and/or student artifacts) for evidence of whether the lesson goals were met. A longer timeline might involve teachers implementing a new teaching technique to address a goal and then collecting data after a few weeks to see how the new technique is affecting student outcomes. However long the timeline, the important point is that there is a feedback loop (Figure 19–7). Goals and action steps are set, monitored, and discussed in a future data conversation. Use the following language to guide teachers to answer the fourth and last guiding question:

FEEDBACK LOOP

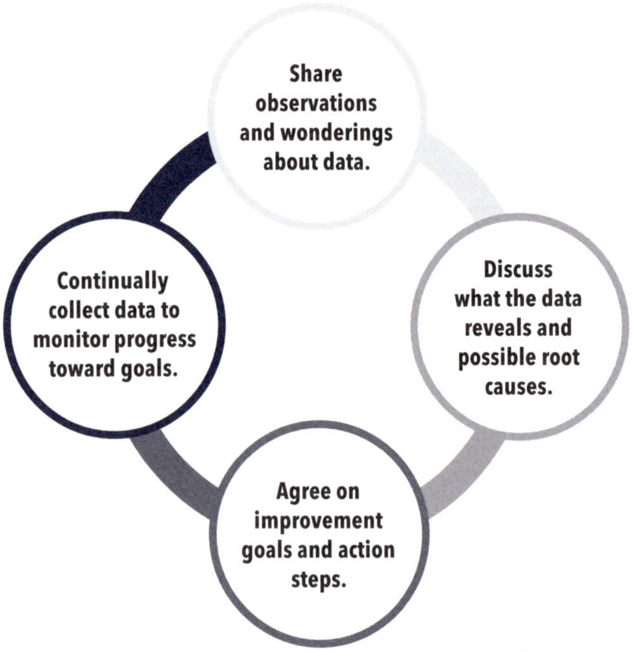

Sample Language: What should we do with what we've learned?

- *How does this information impact your teaching?*
- *What are you thinking you will do next in your teaching?*
- *What are some steps we can take as a school to change ____?*
- *Based on what you have learned, talk about what you see as next steps.*
- *What will you do to get the information you are missing?*
- *What professional learning sessions or materials might help?*
- *What data will you need to collect to monitor your progress toward these goals?*
- *How will you know you are reaching your goals?*

Figure 19-7

A Protocol for Data Conversations

ONLINE RESOURCE 19.1

To guide an effective data conversation, consider using the protocol tool we provide (Figure 19-8; you will find a full-size Protocol Tool: Data Conversations as **OR 19.1** in the Online Resources). There is no need to think about the process as rigid, but the description in the protocol has important reminders for how to stay focused on noticing what the data shows, interpreting what it means, thinking about what is missing, and determining what to do with what you learn. We recommend printing out the tool and keeping it handy in your coaching notebook (Chapter 23) because, as you now know, data conversations are woven into almost every aspect of the professional learning you offer your colleagues.

The Ultimate Goal of Data Conversations

There's no doubt that using data to analyze students' progress is important. But that can't be the sole purpose. It's also important to use data to improve the effectiveness of teaching in the school so that every child can become a skilled language user and a highly literate person. If data does not result in improved teaching, then its value is greatly diminished. Effective assessment allows school leaders and teachers to see the results of instruction and to make valid judgments about what students have learned how to do as readers and writers, what they need to learn how to do next, and what teaching moves will support them.

Effective assessment allows school leaders and teachers to **see the results of instruction . . .**

One of the most important purposes of data conversations is to help teachers continue to build a set of understandings out of which their teaching actions flow and against which they can evaluate their decisions. If assessment is authentic and yields data that documents student learning, then it offers a window on the effects of the most important factors in a high-quality literacy program—the curriculum and the teaching. Analyzing assessment data in the way we have described raises the professional proficiency of the individuals involved.

As a leader of professional learning, help teachers learn to use a laser-like focus to understand, interpret, critically evaluate, and effectively communicate the data—all in the service of informing instruction and driving actions in the classroom.

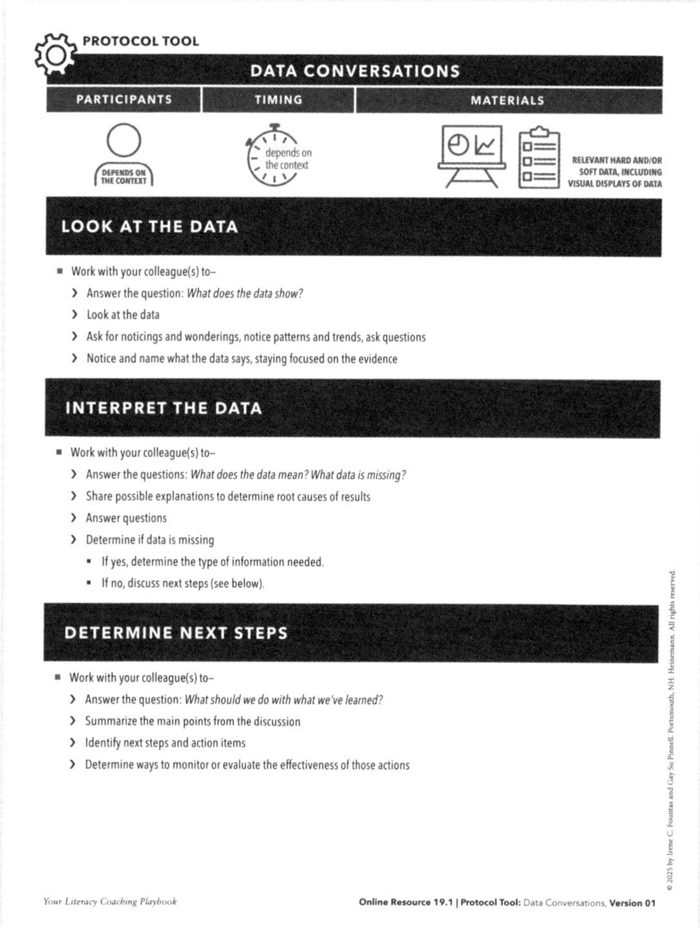
PROTOCOL TOOL

DATA CONVERSATIONS

PARTICIPANTS	TIMING	MATERIALS
DEPENDS ON THE CONTEXT	depends on the context	RELEVANT HARD AND/OR SOFT DATA, INCLUDING VISUAL DISPLAYS OF DATA

LOOK AT THE DATA

- Work with your colleague(s) to–
  - Answer the question: *What does the data show?*
  - Look at the data
  - Ask for noticings and wonderings, notice patterns and trends, ask questions
  - Notice and name what the data says, staying focused on the evidence

INTERPRET THE DATA

- Work with your colleague(s) to–
  - Answer the questions: *What does the data mean? What data is missing?*
  - Share possible explanations to determine root causes of results
  - Answer questions
  - Determine if data is missing
    - If yes, determine the type of information needed.
    - If no, discuss next steps (see below).

DETERMINE NEXT STEPS

- Work with your colleague(s) to–
  - Answer the question: *What should we do with what we've learned?*
  - Summarize the main points from the discussion
  - Identify next steps and action items
  - Determine ways to monitor or evaluate the effectiveness of those actions

Your Literacy Coaching Playbook **Online Resource 19.1 | Protocol Tool:** Data Conversations, **Version 01**

Figure 19-8

Up **Next**

If you're suffering from meeting fatigue—we're talking about meetings you attend and those you lead—Chapter 20 will put a spring in your step. It's a grab bag of tips and advice on how to say goodbye to boredom and make every meeting count.

Chapter 20

The Play: **Break-the-Mold Meetings**

We're pretty sure that in all of recorded history, no one has ever said, "I wish we had more meetings!" Yet, meetings are an inescapable fact of life in most institutions, whether you're talking about a corporation, an agency, or a school, because people simply have to collaborate to make things happen. As a literacy coach, you probably spend more time in meetings than you ever thought you would. But what if they were more purposeful and efficient, less frequent, better planned, and designed to promote active engagement? What if most of the meetings you regularly attend actually worked for you and everyone else in the room?

It's easy to think of meetings as just an add-on to your job, but actually they are an essential part of your coaching role. You are indeed coaching when you attend any one of the many meetings in your already-packed schedule. No doubt, you ask probing questions, share helpful resources to help people think more deeply about an issue at hand, and provide your own unique perspective on what's working in the school and what isn't.

And yet, you *do* spend a lot of time in those meetings, and we know you'd like them to pay off. So don't wait for someone else to take the lead on meeting reform. It's well within your purview to engage school leaders in the important work of improving the quality of meetings for all. In this chapter, you'll learn how to turn the page on "boring" and conduct meetings that break the mold.

Not Every Meeting Needs to Be a Meeting

Have you ever found yourself wondering why the meeting you're sitting through couldn't have been an email instead? Or just a quick huddle in the hallway? Before you put another meeting on your schedule or anybody else's, briefly jot down your goals and ask yourself if there's a better, more efficient way to achieve them.

Reserve the typical meeting format for those topics that truly require live interaction, are time sensitive, or contain content that you know will require more than just a simple explanation to understand. Here are some suggestions for alternative meeting formats you might want to try:

Meetings You Might Attend or Facilitate

In each of the meetings below, you may act as the organizer, facilitator, note-taker, or simply a participant.

- Grade-level team meetings (professional learning communities)
- Data meetings
- Child-study team meetings
- Literacy team meetings
- Multilingual learner team meetings
- Digital team meetings
- Equity/inclusion team meetings

Email: If you typically schedule meetings to provide information or updates on previously discussed topics, consider using email instead. It's much more efficient, and if you are going to ask for comments or input, the conversation thread can serve as notes.

Shared Documents: When you share editable documents with the team, you invite a powerful type of online collaboration. For example, if you'd like teacher input on a report, proposal, or any other kind of document (except those containing personal information about a student, a teacher, or an administrator), emailing a link to a shared file enables participants to review and add comments to the document at their convenience, including at home. We've found that teachers' responses tend to be more thoughtful when they are not distracted by the clamor of the classroom. You might follow up with a meeting to discuss the responses, but you might just find that the shared document and the teachers' notes are enough.

Prerecorded Video Updates: For some presentations or updates that don't require live interaction, a recorded video distributed via text or email might be a better bet. This way, participants can watch it at home or at a more convenient time, pause as needed, and rewatch parts they found confusing. Don't use this format for content that might be upsetting to some people or contains even a hint of controversy.

Group Chat Threads: You probably already have a few group chats on your phone, but do you use them for coaching too? If not, it's easy to start. You'll probably want more than one group, such as the data team, the specialists in the building, or the equity/inclusion team. Launch each group with an introductory message, and let people know they will own the chat and can use it to discuss issues related to their particular team(s). Do check in from time to time so they know you are an active participant, but let the teams do most of the chatting. You'll be surprised by the number of meetings you can shorten or eliminate completely when team members are in regular touch online.

Stand-Up Meetings: In the world of software product development, agile methodology rules the roost. One very effective element of this methodology is the daily stand-up meeting in which all participants, who are able, stand to encourage brevity and focus. The meetings are as short as possible—rarely more than 15 minutes in length. Although the agile daily stand-up is most often used for status meetings, you can use the stand-up model for any meeting that has the potential to run longer than needed or for quick check-ins with teams engaged in school-wide projects. Of course, there will always be times when meetings require an hour or more but consider using stand-up meetings once in a while as a break from the usual.

Plan and Prepare for Meetings

Clear communication is essential in planning and preparing for effective meetings. If you are organizing a meeting, make sure to send reminders to participants at least one week ahead with the date, time, location, and anything they need to bring. It is also helpful to include a brief agenda with a time frame for each topic so participants come prepared to discuss the proposed issues. Send any materials ahead that you would like participants to read or analyze before the meeting.

You Don't Have to Invite Everyone

What's the best group size for a typical meeting? That depends on who really needs to be there. We know you want to be as inclusive as possible, but sometimes inviting people who don't know why they've been asked to join a particular meeting can do more harm than good. It may signal that you don't truly understand people's unique strengths or interests, and that's not helpful.

Be Realistic About the Agenda

We all tend to misjudge how much time it actually takes to discuss agenda items. Especially early in the year when attendees are likely to have more questions. Do your best to limit the agenda to no more than two or three items, depending on their complexity. Then run the check we hope will become a habit: scan the agenda to identify items that don't require live interaction and consider discussing them in a different format, such as email or newsletter. If you think your agenda might be too long, it probably is.

ONLINE RESOURCE 20.1

To keep track of agenda items, consider using Note-Taking Tool: Meeting Notes, which provides space for note-taking and connects the agenda item/topic to an outcome and action plan. Figure 20–1 shows an example of a filled-in template. (You will find a blank, full-size Note-Taking Tool: Meeting Notes as **OR 20.1** in the Online Resources.) Before the meeting, send the agenda to participants with just the first two columns completed. Notice how the facilitator then uses the template as a working document for the course of the meeting.

Break-the-Mold Meetings: What to Say and Do

As the organizer of a meeting, you can decide whether to serve as the facilitator for the meeting yourself or to select a colleague to lead as facilitator. The facilitator leads the team through the agenda and helps them come to consensus on the meeting's outcomes and action items. Consider the following suggestions for what to say and do to keep meetings time-efficient, productive, and action-driven.

Frame Your Meetings

The exact frame you apply to each meeting you host will depend on the topic and what you plan to do. But a few simple guardrails can't hurt. Think in terms of an *introduction*, a *discussion of the agenda items*, and a *summary of action plans*. These three categories are broad enough to suit a variety of meeting topics but not so broad that you'll feel confined by a structure that might not work every time.

NOTE-TAKING TOOL

MEETING NOTES

Date: 10/6
Facilitator: Ms. DiGregorio
Note-taker: Mr. Kimball
Attendees: Mr. O'Leary, Ms. Thomas, Mr. Rodriguez, Ms. Ryan, Mr. Vijek
Meeting: Literacy Leadership Team Meeting

AGENDA/ACTION ITEMS

TOPIC/TIME	PURPOSE/GOAL	ACTION STEPS WITH TIMELINE	PERSON(S) RESPONSIBLE
Status check (10 min.)	Follow-up on action items from last meeting	No action needed. All actions completed from last meeting.	Facilitator
Writing assessment will be held on Nov. 15 (15 min.)	Discuss what prompt and rubric we will use	Next meeting—review prompt and rubric	Ms. Thomas
Professional learning session—Oct. 15 (10 min.)	Determine focus based on teacher feedback received via surveys and from recent learning walk	Focus will be interactive writing. Send reminder and what to bring—one example of interactive writing by Oct. 10	Ms. Thomas
Classroom library ordering (20 min.)	Decide a process for ordering new books for classroom libraries	Complete first inventory of grades K–1 by Dec. 1 Find out budget for libraries by Dec. 1	Mr. O'Leary and Ms. Ryan Ms. Thomas

Notes:

Writing Assessment personal narrative; rubric needs updating

Interactive Writing still needs more support—make it the focus of Oct. 15 PLS

Before ordering more books, need to inventory our classroom libraries. What is the budget for classroom libraries? How diverse are our libraries?

Your Literacy Coaching Playbook **Online Resource 20.1 | Note-Taking Tool:** Meeting Notes, **Version 01**

Figure 20-1

And, if action items were assigned at the last meeting, ask for status updates before jumping into new agenda items.

Start and Stop on Time Every Time

We know you've been in at least a few meetings where the facilitator runs out of time at the end but continues to move through the agenda while participants squirm in their seats. That's always a mistake. Your colleagues will view meetings that consistently run over as a sign that you don't respect their time or their other responsibilities in the school and at home. The same goes for facilitators who show up late or wait until everyone is there. If meetings habitually start ten to fifteen minutes late, then that's when most people will start to show up. Both fixes are easy: If you're running a meeting, be there early. If you don't get through the whole agenda, park items that weren't discussed on a list of items for the next meeting, and let your colleagues get on with their busy lives.

Model Appropriate Meeting Behavior

Whether or not you're aware of it, as a leader of professional learning in your school you are always acting as a role model. When you facilitate meetings, model the behaviors you'd like to see in all participants:

- Maintain an inquiring stance.
- Show respect for diverse opinions and points of view.
- Communicate to everyone in the room that their voices will be acknowledged and heard.
- Come prepared to keep the team engaged.
- Use respectful language at all times.
- Stay focused on the agenda topics.
- When disagreements arise, notice when things are getting heated and call for a few minutes of quiet reflection. Then calmly resume the conversation in a neutral tone.

Maintain Focus

Nothing eats up time more than a person who tends to digress. If you think the conversation is about to go off the rails or already has, you owe it to your colleagues to get back on track quickly. Remember this: every minute spent off topic is a minute of meeting time lost. Don't embarrass the person or call undue attention to the behavior, but do use language such as the following examples.

Sample Language

- *I can see this topic is important to you, so I'll park it in my notes for further discussion at a different meeting.*
- *That's a really good topic. Let's definitely talk about it at our next meeting or the one after. Now, as we were saying . . . .*
- *I want to be respectful of your time, so can we get back to the topic and put that in a parking lot for later.*

Occasionally Use Turn and Talks or Small Breakout Groups

You know how well turn and talk works for students, but do you also use it in your meetings? Especially if problem-solving is on your agenda, giving room for participants to collaborate on solutions or simply to help each other better understand the problem can keep everyone engaged and centered on a topic. Even if your goal is not problem related, turn and talks or breakout groups can re-energize the group when you feel attention beginning to lag. Turn and talk creates a safe structure in which all meeting participants can express their views. This technique has been found to encourage higher participation and engagement in a topic. You can distribute or project prepared prompts if you think they might be needed.

Use Visuals for the Right Reasons

Visuals for the sake of visuals are almost always a bad idea. But do use visuals frequently to synthesize complex data or represent ideas that are easier to communicate graphically. And if a graphic contains text, resist the urge to read from it. Instead, ask participants to read the information themselves so they can process it in their own way.

No Whining, No Complaining

We've all been in a meeting that at some point devolves into a complaint session instead of a working session. Sometimes people legitimately do need time to vent on a specific issue that surfaces in a meeting, so you might not be able to avoid complaining altogether. But assigning a note-taker and a timekeeper can go a long way toward keeping people focused on the desired outcomes of the meeting. So can language like the following.

Sample Language

- *Timekeeper, how much time do we have remaining? Let's use those few minutes to discuss ____.*
- *I can see how upset you are about this, but I can better help you if we meet privately. Can you and I set up a time to talk further about this?*
- *You are bringing up an important issue that needs to be addressed at a different time.*
- *I've captured the issue in my notes, so let's now shift our focus back to where we were in our earlier discussion.*
- *Let's return to our original purpose now because we're almost out of time.*

Above all, remain positive. Do what you can to acknowledge and understand complaints and to visit with those concerned teachers privately. As much as you can, help them resolve their issues without compromising the mission of the school.

Turn Talk into Action

The key to a productive meeting is moving from meaningful discussion to realistic actions. One way to facilitate this process is to pose questions that focus the discussion on action (Figure 20–2). The prompting language you use varies depending on the type of meeting you are facilitating. In Figure 20–3, we offer examples of prompts that lead to action across different types of meetings in addition to examples of action items that might develop from these discussions.

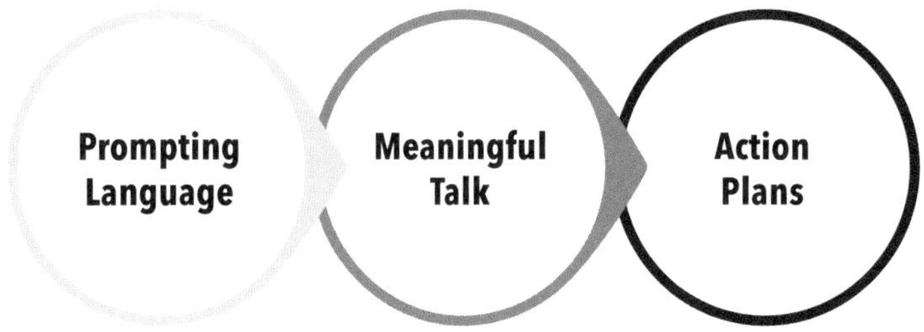

Figure 20-2

MOVE DISCUSSION INTO ACTION

Meeting Type	Prompts	Action Items
Grade-Level Meetings	▪ *How can you work together as a team to improve ____ in your teaching?* ▪ *What effective practices are your colleagues using that you can incorporate into your own teaching and learning experiences?* ▪ *How can I (coach) help you learn more about using ____ in your teaching?* ▪ *What steps might your team take to address (insert a problem of practice)?*	▪ Plan a cluster coaching session around the topic. ▪ Organize peer coaching sessions. ▪ Co-facilitate a professional book club on a topic the grade-level teachers are interested in learning more about. ▪ Visit a lab classroom to watch a lesson on ____. ▪ Plan to co-facilitate a study group to address a problem of practice.
Data Meeting	▪ *In what ways is classroom instruction producing positive learning outcomes for all students? What can we do to promote this?* ▪ *What would be our highest priority action?* ▪ *What can we all do in the short term (long term)?* ▪ *How can we change the status quo?* ▪ *What would we need to do to address those outcomes?* ▪ *Are there disparities in the academic achievement of subgroups of students, and if so, what actions are required to ensure that all children are academically successful?* ▪ *What factors are contributing to the success of high-achieving students, and what can we learn from this to help every child?* ▪ *What patterns do you see in the data?* See Chapter 19 for more information on guiding data conversations.	▪ Plan professional learning sessions that focus on the types of instruction that are producing positive outcomes so all teachers can implement this type of instruction. ▪ Plan a learning walk to look at different ways teachers are allowing students to show their learning. ▪ Plan a classroom environment walk to look at the ways students' identities are being valued in the classroom. ▪ Form a study group to research solutions for achievement disparities.
Child-Study Team Meeting	▪ *What does the evidence show about the student's learning?* ▪ *How can instruction be modified to meet the student's needs?* ▪ *What is needed for further monitoring or intervention?* ▪ *How can we build on these strengths to address the student's needs?* ▪ *What is in the way of the student's success and what can we do about it?*	▪ Create a group with the classroom teacher that reviews the student's work to determine specific strengths and next steps. ▪ Identify assessments that will help further define the problem. ▪ Observe the student so you can think together with the teacher about solutions.

Meeting Type	Prompts	Action Items
Literacy Team Meetings	▪ *Within the school, what practices of effective literacy teaching and learning need to be supported and amplified?* ▪ *What practices of effective literacy teaching and learning do teachers need to begin to take on?* ▪ *What types of school-wide literacy assessments might we want to put into place at regular intervals to inform our practice?*	▪ Plan professional learning sessions followed by coaching for identified instructional contexts. ▪ Ask the data team to look at strengths and challenges in literacy data to determine what literacy teaching should be prioritized. ▪ Implement a writing assessment three times a year and benchmark assessments twice a year.
Multilingual Learners Team Meetings	▪ *What are effective practices for teaching multilingual learners? Which practices are already present in classrooms and need to be supported? Which practices are not yet present and need to be introduced?* ▪ *How can we increase culturally responsive teaching practices that support and honor the languages and cultures of the multilingual students in our school?*	▪ Plan a learning walk to explore the instructional practices already present. ▪ Offer a professional book club focused on culturally responsive teaching. ▪ Create a study group focused on research about culturally responsible teaching. ▪ Investigate ways to form deeper relationships with families.
Digital Team Meetings	▪ *In what ways are we using technology with students to enhance literacy learning?* ▪ *In what ways are we using technology that might be negatively impacting students?* ▪ *What more do we need to learn about using technology–potential and pitfalls–in the classroom?* ▪ *How can we learn to use new technology effectively?*	▪ Ask teachers to begin looking at the balance of time students spend listening to reading on devices vs. reading independently. ▪ Organize a learning walk, focusing on the use of technology during the literacy block. ▪ Create a study group on using technology (including artificial intelligence) with students and have the group report to the whole team.
Equity/Inclusion Team Meetings	▪ *What are systemic inequities that exist in our school?* ▪ *What actions can we take to interrupt the inequities?* ▪ *What subgroups are not achieving excellent outcomes?* ▪ *How well are all of our students represented in the texts used in our literacy curriculum?*	▪ Select three seminal articles on equity and jigsaw-read them at a staff meeting. Then set goals. ▪ Create a monitoring plan for subgroups of students.

Figure 20-3

Summarize Action Plans

Close the meeting with a summary of the action plans, making sure to review or assign who will be responsible for each item. Be sure to assign a time frame for the completion of each action item. As shown in Figure 20–1 (p. 195), work is accomplished between meetings so that initiatives keep moving forward. Spend the last few minutes of the meeting soliciting feedback on the meeting. Ask for suggestions for increased efficiency and productivity, and work together to modify anything that would improve the next meeting. If needed, set the date, time, and location for the next meeting.

ONLINE RESOURCE 20.2

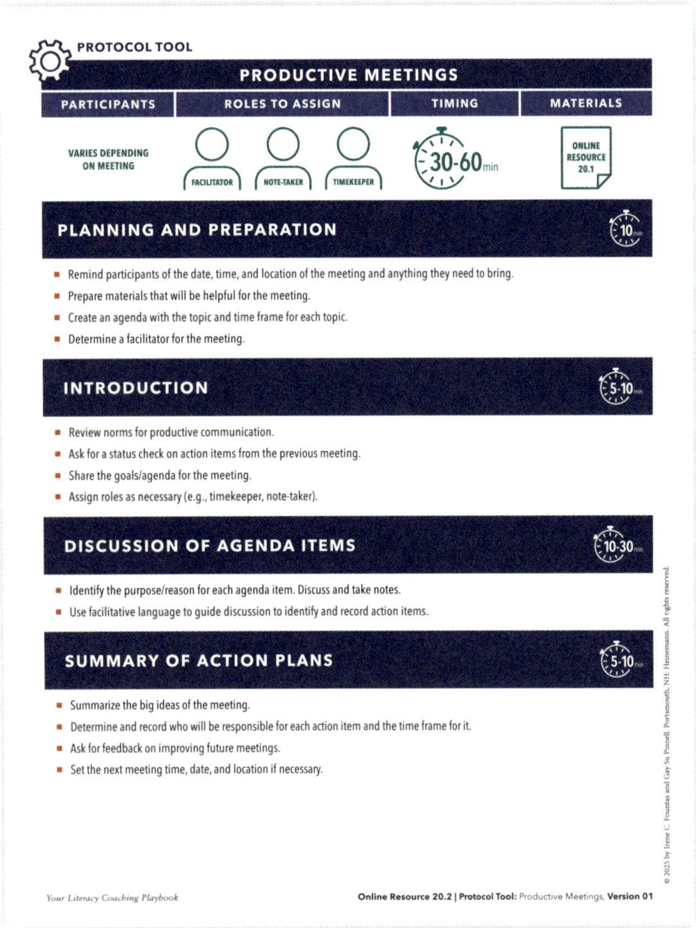

PROTOCOL TOOL

PRODUCTIVE MEETINGS

PARTICIPANTS	ROLES TO ASSIGN	TIMING	MATERIALS
VARIES DEPENDING ON MEETING	FACILITATOR, NOTE-TAKER, TIMEKEEPER	30-60 min	ONLINE RESOURCE 20.1

PLANNING AND PREPARATION — 10 min

- Remind participants of the date, time, and location of the meeting and anything they need to bring.
- Prepare materials that will be helpful for the meeting.
- Create an agenda with the topic and time frame for each topic.
- Determine a facilitator for the meeting.

INTRODUCTION — 5-10 min

- Review norms for productive communication.
- Ask for a status check on action items from the previous meeting.
- Share the goals/agenda for the meeting.
- Assign roles as necessary (e.g., timekeeper, note-taker).

DISCUSSION OF AGENDA ITEMS — 10-30 min

- Identify the purpose/reason for each agenda item. Discuss and take notes.
- Use facilitative language to guide discussion to identify and record action items.

SUMMARY OF ACTION PLANS — 5-10 min

- Summarize the big ideas of the meeting.
- Determine and record who will be responsible for each action item and the time frame for it.
- Ask for feedback on improving future meetings.
- Set the next meeting time, date, and location if necessary.

Your Literacy Coaching Playbook — **Online Resource 20.2 | Protocol Tool:** Productive Meetings, **Version 01**

Figure 20–4

Your role in these meetings is an important one. As the coach, you have a unique perspective and likely a broad view of what happens across classrooms. Value what you bring to meetings and the time you spend in them. Your participation helps you build the collaborative culture that impacts all other professional learning. Indeed, break-the-mold meetings are a play in your playbook not only because they often result in professional learning plans but because the meetings themselves are filled with opportunities for you to support teacher growth as well as impact decisions that ultimately affect student outcomes.

A Protocol Tool for Productive Meetings

Use the Protocol Tool: Productive Meetings (Figure 20–4) to guide meetings. (You will find a full-size version as **OR 20.2** in the Online Resources.) There is no need to think about the process as rigid, but the description in the protocol has important reminders for how to break the mold and produce results in your meetings. We recommend printing it out and keeping it handy in your coaching notebook (Chapter 23).

Up **Next**

Think you can't really accomplish much in ten to thirty minutes? Well, think again. In the next chapter, we introduce you to coaching on the run, a powerful way to put brief pockets of time to work for you and the teachers you serve.

Chapter 21

The Play: **Coaching on the Run**

"There's just not enough time."

That's a common refrain among instructional coaches. You've probably said it, too, as you've come to the realization that many of your colleagues need more one-on-one time than you have to give. We get it. But although you can't do everything you'd like to do, you probably can provide more support than you think in the multiple, short interactions you have "on the run" with colleagues. In this chapter, we encourage you to value the support you give to colleagues in spontaneous conversations across the day.

What Is Coaching on the Run?

We use the term "coaching on the run" to describe the many in-the-moment, informal interactions you have with colleagues in the nooks and crannies of a given school day. With not a minute to lose, coaching on the run allows for short, spontaneous professional conversations that engage you and your colleagues in brief moments of productive thinking about teaching and learning.

From answering a quick question about a book recommendation as you walk down the corridor to the few minutes spent discussing an assessment question in the faculty room at lunch, you respond in ways that position yourself as a generous and ever-available colleague. Through your quick responses, you can make your presence felt throughout the day, the week, and across the year.

BENEFITS OF COACHING ON THE RUN

- Supports professional learning across the school day anytime, anywhere
- Increases the coach's visibility in the school
- Expands the teacher's access to the coach
- Provides quick, efficient responses to teachers
- Builds individual relationships
- Promotes shared problem-solving

Why It Works

A while ago, we were members of a research team conducting a large-scale study on the effects of coaching. At the beginning of the year, coaching began for teachers in eighteen schools in a variety of states. We asked the same single question at the beginning and the end of the year in every participating school: "With whom do you talk about literacy teaching and learning in your school?" At the beginning of the year, data revealed clear silos. Teachers said they sometimes spoke only with other teachers at their own grade level or with just one friend. By the end of the year, the coach was the center of professional talk, and colleagues were all talking with each other—within and across grade levels. And that happened in every school.

When you consistently respond to questions or suggestions with real interest, teachers will begin to seek you out as their thought partner and then do the same with other colleagues. Every short interaction shows your colleagues that you value their thinking, that you work as a team, and that you believe in their competence and good intentions. It demonstrates that you value collective expertise.

> ### *Be Genuinely Curious*
>
> These on-the-run interactions must be real, not contrived, and signal a genuine interest in what is happening in the classroom. You don't want to sound like someone who has only one agenda because you don't want teachers to think, "She only wants to talk with me when she wants to teach me something!" Be a real person, and your colleagues will not only look forward to talking with you but will begin to seek you out.

When you respond to a teacher's question, you have the opportunity to model problem-solving, tentativeness, and the importance of rationales instead of single right answers. Be careful, though, not to get into the advice trap—positioning yourself as the expert with all the answers—because your colleagues will get in the habit of seeking advice instead of seeking a thought partner. Having said that, there will be times when you should just answer the question in a straightforward way.

There is no framework for coaching on the run. Coaching on the run can take place just about anywhere at any time of day. Following is a list of common situations in which you can naturally provide coaching support:

- Stop by a classroom and deliver a children's book that might be appropriate for a writing lesson the teacher is planning.
- Respond to a question about administering an assessment as you encounter a teacher in the corridor.

- Talk over coffee about some writing that students have done.
- Stop by a classroom and talk with a few students during independent reading (later sharing with the classroom teacher what you noticed about the readers' interests or skills).
- Ask a teacher if you can share with grade-level colleagues something you observed in the teacher's classroom that might help others.
- Make a lunch date to discuss a particular student, and volunteer to come and observe later.
- Look at a few books together in the school book room to select one for a lesson.

Throughout this book, we emphasize how your choice of words conveys your stance as a coach and shapes the teacher's self-concept as a problem solver. Coaching on the run responses are no different (Figure 21–1). They are honest, reveal the coach's willingness to learn alongside colleagues, and show the coach's interest in how colleagues are doing with their teaching. The responses have an informal, conversational tone. They are social, even inviting a chat over lunch or coffee. In almost all these examples, the coach empowers the teacher by recognizing the value of the question: "What an important question," "Would you mind sharing that example at our next meeting?" The responses also invite the teacher to be part of the problem-solving process.

Sample Language

- *What an important question.*
- *What were your first thoughts about that?*
- *You were asking about ____. I haven't thought about that, but let's put our heads together and think it through.*
- *I don't really know. I need to think about that, and I will get back to you.*

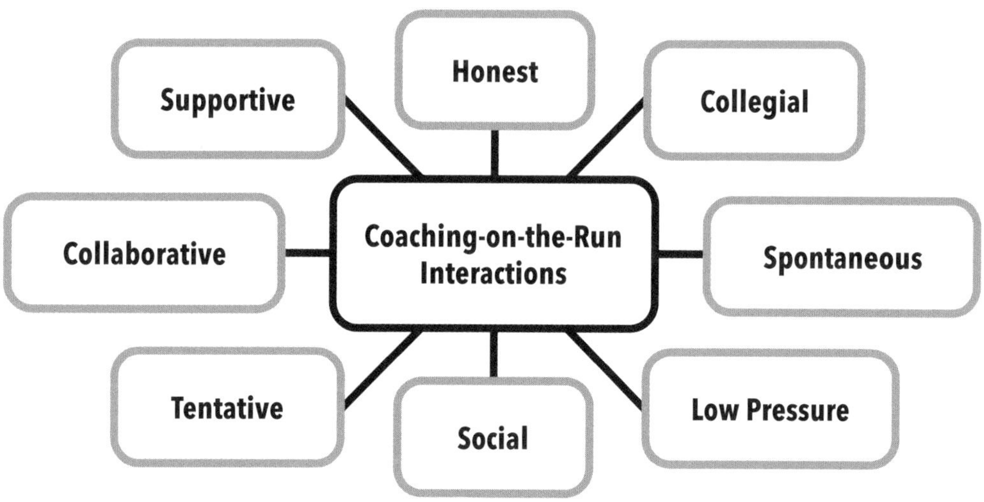

Figure 21-1

- *I will bring my copy of ____, and let's see if we can find something to help us think about that.*
- *We are both wondering about the same thing. Let's sit together at lunch and think about that.*
- *I'm eager to find out how the plan we made is going. How about a chat over coffee?*
- *Would you mind sharing that example at our next meeting? I think others would enjoy discussing it and will learn from the experience.*

Coaching on the Run: What to Say and Do

Every conversation depends on previous conversations. Trust and interdependence build across the time you spend with colleagues in the school. Let's look at a few interactions that illustrate the kind of quick, genuine collaboration and support of teacher learning we expect in coaching on the run.

Example 1: An incidental meeting in the hallway between a coach and third-grade teacher.

Teacher: *I'm glad I ran into you. I'm having trouble getting my guided reading groups up and running.*

Coach: *What do you think is getting in the way?*

Teacher: *I finished assessing all my students, but they are all over the place with their reading levels. I can't figure out how to group them, but I know I need about four groups.*

Coach: *If you want, I could meet with you sometime when you're free, and we could look at your student assessment data together to see if we can come up with some tentative reading groups for you to begin with.*

Teacher: *I'd like that. I don't really feel confident doing that on my own. I want to make sure I get the groups right.*

Coach: *Well, the good news is that we can group the students to get you started, and then if you see that a student is not in the appropriate group, you can always move students around. Groupings are always temporary, and since students will progress differently from each other, you will be moving them as needed.*

Notice in this example that from the start the coach has shown an openness and a willingness to answer questions and enter conversations about anything that provides a challenge. The coach doesn't expect to have the "right" answer quickly. Even with knowledge of the teacher and some of the students in a classroom, the coach doesn't make assumptions or give a pat answer, understanding that more information is needed to form a response. The coach needs to seek the teacher's perspective and do some direct observation. But the teacher's behavior is a great start because the coach has been invited into the classroom for some collaborative work.

Example 2: A special education teacher stops by the coach's room before school.

Teacher: *I'm concerned about one of my students, Kyle. I pull him out of his classroom every day for a small-group specialized reading support, and he does well when he reads with me. However, his classroom teacher doesn't see the same thing from him. She says he is always distracted and doesn't get his work done, and she never sees him reading during independent reading time.*

Coach: *What do you think might be getting in his way in the classroom?*

Teacher: *Well, I do know that he is distracted, but I'm not sure why he won't do any reading in the classroom. I always give him some books that he can read and are on topics he says interest him, but he won't read them in the classroom.*

Coach: *I think it might be good for you, me, and his classroom teacher to sit down and problem-solve together. It sounds like getting Kyle to read in the classroom is your top priority. Why don't I observe Kyle in both settings in the next couple of days, and then the three of us can get together to see what strategies we can come up with to help Kyle be more engaged with reading in his classroom. What do you think about that?*

Teacher: *It's a good idea, I really want him to succeed.*

In this example, too, the coach's first step is to get more information. But the coach also takes concrete action by telling the teacher exactly what the next step will be and, following that, how teamwork will be fostered between the specialist and classroom teacher. The coach's actions confirm the value of collaboration, and the coach's final question confirms that the teacher is making the choice out of caring and concern for the student.

Example 3: A two-minute conversation over coffee in the staff room before school.

Teacher: *I hope I'm going to get everything in during the writers' workshop today. I can't always finish in the time I have.*

Coach: *Can you think back to what seems to eat up the time?*

Teacher: *Well, after the writing lesson, my students just can't seem to settle down to writing quickly. They roam around trying to get their notebooks and writing folders. It seems like by the time they have all their materials and sit down to write, it's time for the group share.*

Coach: *What do you think is preventing them from getting their materials quickly and settling down to write?*

Teacher: *Well, they crowd each other around the writing folders and the shelf where their notebooks are.*

Coach: *Where are the writing folders and notebooks?*

Teacher: *They're in a file box in the front of the room, and the shelf for notebooks is next to it.*

Coach: *Have you thought about having more than one box and placing the folders and notebooks in several places in the room, such as the four corners?*

Teacher: *Good idea. Then the students wouldn't all be crowded in one place and taking so much time.*

Coach: *If you'd like, I can come into your classroom before or after school, and we can take a quick look at the space together.*

Teacher: *Thanks. That would be helpful if that works for you. I know Sarah has had the same issue, so I will invite her to join us.*

Here, the coach confirms the teacher's own analysis of the root problem and offers concrete help. It's also clear that teachers in the school do not hesitate to invite others to collaborate with them in solving problems.

Example 4: After school in a teacher's classroom.

Coach: *I'm just dropping by to give you the book we talked about yesterday. I think your students will really enjoy it. It would also be a good mentor text for teaching how a writer uses metaphor.*

Teacher: *Thanks for this. I've taught a couple of lessons introducing figurative language with some mentor texts, and most of the students seemed to understand and use simile in their writing more easily than metaphor. They seem to understand what a metaphor is, but a few of them have trouble using it in their writing.*

Coach: *That's not really surprising since the art of metaphor is more difficult to master and often hard to sustain in a piece of writing. So how are you thinking you will support those few students so they can achieve that important understanding?*

Teacher: *I do need to think about that. Maybe I'll pull together that small group so they can talk together and discuss whether a metaphor could be appropriate in enhancing their writing.*

Coach: *That's a good idea because there is no point addressing it with all students again.*

Teacher: *I am going to do that. What would you think about my pairing each of them with a peer who has used metaphors successfully? That student could start by reading their writing. Then the partner could read their writing, and they could talk together about when and where a metaphor might enhance the writing.*

Coach: *This sounds like you are really thinking about how to get the writers thinking together and supporting each other. I think when everyone in the class knows each other's writing, it has a big impact on creating a culture of writers in the classroom.*

Once again, you see a coach who radiates confidence in their own thinking and that of their colleagues. The coach does not pretend to be the only one with expertise or to have all the answers, instead acting as a thought partner to colleagues, whether it is in a professional learning session, a coaching session, or a brief conversation in the corridor.

We encourage you to think about facilitating the growth of teachers as your mindset even if your situation affords precious little scheduled time with colleagues. Maximize the opportunities through capturing small moments for big impact. Your presence in the school can be a lever of support all day long.

Up **Next**

This chapter closes out Part 2. Having learned about selecting the type of coaching that best fits your colleagues' needs, you will want to know how to sustain your success as a coach by learning about managing your time and organizing your tasks. Part 3 offers you that information plus how to handle challenges and how to be the coach you want to be. The best part? Our advice is practical and easy to implement right away.

PART 3

Sustain **Success**

Plan your plays

Build your toolbox

Be the coach you want to be

Chapter 22

Plan for the **Time You Have**

Each of the fourteen plays in this playbook is unique in one way or another. That's by design because we know you'll want to provide a wide variety of ways for teachers to build their expertise. But the impact of the individual plays will rest on your ability to stitch them together in a coherent way across weeks and months and the entire school year. The goal is to provide an assortment of learning opportunities that build on one another so professional learning becomes a continuous process. This chapter will help you do that.

First, keep in mind that although we advocate for planning in this chapter, we envision a mostly tentative plan. Sure, there will be some sessions that can—or need—to be scheduled far ahead of time. But remember that your role as a coach is to respond to the developing needs of your colleagues and as shown by the data that informs your decisions. That can't happen if you're bound by a rigid plan. Having said all that, we begin with a look at how you might gain a broad view of your professional learning goals and the offerings that will help you address them.

Start with Your Long Game

First, sketch out a rough plan for the kinds of opportunities you might include in a year of professional learning and approximately how often each might occur. Of course, each year, your plan will look different as teachers grow in expertise. Try to talk with each grade level to determine what they have experienced in their teaching. Help some teachers set up their classrooms and let them talk about their plans. Then, list what you think are necessary first steps and create a timetable. But don't get lost in the weeds with a fully detailed plan that you are determined to stick to. For now, your objective is simply to create a shape for the year. We provide one example of how you might do this (Figure 22-1). Of course, you don't actually

Figure 22-1

need to draw anything unless doing so would help you envision your ideas. Again, these are only examples and not meant to be interpreted as guidelines. Every coach's situation is different.

Construct a Tentative Plan

We hope you now have a better sense of what a year of professional learning might look like in your school. Now it's time to have a long talk with your calendar.

Work with the Time You Have

Time is a constant problem for most coaches because there's never enough of it, especially if your role as leader of professional learning is an add-on to your role as a classroom teacher. Our message to you is simple: You may not have time to do *all* that you envision, but you can always do *something*.

Yearly Planning: A Brief Case Study

One coach we know starts the year by working with the principal to slot the ninety-minute professional learning sessions (PLS) and curriculum days scheduled by their district on a blank calendar. The coach and principal also pencil in one-on-one coaching sessions. We say "pencil" because it's likely that plans will change according to teachers' schedules. They also decide to schedule quarterly lesson studies ahead of time because teachers have found lesson study to be very helpful in creating a spirit of collaboration within the grade-level teams. However, they leave the lesson study topics open for teacher input based on the needs at the time.

You may not have time to do ***all*** that you envision, but you can always do ***something***.

Across the year, the coach uses different structures depending on the needs and interests that surface. For example, one year, this coach and his colleagues were taking a deep dive into learning about interactive writing. He had conducted two professional learning sessions on the topic and followed them up with one-on-one coaching and a visit to the lab classroom, where a teacher demonstrated an interactive writing lesson. His colleagues felt they needed continued support, so they decided to choose a professional book on the topic and held an afterschool professional book club for those who were interested. He also planned a learning walk through several classrooms to observe how interactive writing was being used to reinforce phonics skills. Lastly, he coordinated peer coaching sessions so pairs of teachers could support one another as they tried out their new learning. The scheduled lesson study for the quarter was dedicated to interactive writing.

Our colleague could not have anticipated the need to plan all these rich professional learning experiences at the start of the school year. However, some key planning with his principal at the beginning of the year (i.e., dedicated time for professional learning sessions, lesson study, and one-on-one coaching) provided the structure, time, and flexibility needed to meet the teachers' needs.

No Time Left Behind

You can't make time, but you can use it wisely. It's easy to get overwhelmed, so step back and reflect on your priorities.

- Begin by documenting how you currently use your professional learning time so you and your colleagues can reflect on how to use time wisely going forward.
- Place a high value on the range of formal and informal, short and longer professional learning opportunities you provide. If your plan is varied and flexible, teachers will likely be more flexible about their time.
- Prioritize your school's most urgent goals and the students' greatest needs.
- As often as possible, embed professional learning in the school day so your colleagues will have easier access.
- Leverage video for possible asynchronous opportunities. This makes it very convenient for your colleagues–but emphasize that there is no substitute for in-person learning.
- Enlist the support of your colleagues to advocate for more professional learning time.

Strong Start, Strong Finish

Now let's look at Figure 22-2, which represents some of the ways we have seen various instructional coaches start and finish the school year. We have found commonalities in the ideas and practices across schools for getting professional learning off the ground and ending it with positive energy and anticipation for continued professional growth. Of course, your setup and the structures you plan across the year may be quite different. Nevertheless, the way you start and end each year matters.

Having worked with coaches for several years across many different types of schools and observed a variety of coaching scenarios, we have had the unique opportunity to collect the wisdom of many. We hope some of the wise advice that follows will also be helpful to you.

START STRONG

Before School Opens for Students

- **Meet with your administrator** to discuss school improvement goals and to review the professional learning calendar.
- **Lay out a rough draft of professional learning opportunities** across the year, including scheduled school-wide or district professional learning days.
- **Conduct a morning walk-about** to welcome back your colleagues and introduce yourself to new teachers.
- **Organize and distribute** curriculum and assessment materials.
- **Order any needed materials** for literacy instruction.
- **Support new teachers** as needed to get them up and running.
- **Conduct your start-up meeting** to review school goals, professional learning expectations, and your role in supporting them.
- **Co-plan and support the lab classroom teacher** (if applicable) with classroom setup.
- **Schedule a classroom environment walk** for interested teachers.
- **Provide professional learning sessions** (if applicable).
- **Set up your coaching notebook.**

The First Four Weeks

- **Help teachers schedule and plan** for administering their classroom literacy assessments during the first few weeks of school and for classroom coverage during individual assessments.
- **Continue to get to know your colleagues and establish relationships** (e.g., stop by their classrooms, have lunch with them, engage in casual conversations).
- **Align your own goals with district and school goals.**
- **Talk with teachers about their individual goals.**
- **Attend to organizing curriculum materials** and supplies (as needed).
- **Support individual teachers with building classroom community and establishing management routines** (as requested).
- **Attend scheduled meetings** as your role requires (e.g., child study team meetings, data meetings, literacy team meetings, grade-level team meetings).
- **Plan and facilitate your first professional learning opportunity** (e.g., professional learning session, bite-size professional learning) when applicable and as time allows.
- **Start bi-weekly meetings with your principal.**
- **Schedule and conduct one-on-one coaching sessions** and/or grade-level meetings to review assessment data and set goals.

Figure 22-2 continues

FINISH STRONG

Two Months Before School Ends

- **Support teachers with end-of-the-year assessments** (e.g., help them schedule, problem-solve classroom coverage).
- **Work with your colleagues and administrators to plan summer reading/writing projects** for students to maintain reading and writing.
- **Order any materials** needed to support summer reading/writing projects.
- **Support your colleagues in planning** end-of-the-year reading and writing celebrations for students.

The Last Four Weeks

- **Organize, review, and analyze end-of-the-year, school-wide data** and identify new school-wide goals with team and administrators.
- **Organize and deliver any materials** to support summer reading and writing projects.
- **Work with teachers to launch summer reading/writing projects** for students.
- **Survey teachers about topics for professional learning** that they would like to address in the next school year.
- **Plan professional learning opportunities** with teachers and principal that will take place over the summer or just before the school year begins (e.g., institutes, conferences, free webinars).
- **Evaluate and order materials to support curricular projects and/or plans** for the next school year in case teachers want to bring them home over the summer.
- **Review your coaching notebook** to reflect on successes and areas for improvement.
- **Work with your principal to save dates** for school- or district-wide professional learning for the next school year.

Figure 22-2 continued

NEW TEACHER

Carving out time to work with new teachers during the first few weeks pays dividends all year long. Be sure to leave space in your schedule in the first few weeks to work with each new teacher individually to think about the first days with students. Working on nuts and bolts not only helps new teachers feel confident and prepared but also builds the side-by-side collaborative collegiality you want to establish from the beginning.

Start Early

The best advice we can offer you for a successful year of professional learning is to get started early. One of our coach colleagues, Nikki, finds it helpful to call teachers (especially teachers new to the school) during the summer to introduce herself and invite them to the professional learning sessions she offers before school starts. She finds a way to work with the new teachers for a few days over the summer to introduce them to curriculum, go through instructional routines, discuss the classroom environment, work on schedules, and design classroom setup.

Some teachers, especially new ones, may request or take you up on an offer to go on a classroom environment walk through their colleagues' classrooms during those first few weeks of the year. Invite a few teachers who set up early to open their classrooms and give their interested colleagues a tour, explaining some of the organizational decisions they have made. These informal learning walks can generate exciting discussions about how the physical setup of a room relates to beliefs about teaching and learning, even though the students will have yet to make the space their own with photos of themselves and displays of their work.

Meet with Your Principal Before School Starts

As you saw in the case study we provided earlier in this chapter, it's helpful to meet with your principal before the beginning of every school year to review school improvement goals, mark the calendar, and take the time to clarify your role. When you and your principal have a common understanding of your role, your time can be prioritized for professional learning instead of a lot of other tasks that can eat away at your time.

> *"I learned that my work as an instructional coach began before school ever started. It was important for me to be a first point of contact."*
>
> —EXPERIENCED COACH NIKKI

Identify Your Goals and Clarify Your Role

Meet with your administrator to review improvement goals for the school and professional goals for yourself. Many of these goals might have been established at the end of the previous year using end-of-the-year data. Revisit the data to make sure your goals are aligned. This will make it more likely that you'll receive administrative support across the year. Be sure to clarify the required and optional professional learning opportunities as agreed upon by the team and as consistent with teachers' contracts. Be sure you and your administrator are clear on how the expectations will be communicated.

Finally, to maintain your primary role as a thought partner and a source of support in teachers' professional learning journeys, make sure you are not put in the position of setting the expectations and enforcing attendance agreements. And that goes for all types of professional learning.

Mark the Calendar

Before the school year begins, spend time with your administrator mapping out as much as you can on the calendar so you can plan for professional learning opportunities:

- Dates for required assessments—school, district, and state testing windows
- Dates for required and optional professional learning sessions for teachers new to the school
- Dates for required and optional professional learning sessions for all teachers
- Blocks of time (about three or four one-hour slots per day) for one-on-one or cluster coaching (times for pre-observation conversations and post-observation conversations will need to be arranged with each teacher)
- Availability of coverage if needed for pre-observation conversations, post-observation conversations, and other professional learning opportunities

Setting Goals with Teachers: Keep it Real

Meet with teachers one on one to discuss individual goals. These conversations, which take place over the first few weeks of school, can be quick and casual but are as important as your conversation with the principal. Make the process meaningful by trying any of the following suggestions:

- Provide time for teachers to reflect on their own goals before sharing them with you. Private think time is productive.
- Have teachers, not you, write down their goals in their professional learning notebook.
- Make sure everyone understands that these goals are not intended as a measure for evaluation.
- Invite the teachers to think about how you can support them in reaching their goals.
- Ask them what their teaching would look like if they achieved their goals.

QUICK TIP

Prioritize setting aside blocks of time for one-on-one coaching with each teacher when you set up your schedule for the year to have the greatest impact on the teachers and to link closely with other professional learning opportunities.

- Required meetings you will lead/attend (e.g., literacy team meeting, data meetings, grade-level team meetings, inclusion meetings)

Coach Nikki also finds it helpful to lay out the first month of grade-level team meetings with her principal. For example, they dedicate the first meeting to making sure everyone understands how to administer and score the school's assessments. The next two grade-level meetings are dedicated to helping teachers look at their data and use the information to make instructional decisions. The last meeting of the month is dedicated to having teachers look at the results of their teaching based on the assessments. The bottom line? The more you plan ahead, the more logistical headaches you are likely to avoid and the more meaningful the experiences will be for your colleagues.

Getting and Staying Organized

In the first few weeks of school, consider organizing resources, materials, and supplies to support your colleagues and make your life easier across the year. Organize items such as the following:

- Common spaces (e.g., manipulative bins, text set baskets, book room)
- Assessment materials
- Curriculum materials
- Classroom supplies
- Your coaching notebook
- Digital resources

The more accessible and organized you make things, the more efficient you and the teachers can be.

When it comes to organizing yourself, your coaching notebook is the best place to store useful information and resources. Keeping your own materials in one structured place ensures easy access to what you need when you need it. See Chapter 23 for how to assemble a coaching notebook that works as hard as you do.

Be Present and Available

One of the most important things you can do in those first few weeks of school is to be available. Stop in just to say hello, conduct morning walk-abouts to check in with teachers, and have conversations during lunch and breaks. Each small conversation builds trust in the relationship. Be attentive to the ways you can support your colleagues. You might, for example, spend time problem-solving ways to help them as they administer their beginning-of-the-year assessments. Maybe you can offer to read aloud to a class a few times a week while the teacher assesses individual students. Or, coordinate with two teachers so each teacher takes turns teaching both classes at the same time or taking students out to recess to free their colleague for assessing individuals.

Whatever you do to show your support for your colleagues, make it clear that you want to be helpful to all, especially in those challenging first few weeks.

Plan to Change Your Plan

As you begin to implement your plans for professional learning, be flexible to allow for the on-the-run interactions that support your colleagues. Be prepared to respond to unplanned teacher requests, such as when a teacher asks you for a read-aloud book that connects to the current science or social studies unit. Or, when a teacher asks you to look at a student's assessment data to verify placement in the right instructional group. Or, maybe when another teacher stops you in the hall to get your thoughts on a lesson plan.

If you are a coach who has only a few hours during the week to support teachers, you may find that these brief individual interactions plus your attendance at some weekly grade-level planning meetings and an occasional learning walk make up most of your coaching time. Be assured it is all time well spent because you are responding to your teachers' needs within the limited time you have. And don't forget to save some planning and thinking time for yourself.

Celebrate with Your Students and Colleagues

The end of the year is a perfect time to hold the last reading and writing celebrations of the school year. Some coaches plan school-wide celebrations in which children invite their families and share their writing portfolios, readers' notebooks, etc., while others support teachers in creating small, classroom celebrations.

As your colleagues plan events to celebrate their students' growth, think about ways you can help them celebrate their own development. If possible, use your final coaching sessions to have them look through their reflection journals and think about their professional learning journey across the year. Ask them to write a final reflection about how they have seen themselves grow and to think about their goals for next year.

Responsive Coaching Means Being Open to Change

Sometimes, you enter a coaching situation thinking you will support the teacher one way but end up providing support a different way. For example, you might be prepared for a one-on-one coaching session but then decide, based on the pre-observation conversation, that the time would be better spent exploring a resource or planning a lesson together. Flexibility allows for responsive coaching.

End the Year by Looking Forward

We recommend starting to think about the end of the year two months before school ends. Administering end-of-year assessments at this point gives teachers the data they need to begin planning for next year while also using that data to immediately inform their decisions. Work with your team and administrators to look at end-of-year data to determine goals for the next year. Ask your colleagues to reflect on which professional learning experiences were particularly meaningful for them and which were not as helpful. These conversations inform the type of professional learning you might offer before or at the beginning of the next school year. By starting to think about the following school year early, you can also order supplies and curriculum materials in time for your colleagues to take them home over the summer.

The end of the year is also the time to think about how to help students continue to grow over the summer. Work with your colleagues to brainstorm ideas for summer literacy projects (e.g., summer reading lists, fun ways to engage students and caregivers in reading and writing).

In the end, your professional learning design reflects what you believe about coaching, teaching, and learning. With this mindset, take steps to implement a thoughtful plan for helping your colleagues grow each year from the beginning to the end.

Up **Next**

Every coach needs a fully stocked toolbox, and that's exactly what you'll find in Chapter 23.

Chapter 23:

Build **Your Toolbox**

Can we talk about desks? The ones with teetering towers of observation notes, protocols, records of professional learning sessions, resources you've promised to share, and look-for tools you can't find when you look for them. If this sounds like your desk, it's time to get organized. This chapter will help you do that.

We begin with a tool that we've seen used consistently and to excellent effect in many of the schools we've visited: a well-organized coaching notebook. We'll walk you through how to assemble and maintain a notebook. This will not only help you stay on top of all the work products you've accumulated over time but will also allow you to look back at what you've done in professional learning sessions and coaching, analyze the feedback you've collected, and set goals for your own professional learning and growth.

From there we turn to technology and how it can make your busy life a little easier. If you're already using technology to its fullest extent, go ahead and skip the last part of this chapter. But if you harbor the suspicion that there's more you can be doing on the digital playing field—and really, who doesn't—you'll find plenty of inspiration later in the chapter.

Your Coaching Notebook

Your coaching notebook is a dynamic tool, one that is constantly changing because you continually add to, modify, and improve it. It allows you to keep track of how you spend your time, collect your thinking, record teachers' growth, respond to feedback, and select resources to make the professional learning you offer more effective.

To make a coaching notebook, if you haven't done so already, you can use a binder, a spiral notebook, or a digital notebook. We recommend dividing a physical notebook into sections (Figure 23-1) or, if it is on your computer or tablet, organizing in digital folders. The content of your notebook and the way you organize it is entirely up to you.

We encourage you to make your notebook your own. We have seen everything from strictly utilitarian notebooks to visually creative notebooks and everything in between. We have seen teachers who use a tablet for the notebook and others who maintain a hybrid digital and physical notebook. What they all have in common is that they are organized, are filled with ideas, and allow you to document change over time. We will share an example of sections and forms for collecting and organizing information. We hope you will get ideas from here and then organize your notebook in the way that works for you.

> ***About Tools for Coaching***
>
> Tools for coaching are meant to help you in very practical ways. But if the term *tools* leaves you cold, call them "forms" or "paperwork," but don't decide not to use them. We guarantee that by the end of the year you will be calling them your "gold mine."

Section 1: School Information

Use this section to store important school-wide documents that impact your role and the scheduling of professional learning. We recommend storing a copy of your school's core values for professional learning so you can refer to them with administrators and colleagues as needed (Figure 23-2). You might also want a copy of your school improvement goals handy for meetings and discussions involving the direction of professional learning.

Additionally, you might use this section to keep school-wide calendars and important schedules, such as the following:

- School calendar of professional days and holidays
- Assessment calendar
- Grade-level schedules
    - Dates and times of team meetings
    - Planning times when students are out of the room
    - Lunch schedules
    - Literacy blocks (when teachers typically teach reading, writing, and phonics/word study)

When you know the timing of your colleagues' planning periods, lunches, and curriculum blocks, it facilitates your planning and allows you to stop by to check in, deliver a resource, or simply have a conversation at an appropriate time.

SAMPLE STRUCTURE FOR COACHING NOTEBOOK

SECTION 1: SCHOOL INFORMATION

- Core Values for the School
- School Improvement Goals
- School Calendar
- Assessment Calendar
- Grade-Level Schedules

SECTION 2: AGENDA/ACTION ITEMS

- Meeting Agendas
- Meeting Notes

SECTION 3: RECORD OF PROFESSIONAL LEARNING

- Calendar of Professional Learning
- Record of Coaching Sessions
- Planning Templates and Notes
- Sketch-Notes and Brainstorms

SECTION 4: TEACHER INFORMATION

- Teacher Information
- Professional Learning at a Glance

SECTION 5: RESOURCES

- Protocols
- Look-for Tools
- Prompting Guide
- Professional Resources
- Structured Tools

Figure 23-1

CORE VALUES FOR PROFESSIONAL LEARNING

Every **educator** is a member of an inclusive community that takes collective responsibility for the high achievement of each student in a widely diverse population.

Every **educator** engages in continuous professional learning for the purpose of achieving equitable outcomes for every student in the school.

Every **educator** is committed to implementing the agreed-upon curriculum, assessments, and evidence-based instructional practices to assure coherence in learning opportunities for every child within and across grade levels.

Every **educator** is a member of a team that focuses on assets in students and in colleagues and engages in collaborative problem-solving for continuous improvement.

Every **educator** is responsible for using evidence gained from systematic observation and ongoing assessment data to make sound instructional decisions.

Every **educator** commits to developing professional expertise and supporting the learning of each colleague on the team.

Figure 23-2

Online Calendars for Easy Scheduling

For day-to-day planning, consider using a calendar app that allows you to share your calendar and see the calendars of others. Investigate calendar apps that allow people to sign up for blocks of your time (e.g., for pre- and post-observation conversations, ten-minute coaching consultations). Having access to one another's calendars online can make everyone's life easier and creates a digital footprint of how you are spending your time.

Section 2: Agenda/Action Items

You may find it helpful to have a section of your notebook dedicated to agendas and notes for meetings you lead or attend. For example, this section would be an excellent place to keep some blank copies of Note-Taking Tool: Meeting Notes as well as completed notes (see p. 195). Some coaches choose to keep these notes in a separate notebook, while others have found it valuable to at least have notes from meetings with their principal accessible in their coaching notebook. If you have a physical coaching notebook, you may want to consider using a binder so you can keep only your most current notes and move older ones to a hanging file. Whether physical or digital, the most important thing is to keep all meeting notes dated and organized.

Section 3: Record of Professional Learning

When you record how you spend your time, you have a way to reflect on the balance and effectiveness of the types of professional learning sessions you provide. Keeping a record helps you explain your use of time to administrators, school board members, or community members if needed. It will also help you review priority areas and may serve as a tool for making more efficient use of time. Consider keeping the following in this section:

- **Calendar of Professional Learning:** Some coaches find it helpful to use a calendar template to keep track of all the professional learning they offer over a month (as shown partially in Figure 23-3; a blank, full-size Template Tool: Calendar of Professional Learning is available as **OR 23.1** in the Online Resources). Other coaches keep information in a calendar online. Regardless of how you decide to keep track of your professional learning interactions, maintain an up-to-date schedule to stay organized.

ONLINE RESOURCE 23.1

TEMPLATE TOOL

CALENDAR OF PROFESSIONAL LEARNING

Month: March

MON	TUE	WED	THU	FRI
			1 9–10:30 Coach Ms. Johnson 11–12 Lab classroom 3–4 G4 Team meeting	2 9–11 Lesson study 1–2 PLS planning 3–4 Inclusion mtg
5 9:30–10 G2 Team mtg 10:30–11 Coach Mr. Kolodziej	6 9–10 Coach Ms. Guttierez 11–12 Peer coaching setup 3–4 PLS Writing about reading	7 9–10 Learning walk 11–11:30 Coach Ms. Vitello 1–1:30 Coach Ms. Roche 3–4 G3 Team mtg	8 9–10 Peer coaching setup 11–12 Lab classroom 3–4 G4 Team mtg	9 1–2 G5 Team mtg 2–2:45 Principal Conroy

Figure 23-3

- **Record of Coaching Sessions:** Figure 23-4 shows how one coach uses Template Tool: Record of Coaching Sessions for keeping track of coaching sessions with colleagues. (A blank, full-size template is available full size as **OR 23.2** in the Online Resources.) Use this template to keep track of the topics you have worked on together and whether you have met with a teacher for one-on-one or cluster coaching. Some coaches choose to keep track of these sessions in the teacher information section. Either system works, but having your coaching sessions listed in one place allows you to think about whether you are allocating your time in a way that supports a variety of people in the building instead of only a few of your colleagues.

ONLINE RESOURCE 23.2

- **Planning Templates and Notes:** Another way to keep a record of the professional learning you offer is to keep and organize your planning documents (including planning templates) for professional learning sessions, bite-size professional learning, learning walks, and lesson studies that you will have a record of any reflections or feedback you may have noted after the professional learning experience.

TEMPLATE TOOL

RECORD OF COACHING SESSIONS			
TEACHER NAME	COACHING SESSION DATE	COACHING TOPIC	O = ONE-ON-ONE COACHING C = CLUSTER COACHING
Mrs. Nguyen	10/19	Shared Reading	O
Ms. Roche	10/24	Writing Conferences	O
Mr. Hickman	10/30	Book Clubs	C
Ms. Vitello	10/30	Book Clubs	C
Mrs. Gavaghan	10/30	Book Clubs	C

Figure 23-4

- **Sketch-Notes and Brainstorms:** If you are using a physical notebook or binder, leave some blank pages for brainstorming and sketch-noting. As we have mentioned in other chapters, sketch-noting is a way to make your thoughts visible by using drawings, borders, boxes, and arrows to collect and connect ideas. Literacy coach Stephanie Affinito has a blog dedicated to using sketch-noting in coaching as a way of planning, capturing her ideas for professional learning, and sharing those ideas with others in an engaging way (thecoachingsketchnotebook.com). The process of sketch-noting can be freeing and can sometimes help you think outside the box. If you are using a digital notebook, consider keeping a blank physical notebook handy for sketch-noting. Keep your brainstorming in this section as a record of your planning and thinking, or create a separate section for it.

Section 4: Teacher Information

One way to form strong relationships with teachers is to make sure they feel heard. Capture the conversations and interactions you have with them so you can follow up and build on what you have established. Think about experiences you have had with a doctor. Can you tell the difference between the doctor who has read your chart and knows you and a doctor who comes in cold? Which doctor do you trust more? Which doctor makes you feel heard?

In this section of your notebook, create a tab or digital folder for each teacher you coach. Consider keeping some of the following information in this section:

- **Personal Information:** Get to know your colleagues—their culture, languages, hobbies, favorite books and streaming series, names of their children, and anything else they want you to know about them. You might find it helpful to make note of this information so you can remember and make genuine connections with them.

Keep Your Coaching Notebook Manageable

Establish a place outside of your coaching notebook to confidentially store transcribed lessons from observations within classrooms. If you keep all of these notes within your coaching notebook, it will fill up quickly. Consider storing these notes in hanging folders labeled with the teachers' names. Keep the most recent notes in your coaching notebook until your next coaching session and then file them. Some coaches choose to keep all of their scripted notes in a hanging folder especially if they use a notebook instead of a binder. Then they pull the hanging folder to review before the coaching session.

- **Professional Learning at a Glance:** To record your professional learning contacts with each teacher, use a form such as the one shown in Figure 23-5. (You will find a blank, full-size Template Tool: Professional Learning at a Glance as **OR 23.3** in the Online Resources). The form provides a chronological record of the type of learning and the teachers' goals or any follow-up needed for a school year. You could create a spreadsheet using the information from each teacher's record to summarize your contacts for the year.

ONLINE RESOURCE 23.3

TEMPLATE TOOL

PROFESSIONAL LEARNING AT A GLANCE

Teacher: M. Lourdes

DATE	TYPE	FOCUS
8/14	PLS	Assessment data
8/15	PLS	Linking data to instruction
9/5	LC	Grade 1
9/18	C	Using data to form groups
9/25	PLS	Interactive RA
10/1	C	Interactive RA
10/3	LC (gr. 1)	Interactive RA, Independent rdg
10/9	PLS	Systematic phonics
10/10	CC (gr. 1)	Phonics lesson
10/16	PLS	Phonics lesson
11/4	LW (gr. 1, 2)	Phonics lessons
11/6	PLS	Systematic phonics
11/15	LC	Phonics lesson
11/19	C	Phonics lesson
11/20	C	Phonics lesson
12/3	CC	Phonics lesson
12/4	PC (ML w/MD)	Phonics lesson
12/9	PC (MD w/ML)	Phonics lesson
12/11	PLS	Interactive writing
12/17	C	Interactive writing

TYPE

C: COACHING (ONE-ON-ONE) CC: CLUSTER COACHING LC: LAB CLASSROOM LS: LESSON STUDY LW: LEARNING WALK
PBC: PROFESSIONAL BOOK CLUB PC: PEER COACHING PLS: PROFESSIONAL LEARNING SESSION SG: STUDY GROUP

Your Literacy Coaching Playbook **Online Resource 23.3 | Template Tool:** Professional Learning at a Glance, **Version 01**

Figure 23-5

Section 5: Resources

Here's a quick look at the many resources you can download from the Online Resources and keep in this section of your notebook.

Protocols: All but one of the plays we've provided in this book (in Part 2) have a protocol that summarizes what to do to provide an effective professional learning experience. We recommend that you download or print all protocols and store them in this section of your notebook for easy reference. Having them in one place may also remind you of a play that you might not use frequently but that might be perfect for a particular situation.

Look-for Tools: If you develop look-for tools with your colleagues (see Chapter 13), you might also include them in this section of your notebook so you can refer to them while you coach. Review them with your colleagues to identify particular areas they might want to focus on during a coaching session or a learning walk, for example. You may also want to offer copies to learning partners to ensure more productive peer coaching sessions or to your administrators to make sure everyone is working toward the same goals while supporting teachers.

The fact that look-for tools are developed with your colleagues makes them powerful documents for building cohesion and a common vision for literacy learning across the school. They can be referred to during meetings when needed to keep everyone on the same page. Because you and your colleagues are always developing deeper understandings about instruction, these look-for tools might require revision over time. Your coaching notebook is a dynamic tool, so keep it updated with the most current versions.

QUICK TIP

Overuse of the same prompts can make them seem trite or inauthentic. Vary your responses and questions. Be present and listen. Quick access to the coaching prompting guide in your notebook will help you have better conversations in all of your coaching interactions.

Prompting Guide: We recommend printing out Prompting Guide Tool: Coaching Prompting Guide (Chapter 7) so you have facilitative language prompts at your fingertips in your coaching notebook. We encourage you to add to it and make it your own. The language in the prompting guide ensures a collegial, constructive stance as you conduct coaching conversations. Every coach needs a gentle reminder every so often to rephrase inquiries as open-ended questions that generate reflection and discussion. Scanning the list of facilitative language prompts before entering a coaching experience and identifying a few prompts you might use makes for a more thoughtful discussion. These prompts are designed as a tool to help you, not limit you. Refer back to Chapters 5–7 to read more about the use of facilitative language and this resource. The prompting guide is more meaningful when you understand the rationales behind the carefully worded language.

Professional Resources: One way to keep conversations with your colleagues authentic and rooted in pedagogy is to read and refer to professional resources together. Keep a few seminal journal articles, blog posts, etc., in your coaching notebook (or in a folder online) for easy access, especially to address hot-button topics or those that resurface year after year. When you take teachers into a professional resource, you essentially get out of the way and let the teachers construct their own knowledge. Have these resources readily available to harness momentum and interest in a topic when it arises. Highlight passages and quotes that have been influential.

A Few Structured Tools: As a coach, you grow your colleague's expertise by growing your own. Part of this process is seeking your own opportunities for professional growth through reading, webinars, conferences, etc., and occasionally using structured tools to assess your impact on teachers, students, and the school. You'll find those tools described in Chapter 26. They are available as full-size tools in the Online Resources so you can store them in your notebook if you wish.

Your coaching notebook is a place for you to document your own growth over time. It is a repository of your thinking, a collection of the resources that push your thinking, and a place to document your teachers' growth over time. Once you have set up and used your coaching notebook, take time to, on occasion, review it, reorganize it, clean it out, and keep it fresh. We expect that as you create a new coaching notebook for each new school year, you will have changes to make in the content and organization. The more dynamic your notebook, the more dynamic you will be in your role.

Technology—An Essential Tool in Your Toolbox

There is nothing wrong with holding on to nondigital tools you are accustomed to using. But we do encourage you to think about how you might integrate technology into your daily coaching or simply build on what you are already doing with technology. Here are some of our favorite ways to use technology in coaching and other professional learning opportunities.

The Power of the Video Clip

Let's start with a reliable standby for coaches–the video clip. Now more than ever, it's easy to create a library of go-to video clips. Capturing video segments is a breeze, and so is editing them using today's accessible and user-friendly video editing applications. We encourage you to work with your colleagues to upload labeled video clips of teaching into one secure place for teachers to access.

Having a library of video clips allows you to send links to teachers to demonstrate an idea or follow up on a discussion. (Be sure that these are sent in a safe way and that no one in your group will share them publicly online.) Teachers are often more receptive to new ideas when they see students from their own school in video clips versus a high-production, professional clip. You can also record your own interactions with students, teaching in a lab classroom, or a colleague's teaching (with permission) to send to other teachers. Invite your colleagues to submit video clips as an alternative to live observations when time is limited. There are also apps available that allow you to mark places in a video to make comments to the viewers.

In addition to the benefit to teachers, video clips of your own coaching sessions can help you self-reflect. Use a different lens, such as any of the following suggestions, to think about your coaching.

Video Takes Center Stage

We have highlighted numerous ways to use video across this book. We summarize some of those ways here:

- **Embed video** in slide presentations for professional learning sessions.
- **Ask teachers to submit video clips** for coaching or sharing in groups during professional learning sessions.
- **Follow up professional learning sessions** by asking everyone to record themselves teaching.
- **Create video invitations** to professional learning events, send them via email or post on social media.
- **Advertise a professional book club book** on video and include why teachers should attend.
- **Observe your own coaching videos** for self-reflection.
- **Show videos of you coaching others** to introduce your role and help teachers understand your coaching stance.
- **Create a library of video clips.** Send links to teachers to show a teaching move or teacher language or to introduce a type of teaching.

- Notice and record your coaching language: How does it give the teacher agency? How does it reflect your coaching stance? How does it lift the teacher's thinking?
- Notice your body language and the body language of the teacher: What messages are you sending with your body language, your eye contact? What messages is the teacher sending you through body language and eye contact?
- Notice the balance of talk between you and the teacher.

From demonstrating effective practices to offering inspiration, video plays a significant role in keeping professional learning practical and grounded in the classroom and the behaviors of students.

Invite Digital Feedback and Reflection

Consider using digital surveys or polls to get direction from your colleagues about their needs and interests for professional learning. Use surveys to ask for feedback on professional learning experiences or to collect data. For example, you could offer teachers an electronic survey form to collect quantitative data on a learning walk. Many survey apps allow you to create an easy visual representation of the data.

Using polls to ask teachers questions during a professional learning session keeps them engaged and active during the learning experience. This technique can be particularly effective during virtual professional learning sessions.

You can also create digital whiteboards to collect your colleagues' reflections in one place. For example, after different types of professional learning, ask teachers to post their reflections to a digital whiteboard. We have also seen a coach take pictures of charts teachers made during a professional learning session and post them on a digital whiteboard to preserve the ideas in an efficient way. The coach can then share the work with the group and others in the school.

> **_Other Ways to Consider Using Technology_**
>
> - **Use instant messaging apps** that organize communications into threads for individuals and groups to efficiently communicate with your colleagues.
> - **Use videoconferencing apps** to provide virtual professional learning when you are unable to meet in person.
> - **Use digital bulletin boards** to curate resources, especially images, that you can share with teachers (e.g., pictures of different classroom management systems or setups).
> - **Join coaching networks on social media** to gain ideas and inspiration.
> - **Follow blogs** on both literacy and coaching.
> - **Register for free webinars** offered by professional organizations, authors, researchers, and other professionals in literacy and coaching.
> - **Create your own social media posts** that your teachers can follow. Highlight (with permission) ideas you see in classrooms, student work, and other exciting things going on around the school. Repost interesting ideas from other accounts you follow.

Digital Invitations Offer a Personal Touch

Some coaches use electronic invitation apps to invite and keep track of who is coming to professional learning opportunities. Most invitation apps allow customization. They also allow invitees to RSVP and make comments about the event. Even sending an email with a simple, colorful digital slide to advertise a book club or other professional learning event can attract plenty of interest.

Artificial Intelligence–Learning How to Use It in Your Role

The thing about artificial intelligence (AI) is that it is rapidly evolving. Although we offer a few ideas here to inspire your thinking, you really should do your own research. In fact, if you use one of the generative AI platforms to ask how coaches are using artificial intelligence in their daily coaching experiences, you will get a long list of ideas.

Here are some ideas we have collected (some using AI) to inspire your thinking about how to use AI in your instructional coaching:

- Use it to help you draft emails for teachers, administrators, and parents.
- Ask for professional book recommendations for teachers.
- Ask for book recommendations for students based on interest, previous reading, and grade level.
- Create agendas for meetings.
- Request help to interpret student data.
- Generate ideas and prompts for teachers to reflect on teaching and learning.
- Get ideas for differentiating instruction.
- Ask for classroom management tips and community building ideas.
- Use it to find inspirational quotes to share with your colleagues on specific topics.
- Find tips and ideas for managing stress specific to coaching.
- Use it with your colleagues to generate lesson ideas.
- Get help with aligning lesson plans with state or district curriculum goals.

The tools we've suggested in this chapter will keep you organized, improve your communication, allow you to assess teacher growth, and reflect on your own coaching impact and expertise. Adapt the tools we've suggested here to meet your needs and make them your own, especially your coaching notebook. Use technology according to your own style as a leader and what you think will work best for your teachers. And never forget that the tools in your toolbox all have the same purpose: to help you build a community of learners, working toward a common vision for students' literacy learning.

Up **Next**

Chapter 24 is all about meeting challenges when they arise in your work as professional learning leader. And yes, there will be challenges.

Chapter 24

There Will Be **Challenges**

In our decades of work with coaches, we have found that often they are overwhelmed by the many demands of the job and the complicating factors that exist in their school or district—particularly if they don't feel adequately supported by their principal or district-level administrator. If you're feeling that way, too, take heart. In this chapter, we'll help you work with your principal (or district administrator) to get the support you need so you can move forward in accomplishing the school's goals with optimism and positivity. Please note that for simplicity's sake, we use the term *principal* to mean principal or district-level administrator.

Start with This Quick Exercise

We often use an exercise designed to help coaches recognize their challenges and then find ways to address them constructively. We invite you to give this exercise a try right now to develop your agency in overcoming the barriers that diminish your feelings of job satisfaction and success. We'll guide you through it.

1. Write down two or three ways your principal has shown support for high-quality professional learning in the school.
2. Now write two or three challenges you have experienced in working with your principal to provide high-quality professional learning in the school.
3. Now take a look at Figure 24–1. It shows a sampling of the hundreds of principal-related challenges coaches have shared with us. As you read through the list, think about whether any of the issues resonate with you.
4. Finally, take a minute to think about each challenge listed on the chart, as well as those on your own list. Put a check mark next to each challenge you believe is within your control as the professional learning leader in your school or district.

Common Challenges Involving the Principal

- The principal does not fully understand my role.
- Too many teachers need my support, and I don't have time to coach all of them.
- The principal does not support me when others complain.
- The principal doesn't really know what I do.
- The principal plays favorites with teachers.
- My principal has no time to meet with me or frequently cancels our meetings.
- My principal thinks I can handle everything that comes my way and does not see the need to meet with me to solve problems.
- My principal won't help me schedule time for professional learning.
- My principal continually tries to get me to name teachers who need more support.
- I have to do too many things that aren't really my responsibility, and I have no time for one-on-one coaching.
- I am too often pulled away from my coaching responsibilities to be a substitute teacher, cover lunch duty, attend meetings in place of the principal, or handle other unexpected issues that arise.

Figure 24-1

We expect you to put a check mark next to several items on the list because we're certain you have thought about them and have ideas on how to resolve them. We challenge you to take a positive, problem-solving, "can-do" stance because, in fact, every item on the list is within your control—but only when you see yourself as an advocate for the team and its vision. And that begins by making time for an honest and productive conversation with your principal that will strengthen your partnership.

Work with Your Principal to Resolve Issues

Principals want professional learning to succeed in their schools, and it's important to recognize those positive intentions. Your principal is very busy but really does want to know how you and your colleagues are progressing in your work together as well as what might be getting in the way. Several of the points we make below may echo topics we've discussed in earlier chapters, but they could be the very issues that are behind your current frustrations and concerns. We offer the following supports for your consideration when meeting with your principal.

Take the Lead in Problem-Solving

Don't expect your principal to solve all your problems for you. In fact, it's better if you can begin meetings by bringing up the issues you want to discuss and suggesting whatever tentative solutions you've been thinking about (Figure 24-2). This is what we mean by bringing a can-do attitude to meetings with your principal, and we assure you that attitude will be appreciated. This doesn't mean there

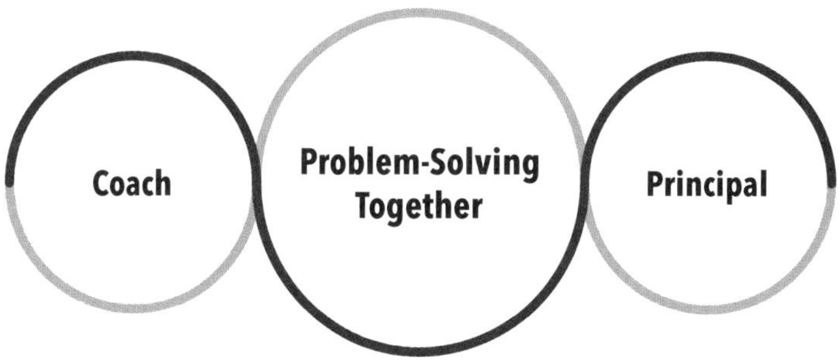

Figure 24-2

won't be a time when you are at a complete loss for a solution to a serious problem. Your principal will want to help you whenever possible.

IF THE ISSUE IS YOUR ROLE

Assume your principal cares about the professional learning of the teachers and the impact on student outcomes. Also assume that the two of you are partners with a common goal. Your early-in-the-year meeting and your regularly scheduled meetings with the principal are ideal times to review your role. If necessary, educate the principal regarding the many aspects of your role by providing a written document of your shared understandings. Revisit it as needed to ensure you are both on the same page.

IF THE ISSUE IS CONFIDENTIALITY

Remind your principal that you are not comfortable talking about teachers by name as your confidentiality best serves the teachers and their growth. But be sure to keep the principal updated on the topics the team is working on in professional learning.

IF THE ISSUE IS YOUR BUDGET

If budget constraints are keeping you from meeting your goals for professional learning, your principal needs to know. We expect there will be some particular resources needed to implement the professional learning design. All schools face difficult financial challenges, so try to prioritize and think of short-term and long-term goals. Put your heads together to brainstorm other possible revenue

sources, like community grants or even a bake sale to raise funds for classroom libraries or to buy a professional book for each teacher.

IF THE ISSUE IS TIME

Time is always a challenge and will likely be a consistent agenda item for your meetings with the principal. Express that you are fully aware of your administrator's commitment to teacher development and that you want to maximize the learning opportunities available for teachers, but your lack of sufficient time to work with all the teachers who need your support is becoming an issue. Explain that you've been thinking about this problem and would like to present a few different plans for professional learning experiences that would require less time than is typically needed.

Another common time issue relates to the common practice of all teachers sharing some duties on a rotating basis, like lunch or recess duty. It is important that you show that you contribute to common needs in the same way as your colleagues, and your principal will appreciate it if you volunteer to pitch in as your schedule allows. But, if you find you are also assigned too many duties that are outside of your coaching responsibilities, prepare to go into the meeting with some constructive suggestions. Share your feelings with your principal and try to problem-solve together.

In your meeting, you might need to remind your principal of the importance of coaching all teachers so they can continue to grow professionally. Explain that the team has committed to continuous professional learning, and leaving any teacher out would be detrimental to the team. If the number of teachers is a challenge, think together about creating a workable list of teachers to begin with, and then cycle to another group. (You might also see Chapters 9 and 10 for the time-saving ideas of cluster coaching and peer coaching, respectively.)

IF THE ISSUE IS LACK OF SUFFICIENT SUPPORT

You may need to express in a kind way that sometimes you don't feel supported in your role. For example, you might use one of the following statements.

Sample Language

- *Our time together makes a critical difference to the professional learning in our school. Can we find another time soon that works better for you?*
- *When you _____, it makes me think we should talk again about how we both see the coaching role.*
- *When you don't have time to meet with me, I find it hard to accomplish all that I know you hope for with our school goals.*

You were chosen for the role of professional learning leader because your principal believes you are highly capable of doing that job. However, your principal may have no idea you are feeling unsupported unless you explicitly state your need for more support. Presume that the principal is well intended and trying to do what is best for students and teachers. But, remember that principals often feel overwhelmed themselves and must attend to multiple important issues every day.

Stay Positive

Throughout this book, we have encouraged you to be clear about your goals, positive in your approach, and enthusiastic about your partnership with your principal. Your tone of positivity and small steps forward will likely ease your frustration and allow you to be effective in your role. You and your principal may need to revisit issues more than once but always with your optimistic "let's figure this out together" attitude. Finally, remember that although your principal may not always be able to support you as much as you'd like in every challenge that comes your way, you certainly can build on your administrator's strengths, continue to relay important information about your work with teachers, and advocate for spending more time together. Even if you don't get all the support you want, you can still make a positive difference.

Up **Next**

In Chapter 25, we move to the topic of teachers who are resistant to professional learning. When you help them understand and commit to the school's agreed-upon values, beliefs, and vision, the issue often works itself out. But when nothing seems to help, you'll need to address the problem head on. In the next chapter we'll help you bring teachers who are still on the sidelines into the huddle.

Chapter 25

When Teachers Aren't "All-in"

At one time or another in your work with teachers, it will probably happen: a teacher will not engage in professional learning opportunities or one-on-one coaching the way the team has envisioned. When that happens (and there's a strong possibility it will), acknowledge the fact that there will always be teachers who find it difficult to change the way they think about professional learning. And the presence of a coach as a new role in the school can feel like a sea change. It's important to remember that although most teachers find their commitment to professional learning exhilarating, some may find it destabilizing. After all, any change can turn the familiar into the unknown overnight, causing feelings of fear, anxiety, or frustration. It's no wonder so many people react to change with resistance and uncertainty.

Most often, resistance manifests at the leading edge of a change process, when people first sense shifting ground beneath their feet. That's when you'll most need to communicate positivity and help your colleagues overcome their feelings of uncertainty. However, while it is true that resistance to professional learning tends to pop up at the beginning of a significant change in a school's expectations about participation in professional learning, it can arise at any time and in any individual.

This chapter will help you recognize resistance to new learning when you see it and be prepared to take steps that will help your colleagues feel more comfortable with you and with the kind of positive change that professional learning opportunities can bring to your school and its teachers. Then, if you keep your eye on the common vision, eventually you will be able to look back at a school that is transformed and take credit for your stance of grace in every professional conversation, your persistent patience, and your unwavering support and belief in the potential of every member of the team.

Analyze Patterns of Behavior

If you have had some experience as a coach, you may immediately call up specific behaviors you have observed in some teachers that cause you concern. Think about what the teachers say or what you see them do, and reflect on these two questions:

1. What do you hear teachers say to you or others that leads you to believe they may not be open to engaging in professional learning?
2. What do they do in front of you or others that implies they are not open to engaging in professional learning?

As we have worked with coaches, they have shared observations of their colleagues' comments and behaviors that have led them to believe that some teachers are not responding positively to the professional learning opportunities in the school. Figure 25-1 shows some of the comments we've heard teachers make and some of the actions they have exhibited during the many coaching or professional learning sessions we have been involved in.

BEHAVIORS OBSERVED

What You Hear Them Say	What You See Them Do
▪ *Are you kidding me? I don't have time to do that.* ▪ *This isn't in our contract.* ▪ *I should be able to decide what I teach and how I teach it in my own classroom.* ▪ *That's not manageable. I don't know how to get all this done.* ▪ *I'm not going to spend time on this–it will be gone soon.* ▪ *Our kids are different. They can't do this.* ▪ *I can't think about this right now–I'm working on my master's and have a lot going on at home.* ▪ *I'm okay. Focus on the new teachers.* ▪ *Just tell me what to do, and I will do it.* ▪ *I don't need a coach.* ▪ *I know my students as readers–I don't need to do benchmark assessments.* ▪ *Please don't give me another thing to learn.* ▪ *I've been teaching for thirty years–I don't know what you could teach me.* ▪ *We've always done it this way.* ▪ *This is a waste of our time.* ▪ *I want to make my own decisions, not do what others want me to do.*	▪ *Cross their arms, make faces, or roll their eyes* ▪ *Constantly make negative or defensive comments* ▪ *Continually make excuses* ▪ *Correct papers during the session* ▪ *Have off-topic side conversations* ▪ *Ignore emails* ▪ *Arrive late at workshops or walk out early* ▪ *Sit through meetings without engaging* ▪ *Blame the district leaders or school principal* ▪ *Interject comments that are the opposite of the message you are trying to convey* ▪ *Ignore or refuse to collaborate with others* ▪ *Show no evidence of planning* ▪ *Teach the same way year after year* ▪ *Use coaching time to complain about other teachers* ▪ *Have no time to discuss issues of equity* ▪ *Avoid regularly analyzing hard and soft data because they think it's the principal's job* ▪ *Continually cancel one-on-one coaching sessions* ▪ *See coaching as implying that they are not good at their jobs*

Figure 25-1

Seek to Understand the Behaviors

Understanding what's behind the behaviors you hear and see is an important first step in reducing resistance to new learning. Let's think together and hypothesize what might be behind such words and actions.

- Teachers fear that if they change what they feel is working for them, then the students may not be as successful.
- They feel that as soon as they get comfortable with an instructional practice or specific curriculum materials, they are asked to try something else.
- They feel they are not being treated like a professional.
- They already work so hard and think the changes will mean they have to work harder.
- They do not have confidence in the capability of the students; they tend to see deficits and not strengths.
- They do not believe the students can succeed in a curriculum that relies on critical thinking.
- They feel they are being told what to do and don't have a voice in making decisions for their own students.
- They fear they won't do well enough or won't be successful.
- They don't trust the coach, the principal, or professional learning experiences because they have had previous negative experiences.
- They don't fully grasp the idea that professional learning is an expectation of their role.
- They don't see themselves as part of a supportive team, perhaps because they've never been part of a team before.
- They are fearful that the coach is an evaluator (or the principal's eye) and don't want to take risks.
- They are overwhelmed and see their learning as one more challenge they can't keep up with.
- They worry that the coach's job is to keep teachers on the "right page of the script."
- They feel defeated by a lack of time or their inability to manage the time they have.
- They have not experienced respectful or productive conversations about new learning.

How to Foster an All-In Attitude

1. Talk about "our students" and "our school."
2. Use "we" often.
3. Ask for help in breaking down grade-level silos.
4. Discourage the formation of cliques among teachers.
5. Remember that you are your school's ambassador to the group, and work to help everyone think of themselves that way.
6. Take pride in all students and all families.
7. Don't stay isolated in your office.
8. Keep the door open to people who are not yet all in.

QUICK TIP

1. Turn resistance into participation.
2. Don't judge.
3. Try to get to the root of a colleague's resistance.
4. Be curious.
5. Be respectful and open-minded.
6. Use neutral language.
7. Find ways to take next steps.
8. Work to get a commitment.

Be Mindful of Your Perceptions

Although you will likely encounter resistance, it's worth taking a moment to look at the situation to be sure the resistance is real. Before assuming that the teacher is resisting your efforts, be mindful of your own thoughts, insecurities, or biases that might be influencing your opinion.

An Ounce of Prevention

So how might you play a role in preventing much of the pushback from occurring, and how might you work constructively to turn it around when it does surface?

Communication is always a major factor in difficult situations. When you think of how you could have prevented much of this behavior, consider all the communication opportunities—those that might have helped you get ahead of the fears, the misinformation, and the feelings of being alone, overwhelmed, and even incompetent. The following are actions that can prevent most of the negativity you might encounter.

NEW TEACHER

Teachers who are new to the profession—or even new to the school—often carry around more anxiety than you'd like to see, and they may bring their worries into coaching sessions. You can boost their confidence and work to develop trusting relationships with them by scheduling brief but frequent check-ins. Often, new teachers just need to know that someone is looking out for them in the intervals between coaching or other professional learning experiences. You might think of these brief interactions as opportunities to mentor new teachers as they learn their way around the school, get to know their colleagues, and become familiar with the literacy curriculum. When time is short, a simple "How are you doing?" might be enough to show your support.

Provide a start-up meeting of the team. When you hold your first coaching conversation of the year (Chapter 4), remind your colleagues of your role and the support that every team member will have. In that meeting, you will also remind them of confidentiality and invite feedback if they have concerns. A tone of transparency and respect goes a long way.

Be sure all teachers understand their collective commitment to professional learning. Remind teachers they work in a school that has an agreed-upon literacy curriculum and broad expectations for their continuous growth and teamwork. Encourage those who may be feeling anxious or uncertain to request a private meeting with you so you can address their specific concerns and they can better understand why ongoing professional learning will benefit both them and their students.

Build trusting relationships every day. Coaching is a relationship. Learning takes risks, so think about how clear it is to your colleagues that you will not judge. How have your conversations with the group and individuals communicated that you are a thinking partner and that each teacher will drive the coaching conversations with your support? Also consider the importance of getting to know each teacher as a person. Begin your relationship with genuine interest in each teacher as a human being. Sit next to different colleagues at meetings or at lunch and show your interest in them in all their uniqueness. Make small gestures of support and appreciation like sending an email or sharing a book or an article or even bringing refreshments as a surprise for the group.

Communicate your role. Although we don't advise providing a detailed job description to your colleagues across the school, it is helpful to review the broad dimensions of your role each year (see Chapter 1) so that everyone understands the range of support you can provide to them. Your just-in-time support can assist them with scheduling, making plans for efficient administration of assessments, and addressing all the issues that concern them in an individual conversation. If they understand this and you are constantly in touch, you can prevent the feelings of being alone and overwhelmed.

Make it clear that you value teachers' thinking. If teachers' voices are not heard, your coaching support will not succeed. Your collaborative stance invites your colleagues' voices in every context. You know well the importance of listening and recognizing various points of view and providing rationales. Your professional learning opportunities need to be built not only on the school's goals but on what teachers see as their individual needs to be successful.

Expect the group to hold themselves accountable. Another key aspect of prevention is getting the team on the same page at the start of each year and continuing to revisit your vision document. This is something the team and you can refer to so everyone will be working in the same direction and better understand the commitments they made to the school and to each other by consensus. Everyone will be "in the know" and can support each other and respond constructively to each other when they make comments that the team believes is misinformation.

Coach individuals as often as possible. When you have the opportunity to coach individuals on a regular basis, you can continue to build the professional relationship and support each individual's specific needs. This will help teachers understand that you are partners in professional learning. You will be able to plan together, co-teach, demonstrate, or engage in any of the menu of supports that are needed.

Construct a set of agreements about working together during sessions. We have found it helpful in the first whole-group professional learning sessions to ask teachers to articulate an agreement on how they can be most productive when working together as a group. Consider taking the time to get everyone's commitment to working well together. Begin by asking your colleagues to think about what they want to honor for themselves and their colleagues to make the best of their time together. After some brief individual thinking and jotting time, invite suggestions and co-generate a short list of guidelines that are then approved by group consensus and revisited at the beginning of sessions for any suggested revisions. They may come up with statements similar to the following:

- Listen to understand your colleagues' thinking.
- Be sure everyone has a chance to speak.
- Give wait time for colleagues to respond.
- Honor each other by being on time and being "present."
- Say what you want to say in our meeting not outside of it.
- Ask questions to understand each other's thinking better and challenge each other's ideas.

Your colleagues will have their own guidelines, but a common working agreement of just a few statements makes the group accountable for the behavior of the group and can make your time together more productive. Consider highlighting one statement to focus on at the start of the meeting. At the end of the session, you might revisit the guidelines to ask the team to reflect on how they did as a group.

Stay in touch. Consider how you can be in frequent touch with every teacher in some way. Whether it is to drop by the classroom, leave a supportive message in a mailbox, or have a brief chat during lunch, make your presence known to every teacher as much as you can. Here is where coaching on the run (Chapter 21) can really support you by making you more visible to all your colleagues.

When It's Time for a Difficult Conversation

We have described a variety of constructive preventive actions, and you will probably think of more. If you didn't attend to them as preventive actions, but you think they might be helpful, you can circle back and revisit them with individuals and with the group in positive, constructive ways.

If you have addressed the concerns in many ways as suggested, and an individual continues to demonstrate behaviors that are a concern, you may need to set up a time with your colleague for a private conversation to problem-solve the situation, but be prepared for what might be a difficult conversation.

How to Handle a Difficult Conversation

First, this is a conversation that must take place in person, in private, and in a neutral space in the school. Avoid meeting in your office, and prioritize meeting in your colleague's space. Wherever you decide to meet, don't talk across a desk but rather in chairs that are in fairly close proximity. This communicates that neither party has the upper hand.

A difficult conversation requires your most empathetic and thoughtful coaching stance. Remember, as you plan for and enter the conversation, that the teacher is your valued colleague; accept comments as expressions of honest frustration, anxiety, or fear. Reflect on the situation, think about what part you may have played in the problem, and identify your goal for the conversation.

During the conversation, try not to argue with the person's view or ignore their concerns. The conversation needs to be a give-and-take so your colleague feels heard and has the chance to express concerns or offer explanations directly to you.

> **Respecting Individual Differences**
>
> As you meet in one-on-one situations, be mindful that your colleagues might have personal or cultural differences that will affect how you conduct the conversation. Some people define personal space differently, so be sure to maintain a comfortable distance. Other people might not be comfortable with establishing or able to establish eye contact because of cultural conventions or for other reasons. Be aware of your own biases. All of us tend to respond better to those like us or who agree with us. Work to understand others' views.

Before the Conversation

Use the time just before the meeting to process the situation and reflect on what might happen when you sit down with the individual. Prepare to speak calmly without becoming defensive and stay conscious of your body language. Be as diplomatic and clear as possible. Finally, keep the conversation brief and to the point. Turn off your phone. Get your head in a positive place by thinking about two or three good qualities of your colleague. And be prepared to present your view of the problematic behavior backed by specific examples that have caused concerns.

Opening the Conversation

Entering a difficult conversation is challenging, so consider the impact of how you do it. Be prepared, but most of all, be honest and sincere.

Share your concern by describing the behavior you observed and explaining the impact it had on you and how you felt. Tell your colleague you think it's important for them to know your concerns about the behavior and refer to the

agreed-upon expectations for the team of educators in the school. Give a few examples and describe the impact of each. Be clear and professional, acknowledging your colleague's point of view but expressing your own view clearly.

Sample Language

- *I hear what you are saying. Can you talk more about why you said that?*
- *Help me better understand how you feel.*
- *Can you talk about why that is so frustrating for you.*

During the Conversation

Continue the conversation from an inquiring stance, showing your curiosity and listening to understand. Invite your colleague to express their perspective on the problem and be sure to recognize and affirm what the person says. Acknowledge the individual's emotions and feelings. Seek more information so you have a good understanding of your colleague's view.

Sample Language

- *I'd like to check in with you about ____.*
- *I was confused by ____.*
- *Help me understand your thinking about that.*
- *What made you think that?*
- *What would make you more comfortable?*
- *When you ____, can you help me understand what you meant?*
- *Talk more about what led you to that conclusion.*

Next, use the skill of paraphrasing to feed back to your colleague your precise understanding.

Sample Language

- *Let me check that I correctly understand your perspective.*
- *Let me check my understanding. You feel ____.*

Be sure to affirm or recognize your colleague's emotions.

Sample Language

- *That is a difficult situation to be in.*
- *You must feel frustrated about that.*
- *I can hear your feelings of anger about that.*

Acknowledge that you accept their feelings or perspective (even though you may not agree with it).

Sample Language

- *I understand what you are saying.*
- *I can see why you feel so strongly about that.*
- *You are sharing a view I had not heard.*

Share your positive intention and think together about what will improve the situation. By the end of the conversation, summarize what you both agree will happen and plan to check in with each other on a specific date.

Sample Language

- *It seems we both understand better now and can move forward with ____.*
- *Let's plan ____.*
- *So let's plan to check in on ____. I will drop by then for a quick chat.*

Know When to Escalate

If you, your principal, and your team have clear expectations for professional learning in your school and have a colleague who still won't engage in spite of your kind and collegial efforts, then the problem becomes an issue of supervision, and your school principal is responsible. Ask your colleague to arrange a meeting with the principal to share the concerns you've discussed. Express your hope that the issue will be resolved soon, and let the teacher know that you will check in after the meeting to see how it went.

Some language that may help at the end of a difficult conversation includes the following.

Sample Language

- *I do appreciate that you took the time for us to think about this issue together. I know you feel very strongly about this. Given my understanding of my role and the school's expectations for participation in coaching and other forms of professional learning, I cannot be more helpful at this point. I suggest you meet with our principal and share your feelings. Would you like me to let her know you want to talk to her about this? Then I will check back with you in a week to see how the conversation went. Please let me know if there are ways I can continue to help.*

Usually, your empathy, understanding, and willingness to problem-solve together will be enough to engage an unwilling colleague. But if your colleague does not promptly request a meeting with the principal, state that this should be done immediately, or you will expect them to engage in the upcoming learning opportunity. Be clear that you will let the principal know a meeting request will be forthcoming. Communicate that between all of you the problem can be solved. You should be able to trust that your principal will uphold the team's agreements for professional learning in the school and that your colleague will be expected to participate in the same ways as others.

Trusting relationships will minimize most challenges with individual colleagues in your school. When you are kind and supportive, but also clear about your role, you can work through the bumps and eventually look back at how your previously resistant colleague is now a full participant in professional learning.

Up **Next**

In our next chapter—which is also our last—we show you how to stay strong, be curious, and continue to grow as a coach. After all, if you do not demonstrate that continuous learning and personal growth are priorities for you, teachers may become complacent. And you really don't want to see that happen.

Chapter 26

Be the **Coach You Want to Be**

When you first took on your current role, you probably had a strong vision of the kind of coach you wanted to be. You may have pictured yourself as a kind and empathetic presence in your school, a builder of knowledge and relationships, a capable problem solver, a skilled observer. There's no reason to think you've fallen short of those ideals, but you can't know for sure unless you spend some purposeful time reflecting on your work with teachers and sifting through the record of your interactions with them and your other colleagues across the school.

To be a strong leader in your school's improvement effort, you'll need to reflect often on your impact. We'll help you do that by providing reflection questions you can use to identify your strengths and a few priorities for your continued growth. We also provide a few structured tools that you may find helpful in considering the many different ways you can assess and reflect on your impact on the administrator, the teachers, the students, and your school.

Reflect on Your Impact

As the leader of professional learning, you're always working toward the goal of increased student achievement. Yet, it's not always easy to see the throughline from your work with teachers to its impact on student outcomes. That's why you need a clear, ongoing view of your impact, and your colleagues and supervisors need the same (Figure 26-1).

You can continually develop the self-awareness needed to assess your impact daily, at regular intervals, and at significant times, such as mid-year and end of year. But you and your team need to take an even longer view by looking at teacher and student performance over several years. It generally takes three to five years to develop a high-performing school, and that's if the majority of staff stays constant.

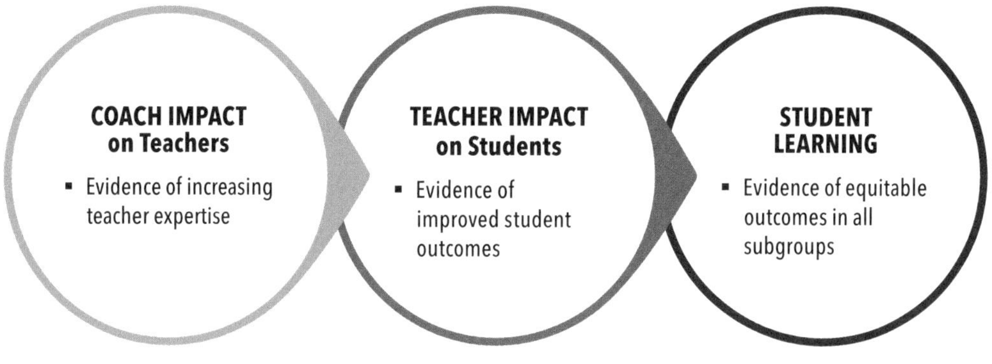

Figure 26-1

Self-assessment of your effectiveness is deeply intertwined with your view of the multiple aspects of your job. Self-reflection helps you develop and validate your vision of a highly effective professional learning leader so you can compare yourself to that vision as objectively as possible. Recognize evidence of small steps toward improvement and areas of strength to address your needs as a learner. After all, if you learn only from others' view of your productivity, you will not develop the internal guidance system you need to be a self-directed member of the school team.

It is important for your work with teachers to move the needle on student achievement, but that can't be your only goal. Schools that are hyper-focused on test scores can become tense and joyless places where instructional coaches (if there are any) lack autonomy and decision-making power. Teachers are isolated and adrift, families forgotten or left out. Students view school as a place they *have* to go, not a place they *want* to go.

Instead, use your position to work with the principal to make your school a place of collaboration: One in which test scores *do* matter, but students are seen as unique human beings, not data points. Where teachers are inspired, children are fully engaged in literacy learning, families are welcomed and appreciated, and all the adults pull in the same direction. Best of all, your school becomes a place where everyone truly is a learner because the culture supports continuous growth for all.

Prompts for Ongoing Self-Reflection

In this section, we provide ten categories with prompts for your ongoing self-reflection (Figure 26–2 on p. 245). Use your journal, date a page, and select a few pertinent categories. Within them there are a few reflection questions to help you list your strengths and areas for improvement. Even if you reflect on only one question in each category, it will help you take stock of where you are. Then review your list and put a star next to two or three current priorities you want to work on.

> **QUICK TIP**
>
> If you are a district-level coach or leader of professional learning and you work with more than one school, you may need to work extra hard to develop strong relationships with multiple principals. Those relationships are key to feeling strong and supported in your role.

1. Reflect on Your Partnership with Your Administrator

The strength of your relationship with your principal will be critical to your success as the leader of professional learning. Ask yourself one or more of these questions to prompt regular reflection on this very important relationship.

- *Do you meet with your administrator regularly to discuss the team's progress?*
- *Do you use language that places yourself as a thought partner with common goals?*
- *Do you listen carefully, ask clarifying questions, and paraphrase to be sure of what the administrator is saying?*
- *Can you communicate highs and lows without naming or blaming teachers?*
- *Can you ask advice without laying the problem on the desk of your administrator?*
- *Do you bring possible solutions for the consideration of your administrator?*
- *Do you demonstrate dedication to the welfare of the children in the solutions you propose?*
- *Do you couch issues in the context of wanting to do your job better rather than your own feeling of being overworked?*
- *Do you communicate a positive and hopeful attitude?*

2. Reflect on Your Collegial Relationships

Coaching is a relationship, and how you nurture your relationships with colleagues can make a big difference in their willingness to receive and apply your help. To reflect on the health of these relationships, ask yourself any of these questions:

- *How would your colleagues in the school describe you?*
- *Do you listen attentively as opposed to leaping to what you want to say next?*
- *How do you respond when colleagues seek you out? Do you actively seek information to help you fully understand? Do you take the action that can be of help?*
- *Are you confident that teachers can reveal their problems and fears to you rather than "putting on a show"?*
- *Do you struggle to understand attitudes of reluctance and fear?*
- *Are you able to work on a problem with a teacher without taking it personally?*
- *Do you engage in professional conversations that are rewarding both to you and your colleagues?*
- *What are your greatest challenges? If you break them down, what is the underlying cause?*
- *Do your colleagues share interesting observations of children or success stories with you? And do you know the children they are talking about?*
- *Do you feel welcome in your colleagues' classrooms? If not, why might that be?*
- *Do you demonstrate an unwavering commitment to the success of all children in the school?*
- *Do you acknowledge the achievements and progress made by individuals, the team, and students?*

10 AREAS FOR SELF-REFLECTION

1. Partnership with Administrator
2. Collegial Relationships
3. Your School Culture
4. Collective Efficacy of Team
5. Use of Shared Leadership
6. Data Analysis
7. Literacy Implementation
8. Equity and Cultural Responsiveness
9. Support of New Teachers
10. Teacher Development

Figure 26-2

3. Reflect on Your School Culture

Earlier in this chapter, we briefly discussed the importance of a healthy and happy school culture. Use any of the reflection questions below to periodically assess the condition of your school's culture.

- *Have you communicated a clear, articulated vision that everyone has contributed to and understands?*
- *Do you model respect, transparency, and other characteristics you want your colleagues to exhibit?*
- *Do you frequently observe teachers sharing their observations of children and entering professional conversations without your help?*
- *Do you and your colleagues talk about children and their families in respectful and positive terms? Does conversation indicate that they value the culture of the families in the school neighborhood?*
- *Do you see evidence that all the educators are committed to each other in accomplishing the school's goals?*

4. Reflect on the Collective Efficacy of Your Team

When groups of teachers pull together as a team, they begin to develop a sense of *collective teacher efficacy,* meaning the cumulative effect of a group working together with increasing effectiveness and agency. Effective teams that work together in a smooth, orchestrated way develop a belief in their own and their colleagues' ability to positively affect student outcomes. Think of it as a "We can do it if we work together" kind of mindset. The questions below will help you reflect on your impact on the collective efficacy of your team of educators.

- *How well do teachers understand that their strength is greater together than as individuals?*
- *Does the team problem-solve together?*
- *Do teachers in the school talk about children across grade levels?*
- *Do you and your colleagues talk about "our goals" and "our students"?*
- *Do teachers readily share with and encourage each other even if they are not on the same grade level?*
- *Does the team show generosity in supporting each other's learning?*
- *What evidence do you see that there is collaboration rather than competition in the teaching in the school?*
- *How strong is the team in their commitment to each other?*

5. Reflect on Your Success in Fostering Shared Leadership

There are teachers in your school who have the competence and confidence or the potential to engage in acts of leadership with you and with their teacher colleagues. Sometimes all you need to do is ask, "Are you interested in expanding your role?" Other times, you may need to invite a few teachers to co-lead a professional learning session such as a professional book club or a learning walk. You might want to use Survey Tool: Leadership Interest Survey (Figure 26-3; a blank, full-size version is available as **OR 26.1** in the Online Resources) with all teachers to capture their leadership interests because some teachers are reticent to volunteer publicly yet have many leadership qualities to offer. Use prompts such as those below to reflect on your efforts to share leadership with your colleagues.

ONLINE RESOURCE 26.1

- *Have you set high expectations for teacher contributions?*
- *Have you set aside time for teachers to perform leadership roles?*
- *Does your principal support compensating teachers who take on extra leadership roles or duties? Have you discussed the possibility?*
- *Have the teachers grown in expertise to take on new roles?*
- *Do you share leadership with colleagues within a climate of trust?*
- *Have you explicitly encouraged promising colleagues to take leadership?*
- *Are there new teachers in the school who show leadership promise? Have you provided professional experiences that will stretch them?*
- *What leadership roles have the teachers taken on?*
- *How successful have you been in mentoring colleagues who have leadership potential?*
- *Have you been able to help some colleagues develop the confidence to engage in acts of leadership with your support?*

SURVEY TOOL

LEADERSHIP INTEREST SURVEY

Please take a few moments to share your interest in taking on leadership roles in the school.

AREAS OF LEADERSHIP

Check any areas of leadership that interest you.

I would like to:

- ☐ Lead a team (e.g., a grade-level team or the data team).
- ☐ Be a member of a team that will address important school improvement goals.
- ☑ Invite colleagues to observe my teaching and think together about our teaching practice.
- ☐ Lead a professional book club.
- ☐ Lead a small group of teachers to investigate a problem, determine causes, and recommend possible solutions.
- ☑ Mentor a new teacher.
- ☐ Represent the school on a district-wide committee.
- ☐ Lead or co-lead a learning walk.
- ☑ Participate in a learning walk.
- ☐ Lead or co-lead a lesson study.
- ☑ Facilitate a study group.

Please share other areas of leadership that interest you or other ways in which you would enjoy leading.

I would enjoy having observers and being invited to observe others—with a particular interest in reading and writing about science.

I would be interested in working with a few colleagues to write a small grant to our community foundation or local businesses to purchase nonfiction books.

AREAS OF EXPERTISE

Share areas in which you feel you have expertise that could benefit other teachers.

Writing across the curriculum—particularly writing in science.

Your Literacy Coaching Playbook **Online Resource 26.1 | Survey Tool:** Leadership Interest Survey, **Version 01**

Figure 26-3

6. Reflect on Your Success in Developing a Data Lens

As an instructional coach, an important part of your role involves educating your colleagues in how to analyze and interpret individual and group data for needs, strengths, and patterns among students and then to take actions based on the evidence. You'll need to share trends in data regularly with faculty, grade-level teams, and individual teachers. And you'll probably also be called upon to submit data-informed recommendations to the school's data team (if there is one) and to school leaders. Use the questions that follow to reflect on your success in helping your colleagues develop a data lens.

- *Does classroom instruction produce positive learning outcomes, as documented by test scores, for all students?*
- *Are there disparities in the academic achievement of particular groups of students (e.g., boys, students of color, students at a particular grade)?*
- *Overall, does the data tell a story of steady improvement across all members of the student community?*
- *In addition to test scores, are you able to observe results, such as the quantity of student reading, quality of engagement in book discussions, or analysis of writing about reading?*
- *Do teachers refer to data (not only from test scores but from their own careful analysis of reading records or writing samples) in their discussion of student learning?*
- *In discussion of student progress, can teachers give explicit examples of reading or writing behaviors?*
- *In your observations, do you notice evidence of teacher decisions that are directly connected to reading records or writing samples?*
- *Do you and your team link the data to student opportunities for learning?*

7. Reflect on the Quality of the Literacy Implementation in the School

A key aspect of your role is to help teachers expand their instructional expertise. As a consistent thought partner, you can help teachers think more analytically about their work, organize their thoughts, reflect on their teaching, set goals, and develop a plan to meet them. Some of the following questions may help you reflect:

- *Do teachers actively seek your help in planning lessons?*
- *Do teachers seek your help in problem-solving?*
- *What components of the adopted literacy curriculum are evident as you visit classrooms? What seems to be harder to implement?*
- *What do teachers say they have the most trouble implementing? What is your plan for helping those who express difficulty?*
- *Do your observations indicate that the practices you have adopted are consistently present in the school (rather than just when you are observing)?*
- *What practices of effective literacy teaching are present within the school that need to be supported and amplified?*
- *How well do teachers understand the rationales for instructional decisions?*
- *How consistent are the teachers in linking rationales and data to their decisions?*

8. Reflect on Equity and Culturally Responsive Teaching Practices

In your role of professional learning leader, you may have a seat on your school's diversity, equity, and inclusion (DEI) team. If so, you will engage in analyzing the educational outcomes and experiences of various groups of students with the goal of identifying and interrupting policies and practices within the school that contribute (in the absence of malice) to inequities in opportunities for particular groups of students. But even if you are not a member of the DEI team, you are a leader in your school, and every educator on the team must identify inequities when they see them and take actions to assure equitable outcomes for all students.

- *What signs of systemic inequities exist in your school?*
- *What actions can you take to interrupt the inequities?*
- *Have you planned professional learning opportunities to strengthen culturally responsive teaching practices?*
- *What do your observations reveal about children who might be neglected in group instruction? Do you need to intervene?*
- *What does your analysis reveal about the school and classroom libraries? Are the resources there to support a multicultural curriculum?*
- *What resources are needed to help your staff implement a curriculum that represents all students and their families?*
- *Do the teachers demonstrate an equity lens in all observations and decisions?*
- *What additional professional learning might be helpful in developing an equity lens?*

9. Reflect on Your Support of New Teachers

All teachers need your guidance, support, and expert-level knowledge of teaching and learning, but new teachers need all that and more. For starters, they may need help with classroom management, lesson planning, and curriculum implementation. They might need emotional support or hands-on practice with analyzing data or integrating technology into the classroom. If you want new teachers to have a strong start, you can't leave their development to chance, so do reflect on the type of support you already provide for new teachers and where you can do more.

- *Do you plan regular learning opportunities just for new teachers?*
- *Do you take on the stance of a mentor when interacting with new teachers?*
- *Do you observe new teachers in action whenever you can?*
- *Do you model effective teaching practices?*
- *Have you invited more experienced teachers to play a significant role in nurturing new teachers?*
- *What evidence do you have that new teachers are taking on new learning? Are they implementing new practices?*
- *Do new teachers consult you about their questions and dilemmas? Do they talk honestly about their classroom challenges? What evidence do you have that they have taken your suggestions?*
- *Do new teachers understand how to use data to guide instructional decisions?*
- *What have you observed about the new teachers' ability to reflect on their teaching experiences?*

10. Reflect on Your Impact on Teacher Development

Your impact on teacher expertise will be the result of the many areas of reflection we have described. You have designed an array of professional learning opportunities to support teacher development, and hopefully you have kept good records in some form of coaching notebook (Chapter 23) to document your work and reflect on the results. Now, think about the results of those opportunities on teacher growth.

Your coaching notebook is the richest source of data on every teacher and every professional learning experience you provided over an entire year, so reflect on your effective use of it. Take time to look back at that data to appreciate the breadth and depth of your impact, and you will uncover areas for improvement in your colleagues and yourself. For example, if you look at your notes on a single teacher from the beginning of the year to the end, what do you notice about development over time? If you do the same thing with your data on additional teachers, do certain patterns begin to emerge?

Keep in mind that your coaching notebook contains both quantitative data (such as the number of one-on-one coaching sessions or professional learning sessions you provided and for how many teachers) and qualitative data (such as what you learn from looking at teacher development, teacher feedback, etc.).

There's no right way or wrong way to reflect on the data about professional learning that you have collected in your coaching notebook, but the following questions may bring some structure and purpose to your reflections.

- *Look through your record of professional learning. How many times have you met with each teacher for one-on-one coaching? For cluster coaching?*
- *Review your reflections on your professional learning offerings. What are your takeaways from your colleagues' feedback?*
- *What types of professional learning have you offered that received the most positive feedback? What was it about those offerings that you think your colleagues responded to?*
- *Review your records of professional learning. How many different ways did you offer professional learning? What additional types might you want to incorporate?*
- *What was your evaluation (and your participants' evaluation) of the quality of offerings? What are your opportunities to learn?*
- *Look in the section on individual teachers. How are you using the data in your coaching notebook to capture and follow up on your colleagues' goals?*
- *What does the journey of expertise look like for each teacher? Do you see any patterns?*
- *How has your coaching notebook helped you with logistical planning? What might you add to your notebook to make planning more useful? What might you take out that you have not used?*

- *Review the resources you have in your coaching notebook. Are there seminal articles missing that you want to add to your collection? Are there stale articles or blog posts that you no longer refer to and could remove and file to use as needed?*
- *How effectively are you using the resources you have in your coaching notebook?*

Structured Tools for Assessing Your Impact

Here we provide five different tools to help you think about the different aspects of your role, your use of language, and your one-on-one coaching experiences. We recommend storing these tools (available in the Online Resources) in the Resources section of your coaching notebook so you can use them throughout the year. Use your reflection time to shape your own goals for next year so you can continue to grow as a coach. Below we provide a brief description of the tools and how to use them.

TOOL #1

Assessing the Impact of Your Role

This first structured tool, called Self-Reflection Tool: Assessing the Impact of Your Role (Figure 26–4), is designed to help you reflect on your multidimensional role. (A blank, full-size version is available as **OR 26.2** in the Online Resources.) The far-left column articulates every aspect of your role as professional learning leader as described in Chapter 1. Choose a few aspects that apply to your specific role. Read the descriptions and briefly note what's going well and what needs improvement. As you work, keep broad questions like these in mind:

ONLINE RESOURCE 26.2

- *What worked? Why were you successful in this area?*
- *What do you need to be more successful?*
- *What have you changed or stopped doing over the years? Why?*
- *What were some specific challenges? How did you deal with those challenges?*
- *What were some of your accomplishments as reflected on your ongoing log?*
- *How many times have you coached each teacher this year?*
- *What professional resources were most helpful to you?*
- *How did you use feedback from others, and how did you address it?*
- *What specific improvements can you make in the next month (quarter, semester)?*

The most important part of this chart is the last column, in which you list your goals for improvement. Limit your goals to an achievable number and prioritize those you believe will be most impactful. You might want to make copies of the blank chart and store them in your coaching notebook to use for jotting notes throughout the year.

SELF-REFLECTION TOOL

ASSESSING THE IMPACT OF YOUR ROLE

	WHAT'S WORKING WELL	WHAT NEEDS IMPROVEMENT	MY PRIORITY GOALS
Teacher of Students Work with students for a few hours, days, or weeks in a colleague's classroom. Alternatively, co-plan and co-teach some lessons with a colleague.	• Taught in several classrooms at 3 grade levels	• Need to teach in intermediate classrooms more frequently	• Solicit 3 teachers I haven't co-taught with • Get weeks on calendar early
Professional Learning Leader Design and implement collaborative, job-embedded, standards-based professional learning opportunities. Create a multi-pronged design for professional learning that includes components such as professional learning sessions, learning walks, book clubs, lesson study, and study groups as well as one-on-one coaching, cluster coaching, and peer coaching. Engage as a thought partner with individual teachers and specialists to support continuous professional growth (one-on-one coaching). Engage as a facilitator of small groups of teachers and specialists to support continuous professional growth (cluster coaching). Provide emails, articles, blogs, newsletters, and other resources to keep teachers updated on cutting-edge research and instructional practices. Maintain records of the professional learning opportunities provided to document and reflect on the impact on teacher development and student outcomes.	• Ambitious plan this year • Prescheduled sessions went well • Coaching sessions felt increasingly productive • Coaching went well • Teachers appreciated resources—lots of comments • Collected good information	• Less is more—need to prioritize • Need more teacher input for study groups • More systematic frequency • Need more cluster coaching • Share more varied resources • Need to reorganize	• Integrate teacher feedback • Get 2–3 topics at year end • More frequent, some shorter sessions • Put cluster session every month on calendar • Invite teachers to suggest • Work on more digital access
Instructional Coach Work directly with teachers through modeling, co-teaching, and observing, and provide feedback for the purpose of improving instruction and promoting teacher knowledge, agency, and independence.			

Your Literacy Coaching Playbook **Online Resource 26.2 | Self-Reflection Tool:** Assessing The Impact of Your Role, page 1 **Version 01**

Figure 26-4 continues

SELF-REFLECTION TOOL

ASSESSING THE IMPACT OF YOUR ROLE *(CONT.)*

	WHAT'S WORKING WELL	WHAT NEEDS IMPROVEMENT	MY PRIORITY GOALS
Partner with School Principal Create a culture of collaboration and teamwork and implement a coherent design for professional learning and school improvement. Update the principal on professional learning, review data, and advocate for materials and policies that support instructional coherence and improvement in student outcomes.	• We agreed on a comprehensive plan early on. • Meetings have been regular & productive.	• Principal needs to suggest agenda items too.	• Link more data to plans • Solicit new agenda items at end of meeting
Coach on the Run Provide teacher support all day in informal, professional conversations, taking advantage of opportunities to interact with teachers in the nooks and crannies of the day.			
Mentor for New Teachers Orient new teachers to the school team, the curriculum, and the assessment materials, and provide an overview of the professional learning opportunities. Assure a strong start for new teachers by meeting regularly to plan and problem-solve. If there are many new teachers, identify additional mentor-teachers and provide support to them.	• New teachers enthusiastic—high energy • Meetings have been productive.	• Work to get all voices • Schedule more regular meetings	• Make notes to invite individuals to play a role • Get on calendar early
Coordinator of Curriculum and Professional Resources Secure, distribute, and coordinate an efficient system for the use of curriculum and assessment materials, the school's book room, manipulatives such as magnetic letters and word cards, and other supplies for literacy teaching. Secure and distribute professional books and other curriculum resources that support the instructional program.			

Your Literacy Coaching Playbook **Online Resource 26.2 | Self-Reflection Tool:** Assessing The Impact of Your Role, page 2 **Version 01**

Figure 26-4 continued

SELF-REFLECTION TOOL

ASSESSING THE IMPACT OF YOUR ROLE *(CONT.)*

	WHAT'S WORKING WELL	WHAT NEEDS IMPROVEMENT	MY PRIORITY GOALS
Data Coach Oversee the administration and interpretation of the school's assessments, including high-stakes literacy assessments, as well as assessments that inform instruction. Manage student achievement data, and help teachers understand, analyze, and use data to identify actions that improve teaching and expand learning opportunities.	• The data is so rich. • The learning is productive and highly relevant.	• Need to develop my expertise so I can lead more effectively • Making specific links to instruction	• Contact our data dept. for consult • Form small ad hoc group to create examples
Curriculum and Instruction Specialist Take responsibility for ensuring coherence and alignment of instruction with school goals. Keep up with the latest research and standards on literacy instruction, read and share professional books, and attend professional learning opportunities for coaches and other school leaders. Work with other school and district curriculum specialists to integrate content-area reading and writing and technology tools, such as AI.			
Learner As a thought leader, position yourself to continually learn more about adult learning, literacy research and practice, coaching skills, and other factors that contribute to sustainable school improvement. As a continuous learner, regularly reflect on the impact of your work on teacher development and student outcomes.	• Realize there's so much to learn • Using a reflection journal	• Keeping up can feel overwhelming • Need to make more time to write and highlight new insights	• Identify one or two specific focus areas for the year • Take 5 minutes at end of all professional learning to write

Your Literacy Coaching Playbook **Online Resource 26.2 | Self-Reflection Tool:** Assessing The Impact of Your Role, page 3 **Version 01**

Figure 26-4 continued

TOOL #2

Assessing the Impact: Effective Use of Language

Throughout this book, we've helped you think about the importance of facilitative language in all aspects of your role as leader of professional learning. As you reflect on your impact, your use of language to accomplish your goals will be an important factor to consider. Think about your language interactions in every aspect of your role whether it is a quick conversation as you coach on the run, a meeting with your principal, or an in-depth one-on-one coaching session.

You can reflect on your language in a variety of ways at different points in time. You can notice the language you used by taking a look at your coaching or session notes or through reviewing video clips or audio recordings of your coaching. You can set up observations by your principal or coach colleagues so they can note your precise language and you can reflect on your strengths and identify areas to refine. Over time, your goal is to internalize facilitative language that is effective in accomplishing your many goals as coach.

To help you assess your use of language, we provide a structured tool (Figure 26-5). This tool contains a series of prompts to stimulate reflection and a section for jotting down your language goals going forward. (You will find a full-size Self-Reflection Tool: Assessing Your Impact: Effective Use of Language as **OR 26.3** in the Online Resources.)

ONLINE RESOURCE 26.3

TOOL #3

A Look-for Tool for One-on-One Coaching Moves

A very important factor in your ability to impact teacher growth is your ability to provide effective one-on-one coaching. When you engage in this type of coaching, you bring together an array of critical moves. Most of the same moves apply to cluster coaching. To help you reflect productively, we have developed a structured tool called Look-for Tool: One-on-One Coaching Moves (shown in Figure 26-6; available full size as **OR 26.4** in the Online Resources).

ONLINE RESOURCE 26.4

As you learned in Chapter 13, a look-for tool can be used to identify observable behaviors before, during, and after observing a high-quality lesson. This particular look-for tool lists the elements of an effective one-on-one coaching session. Use it to reflect on your coaching. Consider making an audio or video recording so you can reflect on your strengths and identify goals. We suggest you select only a few bullets or just one section of the tool as a focus. Over time, you will feel successful in most of the coaching moves and will identify particular areas of strength.

You might invite your principal, another coach, or another school or district leader to observe you in one-on-one coaching using this look-for tool. Prior to the observation, identify specific bullets or an entire section that you're working on. Also, make it clear that no single observation will reveal all the behaviors in the tool. Then spend time thinking together with your colleagues to identify new goals.

SELF-REFLECTION TOOL

ASSESSING YOUR IMPACT: EFFECTIVE USE OF LANGUAGE

CATEGORY	PROMPTS FOR REFLECTION	GOALS GOING FORWARD
Listening	***Do I effectively:*** ▪ *Use listening skills to full advantage (full attention, no interruptions, neutral stance, positive body language)?* ▪ *Attend to the body language of my colleague: facial expressions, tone of voice?* ▪ *Allow for think time through pausing or silence?* ▪ *Listen attentively and empathetically?*	• Slow down the conversation • Notice uptake sooner so colleague not overwhelmed
Asking Effective Questions and Making Statements	***Do I effectively use language to:*** ▪ *Convey collaborative thinking, not judgment?* ▪ *Invite genuine co-inquiry?* ▪ *Ground the talk in data and evidence?* ▪ *Invite honest feedback on our work together?* ▪ *Convey genuine curiosity?* ▪ *Convey tentativeness?* ▪ *Invite analytic thinking?* ▪ *Focus on rationales, not rules?* ▪ *Foster a variety of perspectives?* ▪ *Foster new learning that is generative?* ▪ *Confirm or expand knowledge?* ▪ *Gain new information?* ▪ *Provide helpful information?* ▪ *Lead to an action plan?* ▪ *Support culturally sustaining instructional practices?* ▪ *Honor the unique identities and experiences of each teacher?* ▪ *Foster teacher agency?* ▪ *Promote flexibility?* ▪ *Support teacher self-analysis and reflection?* ▪ *Support collegial problem-solving and inquiry?* ▪ *Show that I was seeking to understand the teacher's precise comments and questions?* ▪ *Focus on the teacher's strengths?* ▪ *Show a particular purpose?* ▪ *Convey intent?* ▪ *Restate my colleague's comments in my own words to show my understanding?* ▪ *Summarize the big ideas or insights and confirm understanding?* ▪ *Prompt the teacher to notice and name literacy behaviors?* ▪ *Support the teacher's ability to reveal the true instructional challenges?*	• Did too much telling—give more wait time • Use prompts to invite teacher to do more of the analysis • Work on making the learning generative • Be sure to invite teacher to recognize own strengths • Don't give up on teacher's ability to identify the true challenges

Your Literacy Coaching Playbook **Online Resource 26.3 | Self-Reflection Tool:** Assessing Your Impact: Effective Use of Language, **Version 01**

Figure 26-5

LOOK-FOR TOOL

ONE-ON-ONE COACHING MOVES

BEFORE THE OBSERVATION

- Assures that the observer has materials for taking notes and relevant professional resources ✓
- Makes brief links to previous coaching sessions and/or professional development sessions
- Involves the teacher in the discussion of precise reading and writing behaviors as evidence of learning strengths and needs
- Listens actively to gain information about the students and identify the teacher's goals
- Reviews data on student reading or writing behaviors (e.g., reading records, writing scores) ✓
- Helps teacher focus on the curriculum goals and the relevant student data
- Listens to the teacher's concerns and requests ✓
- Asks questions to understand the teacher's thinking
- Makes notes on the essential information to guide the observation
- Solicits the teacher's requests for specific observations ✓
- Notices the teacher's use of language, as it reveals understanding
- Discusses appropriateness of lesson goals and materials
- Uses time efficiently
- Formulates questions for self that will guide the observation and follow-up discussion

Notes:

11:00—11:15

- Teacher had resources & notebook
- Prompted teacher for further analysis
- Reviewed data together
- Noted teacher requests

DURING THE OBSERVATION

- Is as unobtrusive as possible
- Observes closely and transcribes teacher-student interactions
- Records time transitions ✓
- Identifies teaching strengths
- Looks for patterns in teaching decisions
- Notes genuine wonderings about teaching and learning ✓
- Identifies a few major coaching points
- Makes notes of the language to use when opening the post-observation conversation (first words) ✓

1:00—1:35

- Took detailed transcription
- Several genuine wonderings
- Jotted first words

AFTER THE OBSERVATION

- Assures the teacher takes notes on the discussion ✓
- Thinks together with the teacher to analyze teaching decisions and their impact on student learning
- Asks open-ended questions
- Pauses frequently or waits to give think time ✓
- Uses evidence of reading or writing behaviors and data to ground discussion
- Notices and builds on teacher's verbal and nonverbal responses
- Listens actively to the teacher's thinking
- Uses effective language skills (e.g., wait time, clarification, paraphrasing, summarizing)
- Facilitates the teacher's self-analysis of interactions during the lesson
- Uses lesson artifacts (e.g., books, writing) to discuss teaching and learning
- Provides rationales for suggestions
- Addresses the teacher's concerns and questions ✓
- Uses discussion time efficiently
- Selects a few especially useful coaching points
- Helps the teacher see the generative value of new insights
- Discusses teaching and learning with clarity and economy of language
- Involves the teacher in setting further goals and specific actions ✓
- Adds brief comments about procedures or other issues (add-ons)
- Engages the teacher in reflecting on and summarizing new learning ✓
- Invites the teacher to evaluate the helpfulness of the coaching session
- Makes notes to inform future coaching sessions and professional learning

2:45—3:15

- Good use of wait time
- Puzzled together about B&R
- Teacher posed questions; got teacher to do thinking first
- Revisited teacher's agenda
- Summarized clearly

Your Literacy Coaching Playbook **Online Resource 26.4 | Look-for Tool:** One-on-One Coaching Moves, **Version 01**

Figure 26-6

Tool #4

Look-for Tool: Coaching Observation

This second tool for assessing your impact in one-on-one coaching is designed to help your principal or trusted colleague know what to look for as they observe you in a coaching session (Figure 26-7). Their observations will help you reflect on your coaching, though you can also use the form for your own self-reflection. The tool has descriptions of relevant coaching moves plus space for notes. (You will find a full-size Look-for Tool: Coaching Observation as **OR 26.5** in the Online Resources). If in-person observation is not possible, consider making an audio or video recording of a coaching session.

ONLINE RESOURCE 26.5

LOOK-FOR TOOL

COACHING OBSERVATION

COACHING MOVES	NOTES
Links conversation to previous coaching and professional learning	Could be more explicit—refer to notes.
Uses coaching elements: • Pre-observation conversation • Observation and transcription • Post-observation conversation (discussion, summary of learning and its generative value, setting of goals, invitation for session feedback)	Set only 2–3 specific goals. Too many seemed overwhelming.
Focuses on complex aspects of the reading/writing process (reading to include concepts about print, phonics, self-monitoring, comprehension, vocabulary, and fluency; writing to include genre, craft, and conventions)	Helped T contemplate the author's deeper message in nonfiction
Uses behavioral data from students to ground the talk	Used last book club comments as evidence
Uses specific teaching interactions as well as lesson artifacts to think together about impact on student learning	T identified S understandings and iimpact of the prompts.
Demonstrates knowledge of instructional practices and their rationales	Beginning to focus on rationales and is thus less anxious about right vs wrong
Shows a strong knowledge base and uses the curriculum and professional resources (texts) to ground thinking, foster independence, and promote further learning	Guided T to places in professional text to revisit
Uses respectful, collegial tone that demonstrates value for the teacher as a thought partner	Sat shoulder to shoulder; T did most of the talking
Listens attentively to understand	Asked questions to clarify
Notices verbal and nonverbal responses	Gave wait time—was helpful
Uses specific language that opens conversation, invites thinking, promotes co-inquiry and analysis, and/or gives information as appropriate	"What was your thinking about that?"
Uses effective language techniques such as clarifying, paraphrasing, asking open-ended questions, and summarizing	Interactions felt comfortable; T shared lots of observations
Selects a few generative and explicit coaching points	Identified 2 prompts that will be useful for discussions

Your Literacy Coaching Playbook **Online Resource 26.5 | Look-for Tool:** Coaching Observation, **Version 01**

Figure 26-7

Tool #5

A Protocol Tool for End-of-Year Feedback on Professional Learning

It will be extremely helpful to reflect on the impact of a year of professional learning. The beauty of the process we describe in Protocol Tool: End-of-Year Feedback on Professional Learning (shown in Figure 26-8; available full size as **OR 26.6** in the Online Resources), sometimes called carousel, is that it harnesses the power (and the anonymity) of the group while also engaging individual teacher voices as teachers think together in a group feedback process. Not only that, but it's a fairly simple and quick way to accumulate data on your performance as a coach. You can accomplish this rich feedback process in about twenty to thirty minutes and have feedback from all your colleagues.

ONLINE RESOURCE 26.6

PROTOCOL TOOL

END-OF-YEAR FEEDBACK ON PROFESSIONAL LEARNING

PARTICIPANTS	ROLES TO ASSIGN	TIMING	MATERIALS
Teachers, Specialists, Administrators	Facilitator, Note-taker, Timekeeper	20-30 min	

PLANNING AND PREPARATION

- Choose date and time to meet.
- Invite educators who have worked with you in professional learning for the year.

INTRODUCTION 5-10 min

- Review norms for productive communication.
- Share the goals for the meeting.
- Form three or four groups; each group selects a facilitator, note-taker, and timekeeper.

FEEDBACK PROCESS 15-20 min

- Have each participant make two columns on a sheet of paper and jot their thoughts on what they think went well in the professional learning for the year and what they'd like to improve for the next year.
- Distribute chart paper and a few markers to each group.
- Have each note-taker make two columns on the chart paper and label the one on the left *What Worked Well*, and the one on the right *What We Would Change*.
- Now have group members share their comments, one person at a time, while the note-taker records them on the chart paper for all to see. Repeat the process for the second column. (Of course, the same process can be done on a shared digital document. Simply combine the documents from the individual groups in a single document for all to read.)
- Invite the groups to walk around the room and read each chart. Then bring them together for a whole-group discussion that ends with a few summary statements you can record on a fresh sheet of chart paper.

AFTER THE SESSION (PROFESSIONAL LEARNING LEADER ONLY)

- When the session is over, remove the charts from the wall (or take a picture of each one on your phone), and review all the feedback you've collected. Look for patterns that indicate areas in which you need to make changes, and plan to address those areas first.

Your Literacy Coaching Playbook **Online Resource 26.6 | Protocol Tool:** End-of-Year Feedback on Professional Learning, **Version 01**

Figure 26-8

The Ten Best Ways to Keep Growing

Your personal growth is not an option—it's a must. How else can you say with confidence that you're always working at the top of your game? In your role as leader of professional learning in your school, you need to keep up with changing times and new instructional practices or refinements of existing ones if you want to stay current. Lastly, let's turn our thinking to how you can use your self-reflections and focus your energy on your journey of continuous growth. Here are the best ways we know to keep you growing all the time.

Your personal growth is not an option —**it's a must**

1. **Seek Out Professional Learning Opportunities**
   The more you practice something, the better you get at doing it. Fortunately, everything you do as a coach is an opportunity to practice your craft. But practice is only one part of the equation. You also need exposure to the continuous flow of research and ideas about literacy teaching and learning. You are not expecting to be perfect—just the best you can be.

   You may already be on mailing lists for upcoming seminars, conferences, workshops, and institutes offered by your district or in neighboring states. If so, do take a few minutes when notices arrive in your mailbox to scan the offerings and decide if there is a session or two you'd like to attend. We know it may mean time away from school or even a trip to another state, but, if you choose carefully, it is a good way to contribute to your professional growth. Such experiences also provide a way to network with other educators.

   The same goes for online courses and webinars, which don't involve travel or big chunks of time. Often, online courses and the like are asynchronous, meaning they don't take place in real time. That allows you to work and receive the learning benefits at a convenient time.

   We suggest that you make it a habit to reserve time for your own professional learning, which will help you feel more confident in your role and better informed about instructional practices and materials. Your expanding competency will be an important factor in the level of trust your colleagues have in you.

2. **Build a Network of Colleagues Who Coach**
   No matter what occupation you have, it helps to spend time with colleagues who "get you." If there are no established networking groups for coaches in your district, consider starting one. All you need is one or two other coaches to make a group, and you may find that you acquire new members as more people hear about it. Alternatively, you could join a virtual coach group online. If there are other literacy coaches in your district, you might set up a few coach-peer visits to watch you coach and vice-versa. The pay-off here is in what happens after the observations as the two of you think together about your coaching.

Maximize Your Growth at Professional Conferences

At any professional conference you attend, you can create your own path of sessions to match your unique goals. Usually, the conference keynotes are designed not only to educate you with cutting-edge thinking but also to inspire you. Perhaps best of all, you are likely to find a diverse array of teachers, researchers, and literacy experts from which to build a network of professional relationships beyond your home base. Here's how to reap maximum rewards from every professional conference you attend.

More Is Better
If your administrator approves, bring one or two colleagues with you to the conference so you can plan together, talk together, go to some of the same sessions or split up, and debrief together. Back home, you can plan together for how best to share your learning with colleagues.

Set Your Goals
Consider the professional learning priorities you have established for yourself and those the team has prioritized. With that lens, spend some time reviewing the offerings and have a tentative plan for your schedule of sessions. Be sure to have a backup for each session you plan to attend. That way, if one is already full when you get to the room, or if you realize the topic wasn't what you anticipated, you'll have another option for that time slot.

Be Prepared
We always find it helpful to get information on the local meal options during the conference in case we decide to set up a lunch with colleagues, which is a wonderful sharing opportunity. Depending on what you learn about the food situation, you might want to bring a few little snacks with you to have in your bag.

During the Conference
Take good notes during sessions to capture key points of each presentation and also to note your thinking about what you saw and heard. Take some time after each session or at day's end to think about and jot down the implications of your learning in your reflection journal.

After the Conference
As soon as you can after the conference, be sure to turn your new learning into an action plan. How will you help your colleagues benefit from your new learning? Consider a short debrief over tea or during lunch and share any pertinent articles or handouts you brought back. Be sure to debrief with your administrator as well.

3. **Try Journaling**
   Writing is thinking made visible, but that's just one reason why you might give journaling a go. Lots of people keep journals to document events of the day, process important experiences, or make personal improvement plans. Others use journaling to collect random and not-so-random thoughts they don't want to lose. We knew a coach who made a habit of sitting with her open journal just before bed and waiting for her accumulated thoughts from the day (mostly about coaching, but not always) to find their way onto the page. Writing helped her fall asleep faster each night because journaling literally allowed her to close the book on her intrusive thoughts and worries from the day so she could more easily drift off.

4. **Up Your AI Game**
   If you have spent any time at all with artificial intelligence (AI) platforms, you know that AI is both powerful and perilous. But don't let fear or suspicion about AI keep you from promoting it as an instructional tool for teachers and for yourself. It's simply too useful to ignore.

Of course, we are well aware of the potential and pitfalls for any new technology, so we encourage you to do some research to arm yourself with suggested guidelines and reasons for using AI. A rapidly growing number of websites, podcasts, blogs, and research reports about the safe and responsible use of AI in schools are available. We also suggest you check with your district for any guidelines that may be available for teachers and school leaders.

When it comes to AI, the genie is out of the bottle. You will not be able to advance in your own career the way you'd like unless you become as knowledgeable as possible about this and other game-changing technologies.

5. **Read Professional Publications**
   You are probably well aware that research journals, and other professional publications (digital or print) can keep you on the cutting edge of your craft by connecting you to studies of effective instructional practices, inspiring stories from the field, and the most current research on coaching and school improvement.
   But if just the mention of a research journal makes you yawn, know this: you don't have to read an entire research report to get the gist. Often, the abstract that comes at the beginning and the summary at the end each provide quick takeaways. Then you can decide to read the full report if the topic is particularly relevant to your work or grabs you for a different reason. However, do read the whole article critically (especially the section called "limitations") before making policy decisions based on it.
6. **Learn from Teachers**
   Don't fall into the trap of thinking you always need to be the smartest or best-informed person in your school. If you find yourself feeling that way, remember that you are only one member of a school community in which everyone is learning all the time. Certainly, you have specific skills and experiences that others may not, but nothing should make you happier than learning something new from a colleague.
7. **Seek Feedback from Teachers**
   Nothing is more important to your professional growth than direct feedback from teachers. To make it easy on them, hand out an index card or paper strip (sometimes referred to as an exit slip) to each teacher at the end of a professional learning or coaching session. Pose a question, and ask teachers to respond in writing. Let the teachers know they can be brief and anonymous in their responses if that might help raise their comfort level. You'll be surprised how much you can learn from just one question. Here are a few to get you started:
   - *What is your biggest takeaway from this professional learning session?*
   - *What is one thing you noticed on our learning walk?*
   - *What is one thing I could do to be more helpful in your learning?*
   - *What is one thing you would change in this learning experience?*

8. **Take Care of Yourself**
   In your decision to become the professional learning leader in your school, you have chosen to do something hard, not something easy. That's why many coaches, especially in the first couple of years, feel intimidated by the scope of their role and overwhelmed by their many responsibilities. If that sounds familiar, it can help to remember that your feelings are normal and to be expected—but only to a point. If you find yourself skipping your morning exercise routine, seeing your friends and family less often than you'd like, not getting enough sleep, or feeling like you're constantly working but never getting as far ahead as you'd like, it might be time for some serious self-care. After all, you can't adequately support teachers if you're not feeling strong yourself. Staying strong means knowing when to lean on your peers, seek support, and take care of your physical and mental health. Here are some ways to accomplish your professional goals without short-changing your personal life or your health.

   1. Think of yourself and your colleagues as if you are on an exciting journey that is ongoing. It's not that you don't have end goals, you just want to enjoy the learning process.
   2. When you notice evidence of progress and success in teachers or in students, make a note of it in your journal or coaching notebook. When you feel like you're not getting anywhere, look back at your notes to remind yourself that you really are having an incremental impact.
   3. Find a trusted person or group who will support you even if they aren't teachers or coaches themselves. Sometimes all you really need is the sympathetic ear of someone who loves and cares about you.
   4. When you can't seem to solve a particular problem, remember that as a first step you *can* get more information. The more you know about a problem, the better able you will be to see your way through it.
   5. Try something to help you relax—yoga, running, knitting, or meditation—anything you can reliably count on to promote relaxation or restore focus.
   6. Turn off the worry machine when you are not in the school. Let your worries rest so you can, too!
   7. Finally, look to the future with optimism knowing that your team of colleagues care very much about the work you are doing together and are proud of the progress they've made so far.

> *"One thing I've learned is that no matter how experienced you are, you always can use coaching. And what I mean is having somebody watch you professionally and having some real dialogue."*
>
> –**JEROD PHILLIPS**
> (2023, 43)

9. **Be Prepared for Conflict**

   The most effective coaches know that conflict is inevitable and are ready to work through it, allowing for different viewpoints. Find a path forward together. Healthy conflict is not personal. It is an opportunity for colleagues to wrestle with ideas and better understand each other's thinking. Conflict makes a team stronger because it engages them in practicing skills they are not often called on to use. One of those skills is the ability to use language effectively when conflicts arise. Here are some useful language stems to help you understand differences and move beyond them.

   - I'm not sure I understand, so can you talk more about why you think that?
   - I understand what you're saying, but have you considered ____?
   - Though I agree with some of the points you made, I need to think about this one idea. Can you say more about that?
   - I don't think I agree about that, but I want to understand your perspective.
   - I think there are other ways to think about that. Would you be open to hearing them?
   - I don't think I agree, but let's keep talking.
   - Before we make a decision about this, let's hear other voices so we can explore multiple factors that may be causing this challenge.

   This language fosters safety in disagreement. If you model it, others might be bolder about disagreeing and come to realize that it gets everyone to a better place. Remember that dissonance is healthy and welcome it for the sake of deeper understandings.

QUICK TIP

Don't be afraid to use humor in your coaching or to laugh at circumstances or yourself instead of complaining.

10. **Find a Coach Just for You**

    So much of your day goes into helping teachers become the teachers you know they want to be. But who is doing that for you? If your answer is "no one," you're missing out on an important way to grow your expertise as a coach.

    Think about other coaches in your school or district. Is there a person you can ask to be your peer coach? If so, consider inviting this professional to coach you in some aspect of your role. For example, the individual could do any of the following:

    - *Attend one of your professional learning sessions and give feedback afterward.*
    - *Participate in problem-solving meetings for the same purpose.*
    - *Observe individual coaching from pre-observation conversation to discussion afterward.*
    - *Respond to a video of a segment of individual coaching.*

    Your partner may be willing to observe a full day of your work as a coach and give feedback on noticings about the ambience in the school or your interactions with teachers. A sensitive person can provide a "second eye" that helps you make your work more effective.

Such assistance might involve an element of assessment; for example, your fellow coach can use protocols developed by your district or select one of our tools as found in the Online Resources for this chapter. Peer coaching by a person you trust can add objectivity to your own self-reflections and give you greater insight into where you need to learn more or to make changes in approaches you tend to lean on.

Plan for Continued Growth

Responsive coaching means creating a professional learning design that builds on teacher strengths and meets your teachers' specific needs. Consider how you spent your time over the year to meet those needs and to grow their expertise: What worked well in building their expertise? What didn't? Identify professional learning goals for the next school year using your colleagues' feedback, data analysis, district and school improvement goals, and your own reflections on coaching (Figure 26–9). Your professional learning design reflects what you believe about effective coaching, teaching, and learning. With this mindset, take steps to implement a thoughtful plan for continuing your own personal growth and that of your colleagues.

Figure 26-9

Be Curious

Curiosity is the beating heart of coaching. It drives you to ask authentic questions, explore new ideas, and look beyond surface-level solutions. Often, curiosity leads to innovation, fosters meaningful connections, and helps you see the potential in every teacher. And, when you display your intellectual curiosity and passion for learning before your colleagues, they begin to see you as a person who is in a constant state of inquiry, problem-solving, and growth and often become more curious themselves.

You're probably curious if you naturally use words and phrases such as as the following:

- *Are there other ways to think about that?*
- *I wonder why that is.*
- *What do you think is happening here?*
- *What if we tried something different?*

Questions and statements like these are characteristic of inquiring minds and communicate to teachers that you are willing to be a partner in uncovering the root causes that may lurk behind problems of practice.

In your role as the professional learning leader in your school, we hope you'll never stop wondering what more you can do, how you can better serve teachers and their students, and where new opportunities for growth might lie. You can be the inspirational example of teaching, leading, and learning.

In this book, we've given you a wealth of ready-to-use resources that will help you create professional learning experiences that your colleagues will want to attend. We've also provided examples of language you can use to shape your conversations, convey your stance, and support teachers in developing new knowledge and understandings about teaching and learning. Along the way, we've provided information to help you succeed in your multidimensional role so teachers will succeed as well. It is our hope that these tools offer the help you need to be the coach you want to be.

References

Aguilar, Elena. 2020. *Coaching for Equity: Conversations That Change Practice*. Hoboken, NJ: Jossey-Bass.

Bates, Celeste C., and Denise N. Morgan. "Literacy Leadership: The Importance of Soft Skills." *The Reading Teacher* 72, no. 3 (November/December 2018): 412–415.

Canaday, Sara. 2023. *Coaching Essentials for Managers: The Tools You Need to Ignite Greatness in Each Employee*. New York: McGraw-Hill.

City, Elizabeth A., Richard F. Elmore, Sarah E. Fiarman, and Lee Teitel. 2009. *Instructional Rounds in Education: A Network Approach to Improving Teaching and Learning*, 6th ed. Cambridge, MA: Harvard Education Press.

Covey, Stephen R. 2020. *The 7 Habits of Highly Effective People*. New York: Simon & Schuster.

Dunne, Faith, Paula Evans, and Gene Thompson-Grove. 2024. "Consultancy Protocol: Framing Consultancy Dilemmas." Center for Leadership and Educational Equity. July 2024. https://www.clee.org/wp-content/uploads/2024/07/consultancy.pdf

Fountas, Irene C., and Gay Su Pinnell. 2009. *Prompting Guide, Part 2, for Comprehension: Thinking, Talking and Writing*. Portsmouth, NH: Heinemann.

——. 2022. *Leading for Literacy: What Every School Leader Needs to Know*. Portsmouth, NH: Heinemann.

—— 2022. *The Literacy Continuum: A Tool for Assessment, Planning, and Teaching*, Second Edition. Portsmouth, NH: Heinemann.

Fullan, Michael, and Clif St. Germain. 2006. *Learning Places: A Field Guide for Improving the Context of Schooling*. Thousand Oaks, CA: Corwin.

Galinsky, Adam, and Maurice Schweitzer. 2015. *Friend & Foe: When to Cooperate, When to Compete, and How to Succeed at Both*. New York: Crown Business.

Hess, Frederick M. "The New Stupid." *Educational Leadership* 66, no. 4 (Dec 2008–Jan 2009): 12–17.

Hicks, Troy, and Misty Sailors. 2018. "Democratizing Professional Growth with Teachers: From Development to Learning." Newark, DE: International Literacy Association. https://literacyworldwide.org/statements

Knowles, Malcolm S., Elwood F. Holton III, Richard A. Swanson, and Petra A. Robinson. 2020. *The Adult Learner: The Definitive Classic in Adult Education and Human Resource Development*, 9th ed. New York: Routledge.

Lipton, Laura, and Bruce Wellman. 2024. *Mentoring Matters: A Practical Guide to Learning-Focused Relationships,* 3rd ed. Bloomington, IN: Solution Tree.

Lyons, Carol, and Gay Su Pinnell. 2001. *Systems for Change in Literacy Education*. Portsmouth, NH: Heinemann.

Phillips, Jerod. "The Collegial Coach." *Principal* 102, no. 3 (January/February 2023): 42–43.

Ray, Katie Wood. 2002. *What You Know by Heart: How to Develop Curriculum for Your Writing Workshop*. Portsmouth, NH: Heinemann.

Renwick, Matt. 2022. *Leading Like a C.O.A.C.H.* Thousand Oaks, CA: Corwin.

Rodgers, Adrian, and Emily M. Rodgers. 2007. *The Effective Literacy Coach*. New York: Teachers College Press.

Sharratt, Lyn D., and Michael Fullan. 2012. *Putting FACES on the Data: What Great Leaders Do!* Thousand Oaks, CA: Corwin.

Showers, Beverly, and Bruce Joyce. "The Evolution of Peer Coaching." *Educational Leadership* 53, no. 6 (March 1996): 12–16.

Singh, Nadira. "Let's Get It Right—Everyone Deserves a Coach." *Coaching* (blog). June 11, 2024. https://learningforward.org/2024/06/11/lets-get-it-right-everyone-deserves-a-coach/

Stanier, Michael Bungay. 2016. *The Coaching Habit: Say Less, Ask More, and Change the Way You Lead Forever*. Vancouver, British Columbia: Page Two.

Stigler, James W., and James Hiebert. 2009. *The Teaching Gap: Best Ideas from the World's Teachers for Improving Education in the Classroom*. New York: Free Press.

Toll, Cathy. 2005. *The Literacy Coach's Survival Guide: Essential Questions and Practical Analyses*. Newark, DE: International Reading Association.

Van Barneveld, Christina. 2008. *Using Data to Improve Student Achievement*. Ontario: Literacy and Numeracy Secretariat.

Index